Asian America

Asian America

A PRIMARY SOURCE READER

EDITED BY

Cathy J. Schlund-Vials

K. Scott Wong

Jason Oliver Chang

Yale UNIVERSITY PRESS

New Haven and London

Published with assistance from the foundation established in memory of
Amasa Stone Mather of the Class of 1907, Yale College.

Yale University Press books may be purchased in quantity for educational, business, or
promotional use. For information, please e-mail sales.press@yale.edu (U.S. office) or
sales@yaleup.co.uk (U.K. office).

Designed by Sonia L. Shannon.
Set in Minion Pro type by Tseng Information Systems, Inc.
Printed in the United States of America.

Library of Congress Control Number: 2016943220
ISBN: 978-0-300-19544-6 (paperback : alk. paper)

A catalogue record for this book is available from the British Library.

This paper meets the requirements of ANSI/NISO Z39.48-1992 (Permanence of Paper).

10 9 8 7 6 5 4 3 2 1

Contents

..

Part II: War and Imperialism

Part III: Race, Rights, and Representation

CONTENTS

Acknowledgments

Asian America: A Primary Source Reader necessarily begins with Sarah Miller at Yale University Press, who had the original vision for this volume; her enthusiasm for such a project, along with her sage advice throughout the entirety of it, inspired us to think always about the possibilities of anthology and field. Ash Lago, along with other members of the Yale University Press editorial team, provided key support at a critical time. To be sure, this volume's scope—along with its final form—is directly attributable to the critical eyes of anonymous readers, who consistently and constructively pushed us to make this a more cohesive, relevant work.

Asian America: A Primary Source Reader is not only a coedited endeavor; its assemblage was collaborative in scope. Indeed, we are thankful to the early efforts of Caryl Nuñez, who helped launch the project via multiple library requests; we are also grateful to Maxine Smestad-Haines and Fe Delos-Santos for their administrative support and encouragement. We are especially indebted to Patrick S. Lawrence, whose careful eye authenticated our transcriptions and who played a keen role in the final stages of the project. Finally, we want to personally acknowledge those who, through their indefatigable support, allow us to do our work:

Cathy is thankful to her family, who have consistently reminded her why Asian American studies *matters:* her parents, Charles and Ginko Schlund; and her twin brother, Charles Raymond Schlund. She is, as ever, grateful to her partner, Christopher Vials, who remains her best friend and colleague.

Scott is grateful to his parents and brothers, who have consistently supported his adventures in academia, as well as Carrie and Sarah, who always remind him what really matters in life. Finally, he is thankful for all of his mentors and friends in Asian American studies, especially Sucheng Chan, for making his path easier to travel through her caring friendship and pioneering work in the field.

Jason thanks his family for their encouragement, particularly his partner, Julie, for her unconditional support while they raise three children together. He also thanks coeditors Cathy and Scott for their generosity, patience, humor, and decisiveness.

Editors' Note

Asian America: A Primary Source Reader is an archival project intended to engender provocative and productive conversations about the many states of "Asian America," a formation on the one hand marked by intersectional histories of immigration and chronicles of conflict. On the other hand, the very legibility of Asian American studies as an interdisciplinary field, along with its enduring relevance in the present, is attributable to its particular relationship to student protest and the mid-twentieth-century activist movements, which stressed self-determination, communal definition, and rights recognition. Correspondingly, *Asian America: A Primary Source Reader* revises—by way of legal documents, legislative acts, political cartoons, newspaper accounts, racialized fictions, antiracist responses, foreign policy declarations, and activist manifestos—Oscar Handlin's 1951 assertion in *The Uprooted* that the history of the United States is the story of immigration. Whereas Handlin's foundational study problematically privileged unilateral migrations across the Atlantic from Europe, *Asian America: A Primary Source Reader* accesses a more expansive, hemispheric imaginary that takes seriously multiple migrations (from East Asia, South Asia, Southeast Asia, and Latin America due to economic circumstance, U.S. imperialism, and American war-making), recollects past and present exclusions (particularly with regard to naturalization restriction and immigration prohibition), and reconsiders the contradictory characterizations of Asian Americans (as "perpetual foreigners" and "model minorities").

Accordingly, the headings of the three sections in this anthology—"Immigration, Migration, and Citizenship"; "War and Imperialism"; and "Race, Rights, and Representation"—reflect these various historical, geographical, political, and cultural "sites" of Asian America. While we initially envisioned a chronological organization for the project that would take readers from eighteenth-century settlements of Filipinos in the Louisiana Territory to post–September 11th discrimination against South Asian Americans, we realized that this tactic potentially replicated a teleological narrative of Asian American history as a story of initial exclusion and eventual assimilation. Whereas we maintain this chronological approach in each of the sections, we encourage readers to consider the relationships between and among different racial, ethnic, classed, and gendered groups. We also urge readers to consider how questions of citizenship intersect with shifting and vexed notions of cultural, social, and political belonging. The excerpts (which have been standardized to ensure grammatical consistency) and working bibliographies included in this book are intended to provoke further scholarly explorations. Most significant, we have endeavored to make this an accessible, usable classroom text. In that exploratory vein, we want to underscore that this is by no means a comprehensive project but instead one intended to foster ongoing conversations about Asian American studies as a dynamic, relevant, and growing field.

Asian America

Asian American History

AN INTRODUCTION

K. Scott Wong, Cathy J. Schlund-Vials, and Jason Oliver Chang
(with Quan Tran)

Early Contexts: Asian Immigration to the United States

Long before scholars and journalists spoke in terms of "the Atlantic world," "the Pacific Rim," "transnationalism," or "globalization," people, goods, and ideas had circulated across national borders in the form of labor, capital, and ideologies that have shaped the contours of Asian American history. The documents and graphics selected for this collection of primary sources for the study of Asians in the Americas touch on themes that run throughout Asian American studies: immigration, migration, and citizenship; war and imperialism; race and civil rights; and representations and the construction of historical narratives, most of which are related to global rather than just national trends of the time periods in which they were created.

Much of Asian American history has been the record of immigration and exclusion. Even before Asians entered the young republic in recognizable numbers, they were denied the possibility of fully engaging in the U.S. political landscape because of the Naturalization Act of 1790, which granted the right of citizenship to only "free White persons." This situation would not fully change until 1952, with the McCarran-Walter Act, which did away with all racial restrictions to citizenship. In between these two landmark legal acts, Asian immigrants and their descendants were subjected to a series of immigration policies intended to deny Asians entrance into the country, based on their class, gender, or "race," as defined by the executive, legislative, and judicial branches of the U.S. government. Although Chinese began immigrating to the Americas in the largest numbers in the mid-nineteenth century, Filipinos were the first Asians to arrive in small numbers. They came to Mexico and areas that would become the American South (Louisiana) in the 1700s because of the Span-

[handwritten: Asians weve trading before the V.S.~Ustarted industrialization /civil.]

ish conquest of the Philippines and the subsequent Manila-Acapulco galleon trade. It is likely that both Filipino and Chinese crew members were among these early Asian pioneers in the "New World."[1] While the Spanish presence in the Pacific and the Caribbean certainly contributed to the European colonization of these areas, British and American imperialism and business concerns in Asia and the islands of the Pacific would have the greatest influence on the development of Asian American history.

Chinese immigrants first came to the United States in appreciable numbers in the mid-nineteenth century because of the California Gold Rush of the 1850s, but the British occupation of India substantially put the trans-Pacific diaspora in motion. From the beginning of British trade with China in the 1830s, the trade balance heavily favored the Chinese. The British went to China wanting a variety of goods (tea, spices, silks, and porcelain), but there was very little the British had to offer that the Chinese desired. Eventually, the British introduced opium grown in their Indian colony to China as a good for trade. The Chinese developed a taste for the drug that would lead to a shift in the trade balance to favor the British as well as the social decay that opium addiction brought to Chinese people of all social classes.

[handwritten: Beginning of the self-victation / Manipulation from the Western.]

In response, the Chinese tried to halt the opium trade by seizing a shipment of opium and setting it afire. The British took this as an act of war and sent their fleet to attack the Chinese navy, which proved no match for the British. The ensuing Treaty of Nanjing (1842) allowed for, among other concessions, more Chinese ports to be open to Western trade. This set the stage for both a greater Western presence in China and the means by which more Chinese could venture to the West. The ships that had increased access to Chinese ports for trade would soon become transport vessels that took Chinese laborers to the Americas in search of gold and the various occupational opportunities found in the American West. These same ships would facilitate the infamous "coolie trade" that took Chinese workers to the Caribbean (Cuba) and Latin America (specifically Peru). In addition, American sugar cane interests and Christian missionaries would soon establish a foothold in Hawai'i, leading to a permanent U.S. colony in the once independent island kingdom (and later, statehood).

Soon after Chinese labor migration to Hawai'i and the American mainland increased and U.S. trade with China became more profitable, Americans broke through Japan's isolationist policy via Commodore Matthew

Perry's 1852–1854 missions to the country. Then as Japan began a program of modernization in the late nineteenth century, Japanese laborers began going to Hawai'i and the United States to seek their fortunes. In addition, Koreans were recruited to work in Hawai'i by American sugar cane plantation owners. Once Japan took full control of Korea (1905,) however, Korean emigration came to a halt because the Japanese did not want Korean workers to compete with Japanese laborers abroad; they wanted Koreans to stay in Korea to work for their Japanese overlords. While the British were engaged in the China trade, they continued their rule of the Indian subcontinent. By the early twentieth century, the British had transformed the cotton-growing area of the Punjab into a commercial agricultural enterprise in which the vast majority of the cotton grown in that area was sent to the mills in England to be processed and manufactured into cloth, thus removing the Indians from that aspect of cotton cloth production and thereby producing a surplus of labor. In response, a large number of men from the Punjab, mainly Sikhs, immigrated to Canada as moving from one part of the British empire to another was easier than trying to enter another country, such as the United States.

Following on the heels of British, American, and Japanese imperialism and their profound effect on Chinese, Japanese, Korean, and Indian emigration to the Americas were the Filipinos—the final group of Asian immigrants to come to the Americas in large numbers before the Second World War. Their emigration history was rooted in the overlapping effects of Spanish and American imperialism. The Spanish began to colonize the archipelago in 1521 with the arrival of Ferdinand Magellan and called this island chain "the Philippine Islands" in honor of King Philip II in 1543. By the late nineteenth century, the people of both the Philippines and Cuba began to resist Spanish colonial rule, and open rebellion broke out. The United States supported the rebels' cause in Cuba and entered the Spanish-American War in 1898. Determined to break Spanish rule in both the Caribbean and the Pacific, the United States opened a two-front war against the Spanish that led to Cuban independence and the U.S. annexation of Puerto Rico, Guam, and the Philippines. However, the Filipino insurgency against the Spanish did not accept U.S. rule, and from 1899 to 1902, the Philippine-American War raged until the Americans finally subdued the resistance. At that point, Filipinos, now American "nationals," were recruited to work in Hawai'i and the U.S. mainland mainly as agricultural workers.

Exclusion, Prohibition, and Discrimination in the Americas

Although actively recruited to work in Hawai'i and the United States, Asian workers encountered strong opposition from American labor, politicians, and the general population. The American hostility to Asian immigrants was rooted in three simultaneous and overlapping issues: race, culture, and economics. Before Asian immigration to the United States, few laws prohibited any specific peoples from entering the country. The Page Act of 1875, however, targeted contract laborers from "China, Japan, or any Oriental country," and anyone, presumably women, who was coming for "lewd and immoral purposes." This act would set the stage for the Chinese Exclusion Act of 1882, which forbade the immigration of Chinese laborers for a period of ten years, barred them from becoming naturalized citizens, and prohibited those already in the United States from bringing their families. Yet, certain groups of Chinese were allowed to enter, including their families. The most important of these "exempt classes" were merchants, who eventually became elites within Chinese American urban communities. These exclusion acts would be renewed a number of times, often becoming more strict or greater in geographical scope. Such prohibitions were by no means limited to the United States; indeed, the Canadian and Mexican governments would, in the ensuing decades, also restrict Asian immigrants.

Nevertheless, and most important, the passage of the Chinese Exclusion Act signaled a fundamental change in the nature of U.S. immigration policy. By targeting a group of aspiring immigrants for exclusion on the basis of their country of origin and socioeconomic status, the United States—for the first time in its history—was "transformed from a nation of immigrants into a gatekeeping nation."[2] By prohibiting many Chinese from immigrating to the United States and by limiting their families' entrance as well, U.S. immigration officials were able to control the size of the Chinese immigrant population and slow down their reproductive rate for more than a generation, ensuring that the political power of the Chinese American community would develop more slowly than that of other immigrant and ethnic groups in this country.

Once the exclusion of Chinese workers was in place, restrictions against other Asian immigrants soon followed. In 1907, the Gentlemen's Agreement was reached between the United States and Japan. Japan agreed to no longer issue passports to its laborers who wanted to go to the United States. Because the U.S. government recognized Korea as a protectorate of

Japan, Koreans fell under the same legal restrictions as Japanese. Within a decade, the Barred Zone Act (1917) was passed, prohibiting immigration from a broad geographical swath of Asia and the Pacific, most notably the Indian subcontinent. Furthermore, by the early 1920s, the fate of Asian immigrants applying for U.S. citizenship was sealed. Two cases that reached the Supreme Court would legally (though ambiguously) codify the meaning of "whiteness" and "race" and effectively create an "oriental race" based on geographical origin and skin color. In 1922, the Supreme Court heard a case in which Takao Ozawa, a Japanese immigrant, petitioned for citizenship on the basis of his "light complexion," thus allowing him to qualify as "white." The court, however, ruled that "white" was synonymous with being "of the Caucasian race," a qualification that did not apply to Ozawa. In the following year, the United States sought to bar Bhagat Singh Thind from citizenship despite his claim that Indians were "Aryan," hence "Caucasian." The court ruled against him, stating that although such terms were unstable and open to various interpretations, the "the average man" could easily see that Thind was not "white." By defining "whiteness" in terms of both "race" and skin color, the Supreme Court set Asians outside the realm of those eligible for U.S. citizenship.

The exclusion acts that prohibited Chinese immigrants from coming to the United States, and the prohibitions with regard to naturalized citizenship in the Ozawa and Thind decisions, set the precedents and parameters for the Johnson-Reed Immigration Act of 1924. This piece of legislation set annual quotas for immigrants from all countries based on 2 percent of their population in the United States as of the 1890 census; it also barred anyone ineligible for U.S. citizenship from immigrating. In a time of increasing nativism, this act severely curtailed the immigration of Asians, and those from Eastern and Southern Europe, many of whom were Jewish or Catholic. This most restrictive immigration act in U.S. history had a particularly tragic connection to the Holocaust: as David S. Wyman provocatively reminds, the 1924 Johnson-Reed Act was used as a way to deny entry to European Jews seeking asylum in the United States during World War II.[3]

Because Filipinos were U.S. nationals, they could not be excluded from immigrating in the same way other Asians were. Nevertheless, during the Great Depression, when Filipinos were competing with poor whites for agricultural jobs in California and other western states, Congress passed the Tydings-McDuffie Act (1934). This act stated that the Philippines would be granted independence in ten years, but in the meantime, Filipino immigration would be cut to fifty people a year. However, the Philippines would not gain independence until after the Second World War, and its immigration quota would then be subject to the limitations of the Johnson-Reed Immigration Act of 1924.

For those Asian immigrants who were able to enter the United States, legally or otherwise, many faced a steady barrage of anti-Asian violence, discriminatory state and local legislation, racist rhetoric, and graphic propaganda. Again, because of their earlier arrival, the Chinese bore the brunt of the early anti-Asian sentiments and actions. Chinese gold miners were driven from the goldfields, subject to the Foreign Miners' Tax, and faced mass violence in race riots in Los Angeles (1871) and Rock Springs, Wyoming (1885). Japanese immigrants and Filipinos would also encounter violence on the West Coast, usually because they were seen as a threat to white labor, as would Sikh workers in Canada and the Pacific Northwest. Coupled with the violence were laws that prevented Asians from testifying in court for or against whites, school segregation, and the denial of certain jobs.

Rhetorical and visual propaganda about Asians took on various forms, such as equating Chinese with rats and questioning the masculinity of Chinese men. In an advertisement for rat poison (included in this book), one can see two common anti-Chinese tropes at work. A stereotypical Chinese man holds a rat as if about to eat it, with the phrase "They Must Go" above him—an obvious reference to the anti-Chinese slogan "The Chinese Must Go!" used extensively by the anti-Chinese activist Denis Kearney. In 1902, the American Federation of Labor published a pamphlet urging Congress to extend the Chinese Exclusion Act with the title *Some Reasons for Chinese Exclusion: Meat vs. Rice. American Manhood against Asiatic Coolieism. Which Shall Survive?* This title encapsulates much of the sentiment embedded in the anti-Asian movement. Accordingly, the American diet, masculinity, and culture were all "at risk" because of the presence of Asian workers in the United States.

Treacherous Subjects and Shifting Allegiances: The Second World War

Nothing, however, would cast Asian America into a state of flux like World War II. With the entrance of the United States into the war after the Japanese attack on Pearl Harbor, American anti-Japanese attitudes reached its zenith, and Chinese Americans would become the "good Asian in the good war." Within weeks after Pearl Harbor, *Life* and *Time* magazines, both owned by Henry Luce, the son of missionaries who spent their careers in China, published short pictorial spreads that aimed to help Americans differentiate between Chinese and Japanese. Titled "How to Tell Japs from the Chinese" and "How to Tell Your Friends from the Japs," these articles cast Japanese—and by extension, Japanese Americans—as the enemy, while the previously reviled Chinese were now "friends." Although these pieces did very little to present any real differences between Japanese and Chinese, they contributed to the hatred directed at Japan and people of Japanese descent and the eventual rehabilitation of the Chinese. Despite the Munson Report (1941), which generally dismissed any anti-American sentiment among Japanese Americans, the war would soon bring about the mass incarceration of the Japanese and Japanese American population (more than 110,000, 70,000 of whom were U.S. citizens) in a string of camps ranging from California to Arkansas, from Texas to North Dakota. Such forced relocations and incarcerations were not limited to the United States; people of Japanese descent in Canada and Latin America (particularly Peru) were also subjected to wartime racial profiling and imprisonment. Throughout the war, Japanese Americans would have to prove their loyalty to the United States, denounce their supposed allegiance to Japan, and effectively lose everything for which they had worked so hard to claim their place in American society.

By contrast, the status of Chinese Americans rose during the war. Because the United States and China were allies against the Axis Powers, there was enough support in Congress for passage of the Magnuson Act (1943), which repealed the Chinese Exclusion Acts and allowed Chinese immigrants to apply for U.S. citizenship. Moreover, the War Brides Act of 1945 allowed either Chinese wives of Chinese immigrants to finally join their husbands in the United States or Chinese American men to go to China to marry. These legislative changes fostered a demographic shift within the Chinese American community as more women and families entered the country, giving Chinese Americans the opportunity to give birth to a belated second generation. The end of the war also brought about the independence of the Philippines and later India; immigrants from these two countries could also become U.S. citizens.

Postwar Legacies and the Cold War

The 1950s continued, to varying degrees and divergent ends, the "opening up" of citizenship to Asian immigrants and the growth of Asian America. Specifically, in 1952, the McCarran-Walter Act did away with racial restrictions to citizenship, giving Japanese and Korean immigrants the chance to finally become citizens. Nevertheless, this act was guided by the restrictive logic of the Cold War, which sought to "contain" threats within and abroad: indeed, the McCarran-Walter Act carried provisions for the exclusion or deportation of people considered subversive, Communist, or homosexual.[4] Despite ostensible citizenship gains, this first decade of the Cold War would prove an unsettling time for many Asian Americans. For example, with the 1949 Communist victory in China, U.S. authorities often saw Chinese American communities as having Communist leanings, and surveillance of Chinatowns increased. Knowing what had happened to Japanese Americans during the Second World War, many Chinese Americans downplayed any sympathies and affinities they may have had with the People's Republic of China. Still reeling from their years of incarceration during the war, Japanese Americans sought to recoup some of the losses they suffered during the conflict and quietly rebuild their lives.

To fully comprehend the ways in which conflicts abroad affected experiences at home, it is important to consider this period through a global lens of decolonization, which dictated the course of U.S. domestic and foreign policies. In particular, the dismantling of the Japanese empire in September 1945 and the withdrawals of various European colonial powers from Asian regions throughout the 1950s prompted new state formations in Asia. Many Asian countries' bids for national independence involved armed conflicts as internal and external power struggles ensued. Emergent Cold War geopolitics—which pitted Communism against democracy and involved China, the Soviet Union, and the United States—further affected these in-country conflicts and national struggles. For example, in 1945 the Allied Powers temporarily divided the Korean peninsula into two occupation zones at the 38th parallel: Soviet troops dominated the northern zone, and U.S. military forces assumed control of the southern zone. In June 1950, assisted by Communist China and the Soviet Union, North Korea invaded South Korea, which the United States and other members of the United Nations defended. The Korean War ended in July 1953 with an armistice that left the peninsula divided into two Koreas (North and South).

In French Indochina, the First Indochina War erupted in 1946 when Viet Minh forces (backed by China and the Soviet Union) confronted the returning French colonial power and Emperor Bao Dai's Vietnamese National Army (supported by the United Kingdom and the United States) to gain control of the country. The war ended in May 1954 with the Viet Minh's victory over the French in the Battle of Dien Bien Phu. The Geneva Accords that followed temporarily divided Vietnam into two zones at the 17th parallel pending a general election for reunification, which never occurred. After successful internal purges, the Communist faction of the Viet Minh led by Ho Chi Minh overtook the northern zone and formed the Democratic Republic of Vietnam. At the same time, the southern part became the Republic of Vietnam under a nationalist government headed by Emperor Bao Dai. The war also affected neighboring Cambodia and Laos, as both were French protectorates. Under the respective leaderships of Norodom Sihanouk and Sisavang Vong, the Kingdom of Cambodia and the Kingdom of Laos gained independence from France in 1953. Cambodian and Laotian national independence struggles were also embroiled in civil conflicts as internal nationalist and Communist forces vied for power under the influences of external Cold War geopolitics. These events ushered in a new era of U.S. intervention in Asian affairs, reflecting not only the military and political interests of the United States in the region, but also U.S. long-term imperialist ambitions.

By the early 1960s, the United States was already embroiled in the Vietnam War (the Second Indochina War) via military and economic aids and other diplomatic measures. U.S. intervention in this war anticipated the so-called domino effect, which, in the context of ongoing Cold War geopolitics, posited that if one country in a region came under the influence of Communism, then nearby countries would follow suit. Spanning the administrations of John F. Kennedy, Lyndon Johnson, and Richard Nixon, the U.S. involvement in the Vietnam War included the U.S. deploying substantial troops in South Vietnam after signing military and economic aid treaties with the governments of Ngo Dinh Diem and subsequent South Vietnamese leaders. Between 1961 and 1969, the number of U.S. troops sent to South Vietnam increased annually, peaking at nearly 540,000 in 1968.[5] Other allied countries, including Australia, South Korea, New Zealand, Thailand, and the Philippines, also sent soldiers to South Vietnam in support of the U.S. and South Vietnamese armies. Meanwhile, the Soviet Union and other Communist countries aided North Vietnam with arms, troops, and economic assistance.

The Vietnam War profoundly polarized U.S. public opinion at home. While some viewed U.S. intervention as a necessity against the expansion of the Soviet Union and Communism, others perceived the war as a racist one that advanced U.S. imperialist agendas at the cost of nonwhite lives. Still others condemned it as a costly mistake that wasted U.S. lives and resources. The antiwar movement in the United States gained momentum, especially in the wake of notable events such as the successful, albeit brief, Tet Offensive launched by Viet Cong troops in January 1968. The surprise attack on several dozen South Vietnamese–controlled regions convinced many Americans that despite its military superiority, the United States could not win the war. Then in November 1968, the brutal mass murder of three hundred to five hundred Vietnamese civilians—mostly unarmed women and children—by U.S. soldiers at My Lai was made public, further inciting even stronger antiwar sentiments both nationally and internationally. The My Lai Massacre also drew attention to other atrocities committed by U.S. troops in Vietnam as well as the human costs and devastating destruction of the war. In the United States, resentment against the war intensified with the introduction of the draft in 1969 to increase U.S. military manpower. The subsequent expansions of the war into Cambodia and Laos also escalated antiwar points of view. Americans who opposed the war were racially, ethnically, socioeconomically, and geographically diverse. They opposed U.S. intervention in the war on moral, legal, political, and pragmatic grounds.

For Asian Americans in particular, the racialized dimension of the Vietnam War was especially disconcerting and transformative. Often lumped together with the "enemy," whose images appeared daily on television news, Asian Americans witnessed and endured blatant racism both at home and abroad. For example, regardless of their ethnicities, enlisted Asian American soldiers (both those who volunteered and those who were drafted) were indiscriminately called "Gooks," "Japs," and "Chinks" during their training and deployment. Worse, because of their physical features, many were singled out by their commanding officers as examples of what the "enemy" looked like and witnessed their own dehumanization in the making. At home, having witnessed the indiscriminant violence inflicted on the Vietnamese people that played out on their televisions, many Asian Americans empathized with their "Asian brothers and sisters" and pointed out the racist nature of the war.[6] As some scholars have noted, the race question set Asian American antiwar protesters apart from mainstream antiwar protesters.[7]

The Civil Rights Movement, Yellow Power, and the Rise of Asian American Studies

Post–World War II domestic developments also heavily shaped the contours of Asian America in the 1960s and 1970s. While the postwar prosperity of the 1950s boosted national morale and offered new opportunities for many Americans, wide-ranging social issues and economic disparities continued, especially for racial minorities across the country. The de jure and de facto discrimination and segregation of the Jim Crow era and widespread racial violence and injustice remained, galvanizing the civil rights movement. Led by African American activists and their allies, this social movement resulted in transformative local and national legal victories such as school desegregation and passage of the Civil Rights Acts of 1964, the Voting Rights Acts of 1965, and the Fair Housing Acts of 1968. Amid these developments, Asian Americans continued to struggle for visibility, equality, equity, and social justice despite the gradual liberalization of discriminatory immigration laws, antimiscegenation laws, land laws, and citizenship and naturalization laws. The civil rights movement thus struck a particular chord with many U.S.-born Asian Americans who, through their own personal and historical experiences of oppression and discrimination, saw their fates entwined with the struggles of other people of color in the United States.

The participation of Asian American activists such as Yuri Kochiyama, Grace Lee Boggs, and others in emerging black revolutionary organizations exemplified this sense of interracial solidarity — as did other multiracial social, political, and labor coalitions formed during this period in various parts of the United States, including the Asian Coalition for Equality in Washington state and the United Farm Workers in California. A notable number of Asian American activists were Japanese Americans who had experienced the injustices of World War II internment and incarceration, but Chinese American, Filipino American, Korean American, and South Asian activists were also at the forefront of the civil rights struggles.

As these groups coalesced, especially on college campuses across the country, they radicalized a young generation of Asian Americans who connected their fates not only with other racialized minorities in the United States, but also with people of color abroad. Besides having a sense of affinity with African Americans, Chicano Americans, and Native Americans, this generation of students was inspired by revolutions for independence and self-determination throughout the so-called Third World. Aware of their own oppression in the United States and grasping the inherent contradictions in the U.S. government's domestic and foreign policies, they especially viewed the U.S. military as the aggressor in the Vietnam War and supported the Vietnamese self-determination and anti-imperialist causes. Their growing sense of self-awareness, their practice of solidarity, and their radical outlook fueled unprecedented coalition-building efforts with African Americans, Chicano Americans, and Native Americans, resulting in proactive student organizations such as the Third World Liberation Front on college campuses in California, such as San Francisco State College and the University of California–Berkeley. Between 1968 and 1969, Third World Liberation Front members held sit-ins and strikes at their campuses to demand reforms in university curricula, minority admissions, and staff to reflect the needs of students of color, whose presence on college campuses had increased notably after World War II. These strikes resulted in the creation of ethnic studies programs, including Asian American studies, and inspired similar efforts at college campuses nationwide.

Asian American activism during the 1960s and 1970s not only contributed to significant social transformations in the United States and raised Asian American consciousness, but also challenged old and new stereotypes of Asian Americans imposed by mainstream society. Whereas American popular culture of the nineteenth and early twentieth centuries had depicted Asian Americans as perpetual foreigners and a "yellow peril" that threatened to destroy Western civilization, the stereotypical repertoire of the late twentieth century honed in on the "model minority" myth that differentiated Asian Americans from other racial minorities. This myth emerged in a post–World War II midcentury context and privileged Asian Americans as an ideal racial group. The myth praised Asian Americans as quiet, passive, hardworking, and law-abiding citizens whose respect for authority and strong family and cultural values intrinsically set them up for success in American society despite a long history of discrimination and social injustice in the United States. In this way, the model minority myth elevated Asian Americans as prime examples of successful integration into American society. Nonetheless, during the 1960s and 1970s the fallacies of this myth were exposed through continued organized and spontaneous public protests by Asian American activists and grassroots coalition-building efforts on college campuses and in communities against local and national forms of institutionalized racism and structural discrimination.

The Making of New Americans: Refugee Policy and Immigrant Acts

Meanwhile, postwar Asian migration to the United States was influenced by expanding U.S. military bases and troops in Japan, Korea, the Philippines, Thailand, and the Pacific Islands throughout the 1950s, and later in Vietnam during the 1960s and 1970s, as well as U.S. economic and cultural diplomacy abroad. Although relatively small in number, Asian-born spouses of U.S. military personnel moved to the United States, as well as refugees under the provisions of the War Brides Act (1945–1948), the Displaced Persons Acts (1948 and 1950), the McCarran-Walter Act (1952), and the Refugee Relief Act of 1953. Through such movements, the Asian American population in the United States diversified during this period. The gradual liberalization of immigration law culminated in the landmark Immigration and Nationality Act of 1965, also known as the Hart-Celler Act, which significantly reshaped the demographics and dynamics of Asian America during the 1960s and 1970s.

Eliminating the quota system as well as the immigration criteria of national origin, race, and ancestry, the Hart-Celler Act opened the gate for immigrants (especially skilled workers) from both East Asia and South Asia. Moreover, the family reunification provision of the 1965 act also enabled a robust era of chain migrations from Asia. Mirroring the domestic postwar "baby boom" of the 1950s, the immigration boom of the 1960s and 1970s increased the population of foreign-born and U.S.-born Asian Americans multifold. According to U.S. census data, the number of Asian Americans and Pacific Islanders increased from 321,033 in 1950 to 980,337 in 1960 and to 1,538,721 in 1970.[8] The majority of this population comprised urban and suburban dwellers, with large concentrations in the metropolitan areas of the mainland U.S. states and in Hawai'i.

Asian America experienced another population surge with the passage of the Indochina Migration and Refugee Assistance Act in May 1975. The Vietnam War had concluded in April 1975 with the victories of the Communist forces of Laos, Cambodia, and North Vietnam over the U.S.-backed nationalist governments of those countries. The end of the war produced a wave of people who fled Indochina and sought refuge primarily in the United States. Most of these individuals had been evacuated by the U.S. military at various points and taken by plane and by ship to U.S. military bases in Guam, Wake Island, and Clark Air Base in the Philippines, though a notable number also fled on their own at the end of the war. The Indochina Migration and Refugee Assistance Act and its amendments subsequently facilitated the migration of approximately 130,000 of these refugees to the United States. Arriving as recognized refugees, these people received financial assistance as well as health, employment, and education services. To ease the stress on local governments, they were initially processed on military bases in California, Florida, Arkansas, and Pennsylvania before being dispersed to various parts of the country.

The late 1970s and well into the 1980s saw another wave of Southeast Asian refugees entering the United States as postwar socialism developed in Indochina, creating multiple social, economic, and political instabilities. Earlier resettlements of Southeast Asian refugees in the United States paved the way for additional ethnic Vietnamese, ethnic Chinese, Hmong, Laotians, and Cambodians, reinforcing the fledging ethnic communities that were forming across the country. The newcomers thus helped to diversify Asian American demographics in terms of socioeconomic composition and the political and cultural landscapes. For instance, given the circumstances of their migration, many Southeast Asian refugees harbor strong anti-Communist sentiments, a political stance that often sets them apart from other Asian Americans, especially those born in the United States, who tend to align with more progressive politics. Asian American landscapes also changed with the establishment and gradual growth of ethnic enclaves, often called "Little Saigons" or "Little Phnom Penhs," in areas with large concentrations of ethnic Vietnamese and Khmer populations, such as Southern California.

From the Cold War to the War on Terror: Contemporary Asian America

Although the 1960s and 1970s were marked by profound shifts with regard to civil rights, the 1980s witnessed a return to conservatism, initially marked by the election of Ronald Reagan as president of the United States. A Hollywood actor-turned-politician, Reagan had previously served as the governor of California (in fact, Reagan's first term as governor coincided with the Third World Liberation Front strikes that led to the founding of Asian American studies as a distinct academic field). During the Reagan administration (1981–1988), gains made during the civil rights movement—particularly with regard to affirmative action and the formation of social welfare programs—were to varying degrees dismantled and defunded. Such austerity-driven domestic agendas intersected with a shift in economic policy toward neoliberalism and wholesale free market principles.

Moreover, as Japan emerged as a viable economic power via its strengths in the automotive and technology industries, and as the manufacturing sector of the U.S. economy shrank dramatically because of global outsourcing, displaced American workers often focused their anxieties and anger upon Asian immigrants and Asian Americans. Such economically driven anti-Asian sentiments were at the forefront of the 1982 brutal beating of Chinese American Vincent Chin at the hands of two unemployed white autoworkers in Detroit, Michigan, who thought the engineer was Japanese. Chin died of his injuries, and the two autoworkers—Ronald Ebens and Michael Nitz—though originally charged with second-degree murder, were found guilty only of manslaughter and were sentenced to three years of probation. This perceived light sentence had a profound effect on Asian Americans, many of whom, along with Chin's mother Lily, rallied for justice on the basis that Ebens and Nitz had committed a hate crime.

In 1988, Congress passed the Civil Liberties Act, a federal law that granted reparations to Japanese Americans who had been forcibly incarcerated during the Second World War. The law was the culmination of more than two decades of activist work and gave surviving internees a onetime reparation payment of $20,000. This would be the most lasting legacy of Reagan's administration regarding Asian Americans. A year later, in 1989, the Berlin Wall fell, signaling the beginning of the demise of the Cold War (its end would be further substantiated by the dissolution of the Soviet Union in 1991). But the United States was by no means a peacetime nation for long; in August 1990, President George H. W. Bush sent U.S. military troops to Kuwait for Operation Desert Shield; this Persian Gulf War came to a quick conclusion in early 1991. In 1992, during the administration of George H. W. Bush, Korean shopkeepers and Korean Americans were disproportionately targeted by rioters in Los Angeles following the acquittal of four white police officers who had been videotaped violently beating Rodney King, a black man. This would serve as a vexed hallmark of President Bush's presidency.

The 1965 Hart-Celler Act—along with the 1975 Indochina Migration and Refugee Assistance Act and the 1980 Refugee Act—dramatically affected the demographic diversity of immigrants and the nation—particularly with regard to Asians. According to U.S. sociologist Pyong Gap Min, between 1965 and 2002, 8.4 million Asian immigrants became permanent residents, a number that represents 34 percent of total immigrants. As a comparison, between 1901 and 1920, only 4 percent of immigrants came from Asia, with 88 percent coming from Europe and 3 percent from Latin America. Between 1980 and 1993, 39 percent of immigrants came from Asia, 43 percent from Latin America and the Caribbean, and only 13 percent hailed from Europe.[9] It can be seen that at the turn of the twenty-first century, former ethnic affiliations had been profoundly overturned.

More recently, a 2012 Pew Research Survey shows that Asian immigrants to the United States are now outpacing their Latin American and Central American counterparts.[10] Indeed, East Asian, South Asian, and Southeast Asian immigrants and refugees have emerged as the fastest-growing immigrant population in the United States. According to U.S. census data, since the 1970s, an estimated forty-eight million immigrants (documented and undocumented) have come to the United States and are currently responsible for the majority of the nation's population growth.[11] Many recent Asian immigrant arrivals, particularly those from South Asia, were recruited by U.S. technology companies and came to the country under the H-1B visa program, which helps employers hire "nonimmigrant aliens" as workers in "specialty occupations."[12]

Yet, the rise in Asian immigration and the growth of Asian America does not necessarily translate into a wholesale acceptance of such individuals within the larger U.S. body politic. The model minority myth continues to have currency, as evidenced in recent antiaffirmative action debates; and the characterization of Asian Americans as perpetual foreigners has gained more popularity in a contemporary imaginary marked by "war on terror" politics. Since the terrorist attacks of September 11, 2001, individuals of South Asian and Arab descent have been profiled, targeted, and discriminated against; such experiences have further been influenced by the Iraq War (2003–2011) and the War in Afghanistan (2001–2014). The rise in deportations following the 9/11 attacks has increasingly involved Southeast Asian refugees, many of whom were children when they migrated and thus have no familiarity with their so-called countries of origin (for instance, Cambodia, Laos, and Vietnam).

The recent state of Asian American affairs speaks to the complexity of Asian America as an entity composed of multiple communities and histories that at times intersect with and at other times diverge from past experiences with exclusion, prohibition, accommodation, and assimilation. Despite these historical differences, Asian Americans have endured war, violence, relocation, incarceration, and legal exclusion to become the nation's fastest growing nonwhite minority. Building on these years of marginalization, Asian Americans will no doubt continue to be an important voice in the cultural, social, and political evolution of American society.

Notes

1. Shelley Sang-Hee Lee, *A New History of Asian America* (New York: Routledge, 2014), 52.

2. Erika Lee, *At America's Gates: Chinese Immigration During the Exclusion Era, 1882–1943* (Chapel Hill: University of North Carolina Press, 2003), 18.

3. David S. Wyman, *The Abandonment of the Jews: America and the Holocaust, 1941–1945* (New York: Pantheon, 1984).

4. Bill Ong Hing, *Defining America Through Immigration Policy* (Philadelphia: Temple University Press, 2004), 73–92.

5. The American War Library, "Vietnam War Allied Troop Levels 1960–73," http://www.americanwarlibrary.com/vietnam/vwatl.htm.

6. Yen Le Espiritu, *Asian American Panethnicity: Bridging Institutions and Identities* (Philadelphia: Temple University Press, 1992), 44.

7. Ibid.

8. Campbell Gibson and Kay Jun, "Historical Census Statistics on Population Totals by Race, 1790 and 1990, and by Hispanic Origin, 1970 to 1990, for the United States, Regions, Divisions, and States," Working Paper No. 56 (U.S. Census Bureau), Internet Release Date: September 2002.

9. Center for Immigration Studies, "Three Decades of Mass Immigration: The Legacy of the 1965 Immigration Act," section titled "Change in Source Countries of Immigrants," http://cis.org/1965ImmigrationAct-MassImmigration.

10. Pew Research Center, "The Rise of Asian Americans," http://www.pewsocialtrends.org/asianamericans/.

11. Campbell Gibson and Kay Jun, "Historical Census Statistics on Population Totals by Race, 1790 and 1990, and by Hispanic Origin, 1970 to 1990, for the United States, Regions, Divisions, and States," Working Paper No. 56 (U.S. Census Bureau), Internet Release Date: September 2002.

12. U.S. Department of Labor, Wage and Hour Division (WHD), "H-1B Program," http://www.dol.gov/whd/immigration/h1b.htm.

PART I

Immigration, Migration, and Citizenship

The Naturalization Act of 1790

Naturalization is a legal process by which individuals not born in the United States obtain U.S. citizenship. The first federal naturalization law, excerpted here, was passed on March 26, 1790. The original law was limited to those who fulfilled the requirement of being a "free white person" and excluded those who fell outside this categorization—for instance, Native Americans, indentured servants, free African Americans, slaves, Asians, and people from Latin America. The racial requirement for naturalized citizenship was amended in 1870 to include those "free white persons" and individuals of "African descent." However, Asian immigrants, who fell between these two racial poles (as being neither white nor black) were deemed "aliens ineligible for citizenship" in a series of Supreme Court cases (Ah Yup, Ozawa, and Thind). Racial restrictions for naturalized citizenship would remain until the passage of the McCarran-Walter Act in 1952. (The Naturalization Act of 1790 [An Act to Establish an Uniform Rule of Naturalization]. Chap. 3; 1 Stat 103. 26 Mar. 1790.)

Section 1. *Be it enacted by the Senate and House of Representatives of the United States of America in Congress assembled,* That any alien, being a free white person, who shall have resided within the limits and under the jurisdiction of the United States for the term of two years, may be admitted to become a citizen thereof, on application to any common law court of record in any one of the states wherein he shall have resided for the term of one year at least, and making proof to the satisfaction of such court, that he is a person of good character, and taking the oath or affirmation prescribed by law, to support the Constitution of the United States, which oath or affirmation such court shall administer; and the clerk of such court shall record such application, and the proceedings thereon; and thereupon such person shall be considered as a citizen of the United States. And the children of such persons so naturalized, dwelling within the United States, being under the age of twenty-one years at the time of such naturalization, shall also be considered as citizens of the United States. And the children of citizens of the United States, that may be born beyond sea, or out of the limits of the United States, shall be considered as natural born citizens: *Provided,* That the right of citizenship shall not descend to persons whose fathers have never been resident in the United States: *Provided also,* That no person heretofore proscribed by any state, shall be admitted a citizen as aforesaid, except by an act of the legislature of the state in which such person was proscribed.

Approved, March 26, 1790.

Saint Malo

A LACUSTRINE VILLAGE IN LOUISIANA

Patrick Lafcadio Hearn

Patrick Lafcadio Hearn (1850–1904) was a writer most known for his works on Japan (which included collections of Japanese myths, legends, and ghost stories). Between 1877 and 1887, Hearn (also known as Koizumi Yakumo) lived in New Orleans and wrote a series of stories focused on the people he encountered in the region. "Saint Malo" details a small fishing village in St. Bernard Parish, Louisiana, the first settlement for Filipinos in the United States. The settlement was originally founded in the mid-eighteenth century; a hurricane destroyed it in 1915. (Originally published in Harper's Weekly, *31 Mar. 1883: 198–99.)*

For nearly fifty years there has existed in the southeastern swamp lands of Louisiana a certain strange settlement of Malay fishermen—Tagalas from the Philippine Islands. The place of their lacustrine village is not precisely mentioned upon maps, and the world, in general, ignored until a few days ago the bare fact of their amphibious existence. Even the United States mail service has never found its way thither, and even in the great city of New Orleans, less than a hundred miles distant, the people were far better informed about the Carboniferous Era than concerning the swampy affairs of this Manila village. Occasionally vague echoes of its mysterious life were borne to the civilized center, but these were scarcely of a character to tempt investigation or encourage belief. Some voluble Italian luggermen once came to town with a short cargo of oysters, and a long story regarding a ghastly "Chinese" colony in the reedy swamps south of Lake Borgne. For many years the inhabitants of the Oriental settlement had lived in peace and harmony without the presence of a single woman, but finally had managed to import an oblique-eyed beauty from beyond the Yellow Sea. Thereupon arose the first dissensions, provoking much shedding of blood. And at last the elders of the people had restored calm and fraternal feeling by sentencing the woman to be hewn in pieces and flung to the alligators of the bayou.

Possible the story is; probable it is not. Partly for the purpose of investigating it, but principally in order to offer *Harper's* artist a totally novel subject of artistic study, the *Times-Democrat* of New Orleans chartered and fitted out an Italian lugger for a trip to the unexplored region in question—to the fishing station of Saint Malo. And a strange voyage it was. Even the Italian sailors knew not whither they were going, none of them had ever beheld the Manila village, or were aware of its location.

Starting from Spanish Fort northeastwardly across Lake Pontchartrain, after the first few miles sailed, one already observes a change in the vegetation of the receding banks. The shore itself sinks, the lowland bristles with rushes and marsh grasses waving in the wind. A little further on and the water becomes deeply clouded with sap green—the myriad floating seeds of swamp vegetation. Banks dwindle away into thin lines; the greenish-yellow of the reeds changes into misty blue. Then it is all water and sky, motionless blue and heaving lazulite, until the reedy waste of Point-aux-Herbes thrusts its picturesque lighthouse far out into the lake. Above the wilderness of swamp grass and bulrushes this graceful building rises upon an open-work of wooden piles. Seven miles of absolute desolation separate the lighthouse keeper from his nearest neighbor. Nevertheless, there is a good piano there for the girls to play upon, comfortably furnished rooms, a good library. The pet cat has lost an eye in fighting with a moccasin, and it is prudent before descending from the balcony into the swamp about the house to reconnoiter for snakes. Still northeast. The sun is sinking above the rushy bank line; the west is crimsoning like iron losing its white heat. Against the ruddy light a cross is visible. There is a cemetery in the swamp. Those are the forgotten graves of lighthouse keepers. Our boat is spreading her pinions for flight through the Rigolets, that sinuous waterway leading to Lake Borgne. We pass by the defenseless walls of Fort Pike, a stronghold without a history, picturesque enough, but almost worthless against modern artillery. There is a solitary sergeant in charge, and a dog. Perhaps the taciturnity of the man is due to his long solitude, the vast silence of the land weighing down upon him. At last appears the twinkling light of the United States custom-house, and the enormous skeleton of the Rigolets Bridge. The custom-house rises on stilts out of the sedge-grass. The pretty daughter of the inspector can manage a skiff as well as most expert oarsmen. Here let us listen a while in the moonless night. From the south a deep sound is steadily rolling up, like the surging of a thousand waves, like the long roaring of breakers. But the huge blind lake is scarcely agitated; the distant glare of a prairie fire illuminates no spurring of "white horses." What, then, is that roar, as of thunder muffled by distance, as of the moaning that seamen hear far inland while dreaming at home of phantom seas? It is only a mighty chorus of frogs, innumerable millions of frogs, chanting in the darkness over unnumbered leagues of swamp and lagoon.

On the eastern side of the Rigolets [bridge] Lake Borgne has scalloped out its grass-fringed bed in the form of a gigantic clover leaf—a shallow and treacherous sea, from which all fishing-vessels scurry in wild terror when a storm begins to darken. No lugger can live in those short chopping waves when Gulf winds are mad. To reach the Manila settlement one must steer due south until the waving bulrushes again appear, this time behind muddy shoals of immense breadth. The chart announces depths varying from six inches to three and a half feet. For a while we grope about blindly along the banks. Suddenly the mouth of a bayou appears—"Saint Malo Pass." With the aid of poles the vessel manages to shamble over a mud-bar, and forthwith rocks in forty feet of green water. We reached Saint Malo upon a leaden-colored day, and the scenery in its gray ghastliness recalled to us the weird landscape painted with words by Edgar Poe—"Silence: a Fragment."

Out of the shuddering reeds and banneretted grass on either side rise the fantastic houses of the Malay fishermen, poised upon slender supports above the marsh, like cranes or bitterns watching for scaly prey. Hard by the slimy mouth of the bayou extends a strange wharf, as ruined and rotted and unearthly as the timbers of the spectral ship in the *Rime of the Ancient Mariner.* Odd craft huddle together beside it, fishing-nets make cobwebby drapery about the skeleton timber-work. Green are the banks, green the water is, green also with fungi every beam and plank and board and shingle of the houses upon stilts. All are built in true Manila style, with immense hat-shaped eaves and balconies, but in wood; for it has been found that palmetto and woven cane could not withstand the violence of the climate. Nevertheless, all this wood had to be shipped to the bayou from a considerable distance, for large trees do not grow in the salty swamp. The highest point of land as far as the "Devil's Elbow," three or four miles away, and even beyond it, is only six inches above the low-water mark, and the men who built those houses were compelled to stand upon ladders, or other wood frame-work, while driving down the piles, lest the quagmire should swallow them up.

Below the houses are patches of grass and pools of water and stretches of gray mud, pitted with the hoof-prints of hogs. Sometimes these hoof-prints are crossed with the tracks of the alligator, and a pig is missing. Chickens there are too — sorry-looking creatures; many have but one leg, others have but one foot: the crabs have bitten them off. All these domestic creatures of the place live upon fish.

Here is the home of the mosquito, and every window throughout all the marsh country must be closed with wire netting. At sundown the insects rise like a thick fog over the lowland; in the darkness their presence is signaled by a sound like the boiling of innumerable caldrons. Worse than these are the great green-headed *tappanoes,* dreaded by the fishermen. Sand-flies attack the colonists in warm weather; fleas are insolent at all hours; spiders of immense growth rival the net-weavers of Saint Malo, and hang their webs from the timbers side by side with seines and fishing-tackle. Wood-worms are busy undermining the supports of the dwellings, and wood-ticks attack the beams and joistings. A marvelous variety of creatures haunt the surrounding swamp — reptiles, insects, and birds. The *prie-dieu* — "pray-god" — utters its soprano note; water-hens and plovers call across the marsh. Numberless snakes hide among the reeds, having little to fear save from the wildcats, which attack them with savage recklessness. Rarely a bear or a deer finds its way near the bayou. There are many otters and musk-rats, minks and raccoons and rabbits. Buzzards float in the sky, and occasionally a bald-eagle sails before the sun.

Such is the land: its human inhabitants are not less strange, wild, picturesque. Most of them are cinnamon-colored men; a few are glossily yellow, like that bronze into which a small portion of gold is worked by the molder. Their features are irregular without being actually repulsive; some have the cheekbones very prominent, and the eyes of several are set slightly aslant. The hair is generally intensely black and straight, but with some individuals it is curly and browner. In Manila there are several varieties of the Malay race, and these Louisiana settlers represent more than one type. None of them appeared tall; the greater number were undersized, but all well-knit, and supple as freshwater eels. Their hands and feet were small; their movements quick and easy, but sailorly likewise, as of men accustomed to walk upon rocking decks in rough weather. They speak the Spanish language; and a Malay dialect is also used among them. There is only one white man in the settlement — the shipcarpenter, whom all the Malays address as "Maestro." He has learned to speak their Oriental dialect, and has conferred upon several the sacrament of baptism according to the Catholic rite; for some of these men were not Christians at the time of their advent into Louisiana. There is but one black man in this lake village—a Portuguese negro, perhaps a Brazilian maroon. The Maestro told us that communication is still kept up with Manila, and money often sent there to aid friends in emigrating. Such emigrants usually ship as seamen on board some Spanish vessel bound for American ports, and desert at the first opportunity. It is said that the colony was founded by deserters—perhaps also by desperate refugees from Spanish justice.

Justice within the colony itself, however, is of a curiously primitive kind, for there are neither magistrates nor sheriffs, neither prisons nor police. Although the region is included within the parish of St. Bernard, no Louisiana official has ever visited it, never has the tax-gatherer attempted to wend thither his unwelcome way. In the busy season a hundred fierce men are gathered together in this waste and watery place, and they must be a law unto themselves. If a really grave quarrel arises, the trouble is submitted to the arbitration of the oldest Malay in the colony, Padre Carpio, and his decisions are usually accepted without a murmur. Should a man, on the other hand, needlessly seek to provoke a difficulty, he is liable to be imprisoned within a fishcar, and left there until cold and hunger have tamed his rage, or the rising tide forces him to terms. Naturally all these men are Catholics; but a priest rarely visits them, for it costs a considerable sum to bring the ghostly father into the heart of the swamp that he may celebrate mass under the smoky rafters of Hilario's house— under the strings of dry fish.

There is no woman in the settlement, nor has the treble of a female voice been heard along the bayou for many a long year. Men who have families keep them at New Orleans, or at Proctorville, or at La Chinche; it would seem cruel to ask any woman to dwell in such a desolation, without comfort and without protection, during the long absence of the fishing-boats. Only two instances of a woman dwelling there are preserved, like beloved traditions, in the memory of the inhabitants. The first of these departed upon her husband's death; the second left the village after a desperate attempt had been made to murder her spouse. In the dead of night the man was unexpectedly assailed; his wife and little boy helped to defend him. The assailant was overcome, tied hand and foot with fish-lines, and fastened to a stake deep driven into the swamp. Next morning they found him dead: the mosquitoes and tappanoes had filled the office of executioner. No excitement was manifested; the Maestro dug a grave deep in the soft gray mud, and fixed above it a rude wooden cross, which still shows its silhouette against the sky just above the reeds.

Such was the narrative which El Maestro related to us with a strange mixture of religious compassion for the unabsolved soul, and marvelous profanity expressed in four different languages. "Only mosquitoes live there now," he added, indicating the decaying edifice where the dead man had dwelt.

But for the possession of modern fire-arms and one most ancient dock, the lake-dwellers of Saint Malo would seem to have as little in common with the civilization of the nineteenth century as had the inhabitants of the Swiss lacustrine settlements of the Bronze Epoch. Here time is measured rather by the number of alligator skins sent to market, or the most striking incidents of successive fishing seasons, than by ordinary reckoning; and did not the Maestro keep a chalk record of the days of the week, none might know Sunday from Monday. There is absolutely no furniture in the place; not a chair, a table, or a bed can be found in all the dwellings of this aquatic village. Mattresses there are filled with dry "Spanish beard," but these are laid upon tiers of enormous shelves braced against the walls, where the weary fishermen slumber at night among barrels of flour and folded sails and smoked fish. Even the clothes (purchased at New Orleans or Proctorville) become as quaint and curiously tinted in that moist atmosphere as the houses of the village, and the broad hats take a greenish and grotesque aspect in odd harmony with the appearance of ancient roofs. All the art treasures of the colony consist of a circus poster immemorially old, which is preserved with much reverence, and two photographs guarded in the Maestro's sea-chest. These represent a sturdy young woman with creole eyes, and a grim-looking Frenchman with wintry beard—the wife and father of the ship-carpenter. He pointed to them with a display of feeling made strongly pathetic by contrast with the wild character of the man, and his eyes, keen and hard as those of an eagle, softened a little as he kissed the old man's portrait, and murmured, "Mon cher vieux père."

And nevertheless this life in the wilderness of reeds is connected mysteriously with New Orleans, where the headquarters of the Manila men's benevolent society are—*La Union Philippina*. A fisherman dies; he is buried under the rustling reeds, and a pine cross planted above his grave; but when the flesh has rotted from the bones, these are taken up and carried by some lugger to the metropolis, where they are shelved away in those curious niche tombs which recall the Roman *columbaria*.

How, then, comes it that in spite of this connection with civilized life the Malay settlement of Lake Borgne has been so long unknown? Perhaps because of the natural reticence of the people. There is still in the oldest portion of the oldest quarter of New Orleans a certain Manila restaurant hidden away in a court, and supported almost wholly by the patronage of Spanish West Indian sailors. Few people belonging to the business circles of New Orleans know of its existence. The *menu* is printed in Spanish and English; the fare is cheap and good. Now it is kept by Chinese, for the Manila man and his oblique-eyed wife, comely as any figure upon a Japanese vase, have gone away. Doubtless his ears, like sea-shells, were haunted by the moaning of the sea, and the Gulf winds called to him by night, so that he could not remain.

The most intelligent person in Saint Malo is a Malay half-breed, Valentine. He is an attractive figure, a supple dwarfish lad almost as broad as tall, brown as old copper, with a singularly bright eye. He was educated in the great city, but actually abandoned a fine situation in the office of a judge to return to his swarthy father in the weird swamps. The old man is still there—Thomas de los Santos. He married a white woman, by whom he had two children, this boy and a daughter, Winnie, who is dead. Valentine is the best pirogue oarsman in the settlement, and a boat bears his name. But opposite the house of Thomas de los Santos rides another graceful boat, rarely used, and whitely christened with the name of the dead Winnie. Latin names prevail in the nomenclature of boats and men: Marcellino, Francesco, Serafino, Florenzo, Victorio, Paosto, Hilario, Marcetto, are common baptismal names. The solitary creole appellation Aristide offers an anomaly. There are luggers and sloops bearing equally romantic names: *Manrico de Aragon, Maravilla, Joven Imperatriz.* Spanish piety has baptized several other with sacred words and names of martyrs.

Of the thirteen or fourteen large edifices on piles, the most picturesque is that of Carpio, old Carpio, who deserts the place once a year to play Monte in Mexico. His home consists of three wooden edifices so arranged that the outer two advance like wings, and the wharf is placed in front of the central structure. Smoked fish black with age hang from the roof, chickens squawk upon the floor, pigs grunt under the planking. Small, squat, swart, dry, and grimy as his smoked fish is old Carpio, but his eye is bright and quick as a lizard's.

It is at Hilario's great *casa* that the Manila men pass stormy evenings, playing monte or a species of Spanish kemo. When the *cantador* (the caller) sings out the numbers, he always accompanies the annunciation with some rude poetry characteristic of fisher life or Catholic faith;

> *Pareja de uno;*
> *Dos piquetes de rivero—*

A pair of one (11); the *two stakes* to which the fish-car is fastened.

> *Número cuatro;*
> *La casa del gato—*

Number 4; the cat's house.

> *Seís con su nuéve;*
> *Arriba y abajo—*

Six with its nine (69); *up and down.*

> *De dos pareja;*
> *Dos paticos en laguna—*

Pair of two (22); two *ducklings* in the lagoon or marsh—the Arabic numerals conveying by their shape this idea to the minds of fishermen. Picturesque? The numbers 77 suggest an almost similar idea—*dos gansos en laguna* (two geese in the lagoon):

> *Tres y parejo*
> *Edad de Cristo—*

thirty-three; the age of Christ.

> *Dos con su cinco;*
> *Buena noche pasado—*

twenty-five (Christmas-eve); the "Good-night" past.

> *Nuéve y parejo;*
> *El mas viejo—*

ninety, "the oldest one." Fifty-five is called the "two boats moored" together, as the figures placed thus 55 convey that idea to the mind—*dos galibos amarrados*. Very musical is the voice of the *cantador* as he continues, shaking up the numbers in a calabash:

Dos y nuéve:
Veinte y nuéve—29
Seís con su cautro;
Sesenta y cuatro—64
Ocho y seís.
Borrachenta y seís—86 (drunken eighty-six)
Nina de quince (a girl of fifteen);
Uno y cinco—15

Polite, too, these sinister-eyed men; there was not a single person in the room who did not greet us with a hearty *buenas noches*. The artist made his sketch of that grotesque scene upon the rude plank-work which serve as a gambling table by the yellow flickering of lamps fed with fish-oil.

There is no liquor in the settlement, and these hardy fishers and alligator-hunters seem none the worse therefor. Their flesh is as hard as oak-wood and sickness rarely affects them, although they know little of comfort, and live largely upon raw fish, seasoned with vinegar and oil. There is but one chimney—a wooden structure—in the village, fires are hardly ever lighted and in the winter the cold and the damp would soon undermine feeble constitutions.

A sunset viewed from the balcony of the Maestro's house seemed to us enchantment. The steel blue of the western horizon heated into furnace yellow, then cooled off into red splendors of astounding warmth and transparency. The bayou blushed crimson, the green of the marsh pools, of the shivering reeds, of the decaying timber-work, took fairy bronze tints, and then, immense with marsh mist, the orange-vermilion face of the sun peered luridly for the last time through the tall grasses upon the bank. Night came with marvelous choruses of frogs; the whole lowland throbbed and laughed with the wild music—a swamp-hymn deeper and mightier than even the surge sounds heard from the Rigolets bank; the world seemed to shake with it!

We sailed away just as the east began to flame again, and saw the sun arise with reeds sharply outlined against the vivid vermilion of his face.

Long fish-formed clouds sailed above him through the blue, green-backed and iridescent-bellied, like the denizens of the green water below. Valentine hailed us from the opposite bank, holding up a struggling *poule-d'eau* which he had just rescued from a wild-cat. A few pirogues were already flashing over the bayou, ribbing the water with wavelets half emerald, half orange gold. Brighter and brighter the eastern fires grew; oranges and vermilions faded out into fierce yellow, and against the blaze all the ragged ribs of Hilario's elfish wharf stood out in black. Somebody fired a farewell shot as we reached the mouth of the bayou; there was waving of picturesque hands and hats, and far in our wake an alligator plashed his scaly body, making for the whispering line of reeds upon the opposite bank.

People v. Hall (1854)

George Hall was originally convicted of murdering a fellow miner; his conviction hinged on the testimonies of three Chinese laborers. At the time of his conviction, California state law dictated that Native Americans and African Americans could not testify against white citizens. Hall challenged his conviction on the grounds that Chinese, as nonwhites, were ineligible to testify; what follows is the state Supreme Court's appeal ruling. (People v. Hall. 4. Cal. 399. Supreme Court of the State of California. 1854.)

Opinion

The appellant, a free white citizen of this State, was convicted of murder upon the testimony of Chinese witnesses.

The point involved in this case is the admissibility of such evidence.

The 394th section of the Act Concerning Civil Cases, provides that no Indian or Negro shall be allowed to testify as a witness in any action or proceeding in which a White person is a party.

The 14th section of the Act of April 16th, 1850, regulating Criminal Proceedings, provides that "No Black or Mulatto person, or Indian, shall be allowed to give evidence in favor of, or against a white man."

The true point at which we are anxious to arrive is the legal signification of the words, "Black, Mulatto, Indian and White person," and whether the Legislature adopted them as generic terms, or intended to limit their application to specific types of the human species.

Before considering this question, it is proper to remark the difference between the two sections of our statute, already quoted, the latter being more broad and comprehensive in its exclusion, by use of the word "Black" instead of Negro.

Conceding, however, for the present, that the word "Black," as used in the 14th section, and "Negro," in 394th, are convertible terms, and that the former was intended to include the latter, let us proceed to inquire who are excluded from testifying as witnesses under the term "Indian."

When Columbus first landed upon the shores of this continent, in his attempt to discover a western passage to the Indies, he imagined that he had accomplished the object of his expedition, and that the Island of San Salvador was one of those Islands of the Chinese Sea, lying near the extremity of India, which had been described by navigators.

Acting upon this hypothesis, and also perhaps from the similarity of features and physical conformation, he gave to the Islanders the name of Indians, which appellation was universally adopted, and extended to the aboriginals of the New World, as well as of Asia.

From that time, down to a very recent period, the American Indians and the Mongolian, or Asiatic, were regarded as the same type of the human species.

In order to arrive at a correct understanding of the intention of our Legislature, it will be necessary to go back to the early history of legislation on this subject, our statute being only a transcript of those of older States.

At the period from which this legislation dates, those portions of Asia which include India proper, the Eastern Archipelago, and the countries washed by the Chinese waters, as far as then known, were denominated the Indies, from which the inhabitants had derived the generic name of Indians.

Ethnology, at that time, was unknown as a distinct science, or if known, had not reached that high point of perfection which it has since attained by the scientific inquiries and discoveries of the master minds of the last half century. Few speculations had been made with regard to the moral or physical differences between the different races of mankind. These were general in their character, and limited to those visible and palpable variations which could not escape the attention of the most common observer.

The general, or perhaps universal opinion of that day was that there were but three distinct types of the human species, which, in their turn, were subdivided into varieties of tribes. This opinion is still held by many scientific writers, and is supported by Cuvier, one of the most eminent naturalists of modern times.

Many ingenious speculations have been resorted to for the purpose of sustaining this opinion. It has been supposed, and not without plausibility, that this continent was first peopled by Asiatics, who crossed Behring's Straits, and from thence found their way down to the more fruitful climates of Mexico and South America. Almost every tribe has some tradition of coming from the North, and many of them, that their ancestors came from some remote country beyond the ocean.

From the eastern portions of Kamtschatka, the Aleutian Islands form a long and continuous group, extending eastward to that portion of the North American Continent inhabited by the Esquimaux. They appear to be a continuation of the lofty volcanic ranges which traverse the two continents, and are inhabited by a race who resemble, in a remarkable degree, in language and appearance, both the inhabitants of Kamtschatka (who are admitted to be of the Mongolian type), and the Esquimaux, who again, in turn, resemble other tribes of American Indians. The similarity of the skull and pelvis, and the general configuration of the two races; the remarkable resemblance in eyes, beard, hair, and other peculiarities, together with the contiguity of the two continents, might well have led to the belief that this country was first peopled by the Asiatics, and that the difference between the different tribes and the parent stock was such as would necessarily arise from the circumstances of climate, pursuits, and other physical causes, and was no greater than that existing between the Arab and the European, both of whom were supposed to belong to the Caucasian race.

Although the discoveries of eminent archeologists, and the researches of modern geologists, have given to this continent an antiquity of thousands of years anterior to the evidence of man's existence, and the light of modern science may have shown conclusively that it was not peopled by the inhabitants of Asia, but that the Aborigines are a distinct type, and as such claim a distinct origin; still, this would not in any degree, alter the meaning of the term, and render that specific which was before generic.

We have adverted to these speculations for the purpose of showing that the name of Indian, from the time of Columbus to the present day, has been used to designate, not alone the North American Indian, but the whole of the Mongolian race, and that the name, though first applied probably through mistake, was afterwards continued as appropriate on account of the supposed common origin.

That this was the common opinion in the early history of American legislation, cannot be disputed, and, therefore, all legislation upon the subject must have borne relation to that opinion.

Can, then, the use of the word "Indian," because at the present day it may be sometimes regarded as a specific, and not as a generic term, alter this conclusion? We think not; because at the origin of the legislation we are considering, it was used and admitted in its common and ordinary acceptation, as a generic term, distinguishing the great Mongolian race, and as such, its meaning then became fixed by law, and in construing statutes the legal meaning of words must be preserved.

Again: the words of the Act must be construed in *pari materia*. It will not be disputed that "White" and "Negro" are generic terms, and refer to two of the great types of mankind. If these, as well as the word "Indian," are not to be regarded as generic terms, including the two great races which they were intended to designate, but only specific, and applying to those whites and Negroes who were inhabitants of this continent at the time of the passage of the Act, the most anomalous consequences would ensue. The European white man who comes here would not be shielded from the testimony of the degraded and demoralized caste, while the Negro, fresh from the coast of Africa, or the Indian of Patagonia, the Kanaka, South Sea Islander, or New Hollander, would be admitted, upon their arrival, to testify against white citizens in our courts of law.

To argue such a proposition would be an insult to the good sense of the Legislature.

The evident intention of the Act was to throw around the citizen a protection for life and property, which could only be secured by removing him above the corrupting influences of degraded castes.

It can hardly be supposed that any Legislature would attempt this by excluding domestic negroes and Indians, who not unfrequently have correct notions of their obligations to society, and turning loose upon the community the more degraded tribes of the same species, who have nothing in common with us, in language, country or laws.

We have, thus far, considered this subject on the hypothesis that the 14th section of the Act Regulating Criminal Proceedings and the 394th section of the Practice Act, were the same.

As before remarked, there is a wide difference between the two. The word "black" may include all negroes, but the term "negro" does not include all black persons.

By the use of this term in this connection, we understand it to mean the opposite of "white," and that it should be taken as contradistinguished from all white persons.

In using the words "no black or mulatto person, or Indian shall be allowed to give evidence for or against a white person," the Legislature, if any intention can be ascribed to it, adopted the most comprehensive terms to embrace every known class or shade of color, as the apparent design was to protect the white person from the influence of all testimony other than that of persons of the same caste. The use of these terms must, by every sound rule of construction, exclude everyone who is not of white blood.

The Act of Congress, in defining what description of aliens may become naturalized citizens, provides that every "free white citizen," etc., etc. In speaking of this subject, Chancellor Kent says that "the Act confines the description to 'white' citizens, and that it is a matter of doubt, whether, under this provision, any of the tawny races of Asia can be admitted to citizenship." (2 Kent's Com. 72.)

We are not disposed to leave this question in any doubt. The word "white" has a distinct signification, which *ex vi termini,* excludes black, yellow, and all other colors. It will be observed, by reference to the first section of the second Article of the Constitution of this State, that none but white males can become electors, except in the case of Indians, who may be admitted by special Act of the Legislature. On examination of the constitutional debates, it will be found that not a little difficulty existed in selecting these precise words, which were finally agreed upon as the most comprehensive that could be suggested to exclude all inferior races.

If the term "white," as used in the Constitution, was not understood in its generic sense as including the Caucasian race, and necessarily excluding all others, where was the necessity of providing for the admission of Indians to the privilege of voting, by special legislation?

We are of the opinion that the words "white," "negro," "mulatto," "Indian," and "black person," wherever they occur in our Constitution and laws, must be taken in their generic sense, and that, even admitting the Indian of this continent is not of the Mongolian type, that the words "black person," in the 14th section, must be taken as contradistinguished from white, and necessarily excludes all races other than the Caucasian. We have carefully considered all the consequences resulting from a different rule of construction, and are satisfied that even in a doubtful case, we would be impelled to this decision on grounds of public policy.

The same rule which would admit them to testify, would admit them to all the equal rights of citizenship, and we might soon see them at the polls, in the jury box, upon the bench, and in our legislative halls.

This is not a speculation which exists in the excited and over-heated imagination of the patriot and statesman, but it is an actual and present danger.

The anomalous spectacle of a distinct people, living in our community, recognizing no laws of this State, except through necessity, bringing with them their prejudices and national feuds in which they indulge in open violation of law; whose mendacity is proverbial; a race of people whom nature has marked as inferior, and who are incapable of progress or intellectual development beyond a certain point, as their history has shown; differing in language, opinions, color, and physical conformation; between whom and ourselves nature has placed an impassable difference, is now presented, and for them is claimed, not only the right to swear away the life of a citizen, but the further privilege of participating with us in administering the affairs of our Government.

These facts were before the Legislature that framed this Act, and have been known as matters of public history to every subsequent Legislature.

There can be no doubt as to the intention of the Legislature, and that if it had ever been anticipated that this class of people were not embraced in the prohibition, then such specific words would have been employed as would have put the matter beyond any possible controversy.

For these reasons, we are of opinion that the testimony was inadmissible.

The judgment is reversed and the case remanded.

Joining the Tracks for the First Transcontinental Railway, Promontory, Utah Territory, 1869

Construction of the first transcontinental railroad began in 1863. The Western Pacific Railroad (WPR) company built the portion of the railroad starting in Oakland, California, headed east; it was built primarily by the labor of Chinese workers, the single largest labor force employed by any of the railroad companies of the time. The WPR held little regard for this vital labor force as demonstrated by the willful endangerment and exploitation of these invited workers through the difficult construction of the railroad

Figure 1.1 "Joining the Tracks for the First Transcontinental Railway, Promontory, Utah Territory, 1869." National Archives and Records Administration, College Park, MD.

line through the Rocky Mountains. The neglect by the railroad company was further exemplified by the absence of Chinese individuals in the celebratory photograph taken at Promontory Point, Utah, marking the railroad's completion on May 10, 1869 (fig. 1.1). The photograph includes railroad employees, managers, owners, and workers other than Chinese, providing the impression that Chinese workers were not of consequence to this industrial feat.

Anti-Chinese Immigration and Naturalization Laws

Chinese immigration to the United States since the mid-nineteenth century provided a vital source of labor for the expansion of mining, agriculture, and railroad construction in the American West. Nevertheless, this group was increasingly demonized and persecuted by a white immigrant working class that consistently cast the Chinese as an economic, social, and racial threat to national integrity. In tandem with such anti-Chinese sentiment, Congress passed a series of laws intended to delimit Chinese migration to the United States. The first, the 1875 Page Act, targeted contracted Chinese laborers and Chinese women who were suspected of prostitution. The Chinese Exclusion Act of 1882 presaged a pattern of immigration reforms that widened immigration restrictions via the prohibition of return migration (the 1888 Scott Act) and included automatic deportation (the 1892 Geary Act). These laws became a pretense for the general persecution and policing of Chinese communities and further authorized mass violence against Chinese residents of the United States. Nevertheless, U.S.-born Chinese, as well as other first-generation immigrants, became key litigants in cases involving naturalization and civil rights. Their legal struggle articulated the juridical exclusion of Asians from being considered white (In re Ah Yup, 1878) yet nevertheless affirmed birthright citizenship (United States v. Wong Kim Ark, 1898).

The Page Act of 1875

(An Act Supplementary to the Acts in Relation to Immigration. Chap. 141; 18 Stat. 477. 3 Mar. 1875.)

Be it enacted by the Senate and House of Representatives of the United States of America in Congress assembled, That in determining whether the immigration of any subject of China, Japan, or any Oriental country, to the United States, is free and voluntary, as provided by section two thousand one hundred and sixty-two of the Revised Code, title "Immigration," it shall be the duty of the consul-general or consul of the United States residing at the port from which it is proposed to convey such subjects, in any vessels enrolled or licensed in the United States, or any port within the same, before delivering to the masters of any such vessels the permit or certificate provided for in such section, to ascertain whether such immigrant has entered into a contract or agreement for a term of service within the United States, for lewd and immoral purposes; and if there be such contract or agreement, the said consul-general or consul shall not deliver the required permit or certificate.

SEC. 2. That if any citizen of the United States, or other person amenable to the laws of the United States shall take, or cause to be taken or transported, to or from the United States any subject of China, Japan, or any Oriental country, without their free and voluntary consent, for the purpose of holding them to a term of service, such citizen or other person shall be liable to be indicted therefor, and, on conviction of such offense, shall be punished by a fine not exceeding two thousand dollars and be imprisoned not exceeding one year; and all contracts and agreements for a term of service of such persons in the United States, whether made in advance or in pursuance of such illegal importation, and whether such importation shall have been in American or other vessels, are hereby declared void.

SEC. 3. That the importation into the United States of women for the purposes of prostitution is hereby forbidden; and all contracts and agreements in relation thereto, made in advance or in pursuance of such illegal importation and purposes, are hereby declared void; and whoever shall knowingly and willfully import, or cause any importation of, women into the United States for the purposes of prostitution, or shall knowingly or willfully hold, or attempt to hold, any woman to such purposes, in pursuance of such illegal importation and contract or agreement, shall be deemed guilty of a felony, and, on conviction thereof, shall be imprisoned not exceeding five years and pay a fine not exceeding five thousand dollars.

SEC. 4. That if any person shall knowingly and willfully contract, or attempt to contract, in advance or in pursuance of such illegal importation, to supply to another the labor of any coolie or other person brought into the United States in violation of section two thousand one hundred and fifty-eight of the Revised Statutes, or of any other section of the laws prohibiting the coolie-trade or of this act, such person shall be deemed guilty of a felony, and, upon conviction thereof, in any United States court, shall be fined in a sum not exceeding five hundred dollars and imprisoned for a term not exceeding one year.

SEC. 5. That it shall be unlawful for aliens of the following classes to immigrate into the United States, namely, persons who are undergoing a sentence for conviction in their own country of felonious crimes other than political or growing out of or the result of such political offenses, or whose sentence has been remitted on condition of their emigration, and women "imported for the purposes of prostitution." Every vessel arriving in the United States may be inspected under the direction of the collector of the port at which it arrives, if he shall have reason to believe that any such obnoxious persons are on board; and the officer making such inspection shall certify the result thereof to the master or other person in charge of such vessel, designating in such certificate the person or persons, if any there be, ascertained by him to be of either of the classes whose importation is hereby forbidden. When such inspection is required by the collector as aforesaid, it shall be unlawful without his permission, for any alien to leave any such vessel arriving in the United States from a foreign country until the inspection shall have been had and the result certified as herein provided; and at no time thereafter shall any alien certified to by the inspecting officer as being of either of the classes whose immigration is forbidden by this section, be allowed to land in the United States, except in obedience to a judicial process issued pursuant to law. If any person shall feel aggrieved by the certificate of such inspecting officer stating him or her to be within either of the classes whose immigration is forbidden by this section, and shall apply for release or other remedy to any proper court or judge, then it shall be the duty of the collector at said port of entry to detain said vessel until a hearing and determination of the matter are had, to the end that if the said inspector shall be found to be in accordance with this section and sustained, the obnoxious person or persons shall be returned on board of said vessel, and shall not thereafter be permitted to land, unless the master, owner or consignee of the vessel shall give bond and security, to be approved by the court or judge hearing the cause, in the sum of five hundred dollars for each such person permitted to land, conditioned for the return of such person, within six months from the date thereof, to the country whence his or her emigration shall have taken place, or unless the vessel bringing such obnoxious person or persons shall be forfeited, in which event the proceeds of such forfeiture shall be paid over to the collector of the port of arrival, and applied by him, as far as necessary, to the return of such person or persons to his or her own country within the said period of six months. And for all violations of this act, the vessel, by the acts, omissions, or connivance of the owners, master, or other custodian, or the consignees of which the same are committed, shall be liable to forfeiture, and may be proceeded against as in cases of frauds against the revenue laws, for which forfeiture is prescribed by existing law.

Approved, March 3, 1875.

In re Ah Yup (1878)

(1 F. Cas. 223; C.C.D. Cal. 1878.)

Naturalization—Chinese—Act 1875.

1. A native of China, of the Mongolian race, is not entitled to become a citizen of the United States under the Revised Statutes as amended in 1875 . . .
2. A Mongolian is not a "white person" within the meaning of the term as used in the naturalization laws of the United States.

Application for naturalization by a native of China.
B. S. Brooks, for petitioner.
S. Heydenfeldt, Jr., contra.
Sawyer, Circuit Judge.

Ah Yup, a native and citizen of the empire of China, of the Mongolian race, presented a petition in writing, praying that he be permitted to make proof of the facts alleged, and upon satisfactory proof being made, and his taking the oath required in such cases, he be admitted as a citizen of the United States. The petition stated all the qualifications required by the statute to entitle the petitioner to be naturalized, provided the statute authorizes the naturalization of a native of China of the Mongolian race. The petitioner was represented by B. S. Brooks, a counsellor of this court. This being the first application made by a native Chinaman for naturalization, the members of the bar were requested by the court to make such suggestions as *amici curiae* as occurred to them upon either side of the question; whereupon S. Heydenfeldt, Jr., argued the case very fully in opposition to the application. Suggestions were also made by other members of the bar present. The only question is, whether the statute authorizes the naturalization of a native of China of the Mongolian race.

In all the acts of Congress relating to the naturalization of aliens, from that of April 14, 1802, down to the Revised Statutes, the language has been "that any alien, being a free white person, may be admitted to become a citizen," etc. After the adoption of the thirteenth and fourteenth amendments to the national Constitution; the former prohibiting slavery, and the latter declaring who shall be citizens, Congress in the act of July 14, 1870, amending the naturalization laws, added the following provision: "That the naturalization laws are hereby extended to aliens of African nativity, and to persons of African descent." 16 Stat. 256, § 7. Upon the revision of the statutes, the revisors, probably inadvertently, as Congress did not contemplate a change in the laws in force, omitted the words "white persons;" section 2165 of the Revised Statutes, being the section conferring the right, reading: "An alien may be admitted to become a citizen," etc., etc. The provision relating to Africans of the act of 1870, is carried into the Revised Statutes in a separate section, which reads as follows: "The provisions of this title shall apply to aliens of African nativity, and to persons of African descent." Section 2169. This section was amended by the "act to correct errors and to supply omissions in the Revised Statutes of the United States," of February 18, 1875, so as to read: "The provisions to this title shall apply to aliens being free white persons, and to aliens of African nativity, and to persons of African descent." Rev. St. (1st Ed.) p. 1435; 18 Stat 318. And so the statute now stands.

The questions are: 1. Is a person of the Mongolian race a "white person" within the meaning of the statute? 2. Do these provisions exclude all but white persons and persons of African nativity or African descent? Words in a statute, other than technical terms, should be taken in their ordinary sense. The words "white person," as well argued by petitioner's counsel, taken in a strictly literal sense, constitute a very indefinite description of a class of persons, where none can be said to be literally white and those called white may be found of every shade from the lightest blonde to the most swarthy brunette. But these words in this country, at least, have undoubtedly acquired a well-settled meaning in common popular speech, and they are constantly used in the sense so acquired in the literature of the country, as well as in common parlance. As ordinarily used everywhere in the United States, one would scarcely fail to understand that the party employing the words "white person" would intend a person of the Caucasian race.

In speaking of the various classifications of races, Webster in his dictionary says, "The common classification is that of Blumenbach, who makes five. "1. The Caucasian, or white race, to which belong the greater part of the European nations and those of Western Asia; 2. The Mongolian, or yellow race, occupying Tartary, China, Japan, etc.; 3. The Ethiopian or Negro (black) race, occupying all Africa, except the north; 4. The American, or red race, containing the Indians of North and South America; and, 5. The Malay, or Brown race, occupying the islands of the Indian Archipelago," etc. This division was adopted from Buffon, with some changes in names, and is founded on the combined characteristics of complexion, hair and skull. Linnaeus makes four divisions, founded on the color of the skin: "1. European, whitish; 2. American, coppery; 3. Asiatic, tawny; and, 4. African, black." Cuvier makes three: Caucasian, Mongol, and Negro. Others make many more, but no one includes the white, or Caucasian, with the Mongolian or yellow race; and no one of those classifications recognizing color as one of the distinguishing characteristics includes the Mongolian in the white or whitish race. See New American Cyclopedia, tit. "Ethnology."

Neither in popular language in literature, nor in scientific nomenclature, do we ordinarily, if ever, find the words "white person" used in a sense so comprehensive as to include an individual of the Mongolian race. Yet, in all, color, notwithstanding its indefiniteness as a word of description, is made an important factor in the basis adopted for the distinction and classification of races. I am not aware that the term "white person," as used in the statutes as they have stood from 1802 till the late revision, was ever supposed to include a Mongolian. While I find nothing in the history of the country, in common or scientific usage, or in legislative proceedings, to indicate that Congress intended to include in the term "white person" any other than an individual of the Caucasian race, I do find much in the proceedings of Congress to show that it was universally understood in that body, in its recent legislation, that it excluded Mongolians. At the time of the amendment, in 1870, extending the naturalization laws to the African race, Mr. Sumner made repeated and strenuous efforts to strike the word "white" from the naturalization laws, or to accomplish the same object by other language. It was opposed on the sole ground that the effect would be to authorize the admission of Chinese to citizenship. Every senator who spoke upon the subject, assumed that they were then excluded by the term "white person," and that the amendment would admit them, and the amendment was advocated on the one hand, and opposed on the other, upon that single idea. Senator Morton, in the course of the discussion said: "This amendment involves the whole Chinese problem . . . The country has just awakened to the question and to the enormous magnitude of the question, involving a possible immigration of many millions, involving another civilization, involving labor problems that no intellect can solve without study and time. Are you now prepared to settle the Chinese problem, thus in advance inviting that immigration?" Congressional Globe, pt. 6, 1869–70, p. 5122. Senator Sumner replied: "Senators undertake to disturb us in our judgment by reminding us of the possibility of large numbers swarming from China; but the answer to all this is very obvious and very simple. If the Chinese come here they will come for citizenship, or merely for labor. If they come for citizenship then in this desire do they give a pledge of loyalty to our institutions, and where is the peril in such vows? They are peaceful and industrious; how can their citizenship be the occasion of solicitude?" Id. 5155.

Many other senators spoke pro and con on the question, this being the point of the contest, and these extracts being fair examples of the opposing opinions. Id. 5121–5177. It was finally defeated, and the amendment cited, extending the right of naturalization to the African only, was adopted. It is clear, from these proceedings that Congress retained the word "white" in the naturalization laws for the sole purpose of excluding the Chinese from the right of naturalization. Again, when it was found that the term "white person" had been omitted in the Revised Statutes it was restored by the act passed "to correct errors and to supply omissions" in the Revised Statutes before cited . . . Thus, whatever latitudinarian construction might otherwise have been given to the term "white person," it is entirely clear that Congress intended by this legislation to exclude Mongolians from the right of naturalization. I am, therefore, of the opinion that a native of China, of the Mongolian race, is not a white person within the meaning of the act of Congress.

The second question is answered in the discussion of the first. The amendment is intended to limit the operation of the provision as it then stood in the Revised Statutes. It would have been more appropriately inserted in section 2165, than where it is found in section 2109. But the purpose is clear. It was certainly intended to have some operation, or it would not have been adopted. The purpose undoubtedly was to restore the law to the condition in which it stood before the revision, and to exclude the Chinese. It was intended to exclude some classes, and as all white aliens and those of the African race are entitled to naturalization under other words, it is difficult to perceive whom it could exclude unless it be the Chinese. It follows that the petition must be denied, and it is so ordered.

The Chinese Exclusion Act (1882)

(An Act to Inaugurate Certain Treaty Stipulations Relating to Chinese. Chap. 126; 22 Stat. 58. 6 May 1882.)

Preamble. Whereas, in the opinion of the Government of the United States the coming of Chinese laborers to this country endangers the good order of certain localities within the territory thereof: Therefore,

Be it enacted by the Senate and House of Representatives of the United States of America in Congress assembled, That from and after the expiration of ninety days next after the passage of this act, and until the expiration of ten years next after the passage of this act, the coming of Chinese laborers to the United States be, and the same is hereby, suspended; and during such suspension it shall not be lawful for any Chinese laborer to come, or, having so come after the expiration of said ninety days, to remain within the United States.

SEC. 2. That the master of any vessel who shall knowingly bring within the United States on such vessel, and land or permit to be landed, any Chinese laborer, from any foreign port or place, shall be deemed guilty of a misdemeanor, and on conviction thereof shall be punished by a fine of not more than five hundred dollars for each and every such Chinese laborer so brought, and may be also imprisoned for a term not exceeding one year.

SEC. 3. That the two foregoing sections shall not apply to Chinese laborers who were in the United States on the seventeenth day of November, eighteen hundred and eighty, or who shall have come into the same before the expiration of ninety days next after the passage of this act, and who shall produce to such master before going on board such vessel, and

45

shall produce to the collector of the port in the United States at which such vessel shall arrive, the evidence hereinafter in this act required of his being one of the laborers in this section mentioned; nor shall the two foregoing sections apply to the case of any master whose vessel, being bound to a port not within the United States by reason of being in distress or in stress of weather, or touching at any port of the United States on its voyage to any foreign port of place: *Provided,* That all Chinese laborers brought on such vessel shall depart with the vessel on leaving port.

SEC. 4. That for the purpose of properly identifying Chinese laborers who were in the United States on the seventeenth day of November, eighteen hundred and eighty, or who shall have come into the same before the expiration of ninety days next after the passage of this act, and in order to furnish them with the proper evidence of their right to go from and come to the United States of their free will and accord, as provided by the treaty between the United States and China dated November seventeenth, eighteen hundred and eighty, the collector of customs of the district from which any such Chinese laborer shall depart from the United States shall, in person or by deputy, go on board each vessel having on board any such Chinese laborer and cleared or about to sail from his district for a foreign port, and on such vessel make a list of all such Chinese laborers, which shall be entered in registry-books to be kept for that purpose, in which shall be stated the name, age, occupation, last place of residence, physical marks or peculiarities, and all facts necessary for the identification of each of such Chinese laborers, which books shall be safely kept in the custom-house; and every such Chinese laborer so departing from the United States shall be entitled to, and shall receive, free of any charge or cost upon application therefore, from the collector or his deputy, at the time such list is taken, a certificate, signed by the collector or his deputy and attested by his seal of office, in such form as the Secretary of the Treasury shall prescribe, which certificate shall contain a statement of the name, age, occupation, last place of residence, personal description, and fact of identification of the Chinese laborer to whom the certificate is issued, corresponding with the said list and registry in all particulars. In case any Chinese laborer after having received such certificate shall leave such vessel before her departure he shall deliver his certificate to the master of the vessel, and if such Chinese laborer shall fail to return to such vessel before her departure from port the certificate shall be delivered by the master to the collector of customs for cancellation. The certificate herein provided for shall entitle the Chinese laborer to whom the same is issued to return to and re-enter the United States upon producing and de-livering the same to the collector of customs of the district at which such Chinese laborer shall seek to re-enter; and upon delivery of such certifi-cate by such Chinese laborer to the collector of customs at the time of re-entry in the United States, said collector shall cause the same to be filed in the custom house and duly canceled.

SEC. 5. That any Chinese laborer mentioned in section four of this act being in the United States, and desiring to depart from the United States by land, shall have the right to demand and receive, free of charge or cost, a certificate of identification similar to that provided for in section four of this act to be issued to such Chinese laborers as may desire to leave the United States by water; and it is hereby made the duty of the collec-tor of customs of the district next adjoining the foreign country to which said Chinese laborer desires to go to issue such certificate, free of charge or cost, upon application by such Chinese laborer, and to enter the same upon registry-books to be kept by him for the purpose, as provided for in section four of this act.

SEC. 6. That in order to the faithful execution of articles one and two of the treaty in this act before mentioned, every Chinese person other than a laborer who may be entitled by said treaty and this act to come within the United States, and who shall be about to come to the United States, shall be identified as so entitled by the Chinese Government in each case, such identity to be evidenced by a certificate issued under the authority of said government, which certificate shall be in the English language or (if not in the English language) accompanied by a translation into English, stat-ing such right to come, and which certificate shall state the name, title, or official rank, if any, the age, height, and all physical peculiarities, former and present occupation or profession, and place of residence in China of the person to whom the certificate is issued and that such person is en-titled conformably to the treaty in this act mentioned to come within the United States. Such certificate shall be *prima-facie* evidence of the fact set forth therein, and shall be produced to the collector of customs, or his deputy, of the port in the district in the United States at which the person named therein shall arrive.

SEC. 7. That any person who shall knowingly and falsely alter or sub-stitute any name for the name written in such certificate or forge any such certificate, or knowingly utter any forged or fraudulent certificate, or falsely personate any person named in any such certificate, shall be deemed guilty of a misdemeanor; and upon conviction thereof shall be fined in a sum not exceeding one thousand dollars, and imprisoned in a penitentiary for a term of not more than five years.

SEC. 8. That the master of any vessel arriving in the United States from any foreign port or place shall, at the same time he delivers a manifest of the cargo, and if there be no cargo, then at the time of making a report of the entry of the vessel pursuant to law, in addition to the other matter required to be reported, and before landing, or permitting to land, any Chinese passengers, deliver and report to the collector of customs of the district in which such vessels shall have arrived a separate list of all Chinese passengers taken on board his vessel at any foreign port or place, and all such passengers on board the vessel at that time. Such list shall show the names of such passengers (and if accredited officers of the Chinese Government traveling on the business of that government, or their servants, with a note of such facts), and the name and other particulars, as shown by their respective certificates; and such list shall be sworn to by the master in the manner required by law in relation to the manifest of the cargo. Any willful refusal or neglect of any such master to comply with the provisions of this section shall incur the same penalties and forfeiture as are provided for a refusal or neglect to report and deliver a manifest of cargo.

SEC. 9. That before any Chinese passengers are landed from any such vessel, the collector, or his deputy, shall proceed to examine such passengers, comparing the certificates with the list and with the passengers; and no passenger shall be allowed to land in the United States from such vessel in violation of law.

SEC. 10. That every vessel whose master shall knowingly violate any of the provisions of this act shall be deemed forfeited to the United States, and shall be liable to seizure and condemnation on any district of the United States into which such vessel may enter or in which she may be found.

SEC. 11. That any person who shall knowingly bring into or cause to be brought into the United States by land, or who shall knowingly aid or abet the same, or aid or abet the landing in the United States from any vessel of any Chinese person not lawfully entitled to enter the United States, shall be deemed guilty of a misdemeanor, and shall, on conviction thereof, be fined in a sum not exceeding one thousand dollars, and imprisoned for a term not exceeding one year.

SEC. 12. That no Chinese person shall be permitted to enter the United States by land without producing to the proper officer of customs the certificate in this act required of Chinese persons seeking to land from a vessel. And any Chinese person found unlawfully within the United States shall be caused to be removed therefrom to the country from whence he came, by direction of the United States, after being brought before some justice, judge, or commissioner of a court of the United States and found to be one not lawfully entitled to be or remain in the United States.

SEC. 13. That this act shall not apply to diplomatic and other officers of the Chinese Government traveling upon the business of that government, whose credentials shall be taken as equivalent to the certificate in this act mentioned, and shall exempt them and their body and household servants from the provisions of this act as to other Chinese persons.

SEC. 14. That hereafter no State court or court of the United States shall admit Chinese to citizenship; and all laws in conflict with this act are hereby repealed.

SEC. 15. That the words "Chinese laborers," whenever used in this act, shall be construed to mean both skilled and unskilled laborers and Chinese employed in mining.

Approved, May 6, 1882.

The Scott Act of 1888

(An Act to Prohibit the Coming of Chinese Laborers to the United States. Chap. 1015; 25 Stat. 476. 18 Sept. 1888.)

Entry of Chinese unlawful, except as provided.

Be it enacted, &c., That from and after the date of the exchange of ratifications of the pending treaty between the United States of America and His Imperial Majesty the Emperor of China, signed on the twelfth day of March, Anno Domini eighteen hundred and eighty-eight, it shall be unlawful for any Chinese person, whether a subject of China or of any other power, to enter the United States, except as hereinafter provided . . .

Classes of Chinese permitted to enter; certificates of identity.

SEC. 2. That Chinese officials, teachers, students, merchants, or travelers for pleasure or curiosity, shall be permitted to enter the United States, but in order to entitle themselves to do so, they shall first obtain the permission of the Chinese Government, or other government of which they may at the time be citizens or subjects. Such permission and also their personal identity shall in such case be evidenced by a certificate to be made out by the diplomatic representative of the United States in the country, or of the consular representative of the United States at the port or place from which the person named therein comes. The certificate shall contain a full description of such person, of his age, height, and general physical features, and shall state his former and present occupation or profession and place of residence, and shall be made out in duplicate. One copy shall be delivered open to the person named and described, and the other copy shall be sealed up and delivered by the diplomatic or consular officer as aforesaid to the captain of the vessel on which the person named in the certificate sets sail for the United States, together with the sealed certificate, which shall be addressed to the collector of customs at the port where such person is to land. There shall be delivered to the aforesaid captain a letter from the consular officer addressed to the collector of customs aforesaid, and stating that said consular officer has on a certain day delivered to the said captain a certificate of the right of the person named therein to enter the United States as a Chinese official, or other exempted person, as the case may be. And any captain who lands or attempts to land a Chinese person in the United States, without having in his possession a sealed certificate, as required in this section, shall be liable to the penalties prescribed in section nine of this act . . .

Persons to whom act applicable; "Chinese laborers" defined.

SEC. 3. That the provisions of this act shall apply to all persons of the Chinese race, whether subjects of China or other foreign power, excepting Chinese diplomatic or consular officers and their attendants; and the words "Chinese laborers," whenever used in this act, shall be construed to mean both skilled and unskilled laborers and Chinese employed in mining . . .

Lists of Chinese passengers to be delivered by masters of vessels arriving from foreign ports; contents; landing diplomatic and consular officers, etc.; penalties.

SEC. 4. That the master of any vessel arriving in the United States from any foreign port or place with any Chinese passengers on board shall, when he delivers his manifest of cargo, and if there be no cargo, when he makes legal entry of his vessel, and before landing or permitting to land any Chinese person (unless a diplomatic or consular officer, or attendant of such officer), deliver to the collector of customs of the district in which the vessel shall have arrived the sealed certificates and letters as aforesaid, and a separate list of all Chinese persons taken on board of his vessel at any foreign port or place, and of all such persons on board at the time of arrival as aforesaid. Such list shall show the names of such persons and other particulars as shown by their open certificates, or other evidences required by this act, and such list shall be sworn to by the master in the manner required by law in relation to the manifest of the cargo. The master of any vessel as aforesaid shall not permit any Chinese diplomatic or consular officer or attendant of such officer to land without having first been informed by the collector of customs of the official character of such officer or attendant . . .

Conditions under which Chinese laborers may return.

SEC. 6. That no Chinese laborer within the purview of the preceding section shall be permitted to return to the United States unless he has a lawful wife, child, or parent in the United States, or property therein of the value of one thousand dollars, or debts of like amount due him and pending settlement. The marriage to such wife must have taken place at least a year prior to the application of the laborer for a permit to return to the United States, and must have been followed by the continuous cohabitation of the parties as man and wife. If the right to return be claimed on the ground of property or of debts, it must appear that the property is bona fide and not colorably acquired for the purpose of evading this act, or that the debts are unascertained and unsettled, and not promissory notes or other similar acknowledgments of ascertained liability . . .

Identification of Chinese laborers claiming right to leave and return; certificates; limitation of time for return; ports at which Chinese may enter.

SEC. 7. That a Chinese person claiming the right to be permitted to leave the United States and return thereto on any of the grounds stated in the foregoing section, shall apply to the collector of customs of the district from which he wishes to depart at least a month prior to the time of his departure, and shall make on oath before the said collector a full statement descriptive of his family, or property, or debts, as the case may be, and shall furnish to said collector such proofs of the facts entitling him to return as shall be required by the rules and regulations prescribed from time to time by the Secretary of the Treasury, and for any false swearing in relation thereto he shall incur the penalties of perjury. He shall also permit the collector to take a full description of his person, which description the collector shall retain and mark with a number. And if the collector after hearing the proofs and investigating all the circumstances of the case, shall decide to issue a certificate of return, he shall at such time and place as he may designate, sign and give to the person applying a certificate containing the number of the description last aforesaid, which shall be the sole evidence given to such person of his right to return. If this last named certificate be transferred, it shall become void, and the person to whom it was given shall forfeit his right to return to the United States. The right to return under the said certificate shall be limited to one year; but it may be extended for an additional period, not to exceed a year, in cases where, by reason of sickness or other cause of disability beyond his control, the holder thereof shall be rendered unable sooner to return, which facts shall be fully reported to and investigated by the consular representative of the United States at the port or place from which such laborer departs for the United States, and certified by such representative of the United States to the satisfaction of the collector of customs at the port where such Chinese person shall seek to land in the United States, such certificate to be delivered by said representative to the master of the vessel on which he departs for the United States. And no Chinese laborer shall be permitted to reenter the United States without producing to the proper officer of the customs at the port of such entry the return certificate herein required. A Chinese laborer possessing a certificate under this section shall be admitted to the United States only at the port from which he departed therefrom, and no Chinese person, except Chinese diplomatic or consular officers, and their attendants, shall be permitted to enter the United States except at the ports of San Francisco, Portland, Oregon, Boston, New York, New Orleans, Port Townsend, or such other ports as may be designated by the Secretary of the Treasury . . .

The Geary Act of 1892

(An Act to Prohibit the Coming of Chinese Persons into the United States. Chap 60; 27 Stat. 25. 5 May 1892.)

    Be it enacted by the Senate and House of Representatives of the United States of America in Congress assembled, That all laws now in force prohibiting and regulating the coming into this country of Chinese persons and persons of Chinese descent are hereby continued in force for a period of ten years from the passage of this act.

SEC. 2. That any Chinese person or person of Chinese descent, when convicted and adjudged under any of said laws to be not lawfully entitled to be or remain in the United States, shall be removed from the United States to China, unless he or they shall make it appear to the justice, judge, or commissioner before whom he or they are tried that he or they are subjects or citizens of some other country, in which case he or they shall be removed from the United States to such country: Provided, That in any case where such other country of which such Chinese person shall claim to be a citizen or subject shall demand any tax as a condition of removal of such person to that country, he or she shall be removed to China.

SEC. 3. That any Chinese person or person of Chinese descent arrested under the provisions of this act or the acts hereby extended shall be adjudged to be unlawfully within the United States unless such person shall establish, by affirmative proof, to the satisfaction of such justice, judge, or commissioner, his lawful right to remain in the United States.

SEC. 4. That any Chinese person or person of Chinese descent convicted and adjudged to be not lawfully entitled to be or remain in the United States shall be imprisoned at hard labor for a period of not exceeding one year and thereafter removed from the United States, as hereinbefore provided.

SEC. 5. That after the passage of this act on an application to any judge or court of the United States in the first instance for a writ of *habeas corpus,* by a Chinese person seeking to land in the United States, to whom that privilege has been denied, no bail shall be allowed, and such application shall be heard and determined promptly without unnecessary delay.

SEC. 6. And it shall be the duty of all Chinese laborers within the limits of the United States, at the time of the passage of this act, and who are entitled to remain in the United States, to apply to the collector of internal revenue of their respective districts, within one year after the passage of this act, for a certificate of residence, and any Chinese laborer, within the limits of the United States, who shall neglect, fail, or refuse to comply with the provisions of this act, or who, after one year from the passage hereof, shall be found within the jurisdiction of the United States without such certificate of residence, shall be deemed and adjudged to be unlawfully within the United States, and may be arrested, by any United States customs official, collector of internal revenue or his deputies, United States marshal or his deputies, and taken before a United States judge, whose duty it shall be to order that he be deported from the United States as hereinbefore provided, unless he shall establish clearly to the satisfaction of said judge, that by reason of accident, sickness or other unavoidable cause, he has been unable to procure his certificate, and to the satisfaction of the court, and by at least one credible white witness, that he was a resident of the United States at the time of the passage of this act; and if upon the hearing, it shall appear that he is so entitled to a certificate, it shall be granted upon his paying the cost. Should it appear that said Chinaman had procured a certificate which has been lost or destroyed, he shall be detained and judgment suspended a reasonable time to enable him to procure a duplicate from the officer granting it, and in such cases, the cost of said arrest and trial shall be in the discretion of the court. And any Chinese person other than a Chinese laborer, having a right to be and remain in the United States, desiring such certificate as evidence of such right may apply for and receive the same without charge.

SEC. 7. That immediately after the passage of this act, the Secretary of the Treasury shall make such rules and regulations as may be necessary for the efficient execution of this act, and shall prescribe the necessary forms and furnish the necessary blanks to enable collectors of internal revenue to issue the certificates required hereby, and make such provisions that certificates may be procured in localities convenient to the applicant, and shall contain the name, age, local residence, and occupation of the applicants, such other description of the applicant as shall be prescribed by the Secretary of the Treasury, and a duplicate thereof shall be filed in the office of the collector of internal revenue for the district within which such Chinaman makes application.

SEC. 8. That any person who shall knowingly and falsely alter or substitute any name for the name written in such certificate or forge such certificate, or knowingly utter any forged or fraudulent certificate, or falsely personate any person named in such certificate, shall be guilty of a misdemeanor, and upon conviction thereof shall be fined in a sum not exceeding one thousand dollars or imprisoned in the penitentiary for a term of not more than five years.

SEC. 9. The Secretary of the Treasury may authorize the payment of such compensation in the nature of fees to the collectors of internal revenue, for services performed under the provisions of this act in addition to salaries now allowed by law, as he shall deem necessary, not exceeding the sum of one dollar for each certificate issued.

Approved, May 5, 1892.

United States v. Wong Kim Ark (1898)

(169 U.S. 649. Supreme Court of the United States. 1898.)

Appeal from the District Court of the United States for the Northern District of California

> A child born in the United States, of parents of Chinese descent, who, at the time of his birth, are subjects of the Emperor of China, but have a permanent domicile and residence in the United States, and are there carrying on business, and are not employed in any diplomatic or official capacity under the Emperor of China, becomes at the time of his birth a citizen of the United States, by virtue of the first clause of the Fourteenth Amendment of the Constitution: "All persons born or naturalized in the United States, and subject to the jurisdiction thereof, are citizens of the United States and of the State wherein they reside."

Statement of the Case

This was a writ of *habeas corpus* issued October 2, 1895, by the District Court of the United States for the Northern District of California to the collector of customs at the port of San Francisco, in behalf of Wong Kim Ark, who alleged that he was a citizen of the United States, of more than twenty-one years of age, and was born at San Francisco in 1873 of parents of Chinese descent and subjects of the Emperor of China, but domiciled residents at San Francisco; and that, on his return to the United States on the steamship Coptic in August 1895, from a temporary visit to China, he applied to said collector of customs for permission to land, and was by the collector refused such permission, and was restrained of his liberty by the collector, and by the general manager of the steamship company acting under his direction, in violation of the Constitution and laws of the United States, not by virtue of any judicial order or proceeding, but solely upon the pretence that he was not a citizen of the United States.

At the hearing, the District Attorney of the United States was permitted to intervene in behalf of the United States in opposition to the writ, and stated the grounds of his intervention in writing as follows:

"That, as he is informed and believes, the said person in whose behalf said application was made is not entitled to land in the United States, or to be or remain therein, as is alleged in said application, or otherwise.

"Because the said Wong Kim Ark, although born in the city and county of San Francisco, State of California, United States of America, is not, under the laws of the State of California and of the United States, a citizen thereof, the mother and father of the said Wong Kim Ark being Chinese persons and subjects of the Emperor of China, and the said Wong Kim Ark being also a Chinese person and a subject of the Emperor of China.

"Because the said Wong Kim Ark has been at all times, by reason of his race, language, color and dress, a Chinese person, and now is, and for some time past has been, a laborer by occupation.

"That the said Wong Kim Ark is not entitled to land in the United States, or to be or remain therein, because he does not belong to any of the privileged classes enumerated in any of the acts of Congress, known as the Chinese Exclusion Acts, which would exempt him from the class or classes which are especially excluded from the United States by the provisions of the said acts.

"Wherefore the said United States Attorney asks that a judgment and order of this honorable court be made and entered in accordance with the allegations herein contained, and that the said Wong Kim Ark be detained on board of said vessel until released as provided by law, or otherwise to be returned to the country from whence he came, and that such further order be made as to the court may seem proper and legal in the premises."

The case was submitted to the decision of the court upon the following facts agreed by the parties:

"That the said Wong Kim Ark was born in the year 1873, at No. 751 Sacramento Street, in the city and county of San Francisco, State of California, United States of America, and that his mother and father were persons of Chinese descent and subjects of the Emperor of China, and that said Wong Kim Ark was and is a laborer.

"That, at the time of his said birth, his mother and father were domiciled residents of the United States, and had established and enjoyed a permanent domicile and residence therein at said city and county of San Francisco, State aforesaid.

"That said mother and father of said Wong Kim Ark continued to reside and remain in the United States until the year 1890, when they departed for China.

"That during all the time of their said residence in the United States as domiciled residents therein, the said mother and father of said Wong Kim Ark were engaged in the prosecution of business, and were never engaged in any diplomatic or official capacity under the Emperor of China.

"That ever since the birth of said Wong Kim Ark, at the time and place hereinbefore stated and stipulated, he has had but one residence, to wit, a residence in said State of California, in the United States of America, and that he has never changed or lost said residence or gained or acquired another residence, and there resided claiming to be a citizen of the United States.

"That, in the year 1890 the said Wong Kim Ark departed for China upon a temporary visit and with the intention of returning to the United States, and did return thereto on July 26, 1890, on the steamship Gælic, and was permitted to enter the United States by the collector of customs upon the sole ground that he was a native-born citizen of the United States.

"That after his said return, the said Wong Kim Ark remained in the United States, claiming to be a citizen thereof, until the year 1894, when he again departed for China upon a temporary visit, and with the intention of returning to the United States, and did return thereto in the month of August, 1895, and applied to the collector of customs to be permitted to land, and that such application was denied upon the sole ground that said Wong in Ark was not a citizen of the United States.

"That said Wong Kim Ark has not, either by himself or his parents acting for him, ever renounced his allegiance to the United States, and that he has never done or committed any act or thing to exclude him therefrom."

The court ordered Wong Kim Ark to be discharged, upon the ground that he was a citizen of the United States. 71 Fed. Rep. 382. The United States appealed to this court, and the appellee was admitted to bail pending the appeal. . . .

Opinion of the Court

Mr. Justice Gray, after stating the case, delivered the opinion of the court.

The facts of this case, as agreed by the parties, are as follows: Wong Kim Ark was born in 1873 in the city of San Francisco, in the State of California and United States of America, and was and is a laborer. His father and mother were persons of Chinese descent, and subjects of the Emperor of China; they were at the time of his birth domiciled residents of the United States, having previously established and still enjoying a permanent domicile and residence therein at San Francisco; they continued to reside and remain in the United States until 1890, when they departed for China, and during all the time of their residence in the United States, they were engaged in business, and were never employed in any diplomatic or official capacity under the Emperor of China. Wong Kim Ark, ever since his birth, has had but one residence, to-wit, in California, within the United States, and has there resided, claiming to be a citizen of the United States, and has never lost or changed that residence, or gained or acquired another residence, and neither he nor his parents acting for him ever renounced his allegiance to the United States, or did or committed any act or thing to exclude him therefrom. In 1890 (when he must have been about seventeen years of age), he departed for China on a temporary visit and with the intention of returning to the United States, and did return thereto by sea in the same year, and was permitted by the collector of customs to enter the United States upon the sole ground that he was a native-born citizen of the United States. After such return, he remained in the United States, claiming to be a citizen thereof, until 1894, when he (being about twenty-one years of age, but whether a little above or a little under that age does not appear) again departed for China on a temporary visit and with the intention of returning to the United States, and he did return thereto by sea in August, 1895, and applied to the collector of customs for permission to land, and was denied such permission upon the sole ground that he was not a citizen of the United States.

It is conceded that, if he is a citizen of the United States, the acts of Congress, known as the Chinese Exclusion Acts, prohibiting persons of the Chinese race, and especially Chinese laborers, from coming into the United States, do not and cannot apply to him.

The question presented by the record is whether a child born in the United States, of parents of Chinese descent, who, at the time of his birth, are subjects of the Emperor of China, but have a permanent domicil[e] and residence in the United States, and are there carrying on business, and are not employed in any diplomatic or official capacity under the Emperor of China, becomes at the time of his birth a citizen of the United States by virtue of the first clause of the Fourteenth Amendment of the Constitution: "All persons born or naturalized in the United States, and subject to the jurisdiction thereof, are citizens of the United States and of the State wherein they reside."

I. In construing any act of legislation, whether a statute enacted by the legislature or a constitution established by the people as the supreme law of the land, regard is to be had not only to all parts of the act itself, and of any former act of the same lawmaking power of which the act in question is an amendment; but also to the condition and to the history of the law as previously existing, and in the light of which the new act must be read and interpreted.

The Constitution of the United States, as originally adopted, uses the words "citizen of the United States," and "natural-born citizen of the United States." By the original Constitution, every representative in Congress is required to have been "seven years a citizen of the United States," and every Senator to have been "nine years a citizen of the United States;" and "no person except a natural-born citizen, or a citizen of the United States at the time of the adoption of this Constitution, shall be eligible to the office of President." The Fourteenth Article of Amendment, besides declaring that "all persons born or naturalized in the United States, and subject to the jurisdiction thereof, are citizens of the United States and of the State wherein they reside," also declares that "no State shall make or enforce any law which shall abridge the privileges or immunities of citizens of the United States; nor shall any State deprive any person of life, liberty or property, without due process of law; nor deny to any person within its jurisdiction the equal protection of the laws." And the Fifteenth Article of Amendment declares that "the right of citizens of the United States to vote shall not be denied or abridged by the United States, or by any State, on account of race, color, or previous condition of servitude."

The Constitution nowhere defines the meaning of these words, either by way of inclusion or of exclusion, except insofar as this is done by the affirmative declaration that "all persons born or naturalized in the United States, and subject to the jurisdiction thereof, are citizens of the United States." In this as in other respects, it must be interpreted in the light of the common law, the principles and history of which were familiarly known to the framers of the Constitution. . . .

Dissenting Opinion: Chief Justice Fuller and Justice Harlan

. . . It is not to be admitted that the children of persons so situated become citizens by accident of birth. On the contrary, I am of the opinion that the President and Senate by treaty, and the Congress by naturalization, have the power, notwithstanding the Fourteenth Amendment, to prescribe that all persons of a particular race, or their children, cannot become citizens, and that it results that the consent to allow such persons to come into and reside within our geographical limits does not carry with it the imposition of citizenship upon children born to them while in this country under such consent, in spite of treaty and statute.

In other words, the Fourteenth Amendment does not exclude from citizenship by birth children born in the United States of parents permanently located therein, and who might themselves become citizens; nor, on the other hand, does it arbitrarily make citizens of children born in the United States of parents who, according to the will of their native government and of this Government, are and must remain aliens.

Tested by this rule, Wong Kim Ark never became and is not a citizen of the United States, and the order of the District Court should be reversed. . . .

The 1902 Scott Act

Passed by Congress on April 29, the Scott Act of 1902 drew upon and made more restrictive the various provisions at the forefront of the 1892 Geary Act. In particular, whereas the Geary Act had extended the ban on Chinese immigration for ten years, the Scott Act extended it indefinitely. It also expanded exclusion to U.S. island territories (such as Hawai'i, Puerto Rico, and Guam). This ban would persist until 1943, when Congress repealed all Chinese exclusion laws as a response to the fact that China was a U.S. ally during World War II. (An Act to Prohibit the Coming into and to Regulate the Residence Within the United States, Its Territories, and All Territory Under Its Jurisdiction, and the District of Columbia, of Chinese and Persons of Chinese Descent. Chap 641; 32 Stat. 176. 29 Apr. 1902.)

Be it enacted by the Senate and House of Representatives of the United States of America in Congress assembled, That all laws now in force prohibiting and regulating the coming of Chinese persons, and persons of Chinese descent, into the United States, and the residence of such persons therein, including sections five, six, seven, eight, nine, ten, eleven, thirteen, and fourteen of the Act entitled, "An Act to prohibit the coming of Chinese laborers into the United States" approved September thirteenth, eighteen hundred and eighty-eight, be, and the same are hereby, re-enacted, extended, and continued so far as the same are not inconsistent with treaty obligations, until otherwise provided by law, and said laws shall also apply to the island territory under the jurisdiction of the United States, and prohibit the immigration of Chinese laborers, not citizens of the United States, from such island territory to the mainland territory of the United States, whether in such island territory at the time of cession or not, and from one portion of the island territory of the United States to another portion of said island territory: *Provided, however,* That said laws shall not apply to the transit of Chinese laborers from one island to another island of the same group; and any islands within the jurisdiction of any state or the District of Alaska shall be considered as a part of the mainland under this section.

SEC. 2. That the Secretary of the Treasury is hereby authorized and empowered to make and prescribe, from time to time to change, such rules and regulations not inconsistent with the laws of the land as he may deem necessary and proper to execute the provisions of this Act and of the Acts hereby extended and continued and of the treaty of December eighth, eighteen hundred and ninety-four, between the United States and China, and with the approval of the President to appoint such agents as he may deem necessary for the efficient execution of said treaty and said Acts . . .

Approved, April 29, 1902.

Gentlemen's Agreement of 1907

The "Gentlemen's Agreement of 1907" refers to an informal arrangement between the United States and Japan about future Japanese immigration. Specifically, the United States (as suggested by President Theodore Roosevelt's letter to Secretary of Commerce and Labor Victor Howard Metcalf; below and fig. 1.2) would not impose overt immigration restriction; Japan would correspondingly not allow further immigration to the United States. The agreement was in response to increased tensions involving Japanese immigrants following Japan's 1905 victory in the Japan-Russo War. That same year, in San Francisco, the Japanese and Korean Exclusion League was formed with the intent to extend the Chinese Exclusion Act to include Japanese and Koreans (who were considered imperial Japanese subjects), facilitate the nonhiring of Japanese employees by league members, push the San Francisco School Board to segregate Japanese children from their white counterparts, and launch a federal- and congressional-level anti-Japanese campaign. The following year, after the earthquake of April 18, 1906, destroyed much of the city, the San Francisco School Board forced ninety-three students of Japanese descent to attend "The Oriental Public School for Chinese, Japanese, and Koreans." In response, President Roosevelt sent Metcalf to investigate the situation and persuade the School Board to rescind such segregation. Local officials were not persuaded and insisted on exclusion: if the president could assure the cessation of Japanese immigration to the United States, the San Francisco School Board would allow Japanese American students to attend the city's public schools. Aimed to reduce tensions between the two nations, the "gentlemen's agreement" was never ratified by Congress. The agreement came to a dramatic end in 1924, with the passage of the Johnson-Reed Immigration Act (see below).

My Dear Secretary Metcalf:

Let me begin by complimenting you upon the painstaking thoroughness and admirable temper with which you have been going into the case of the treatment of the Japanese on the coast. If our treaty contains no "most favored nation" clause then I am inclined to feel as strongly as you do that we had better take no action to upset the action of the Board of Education of the City of San Francisco. I had a talk with the Japanese Am-

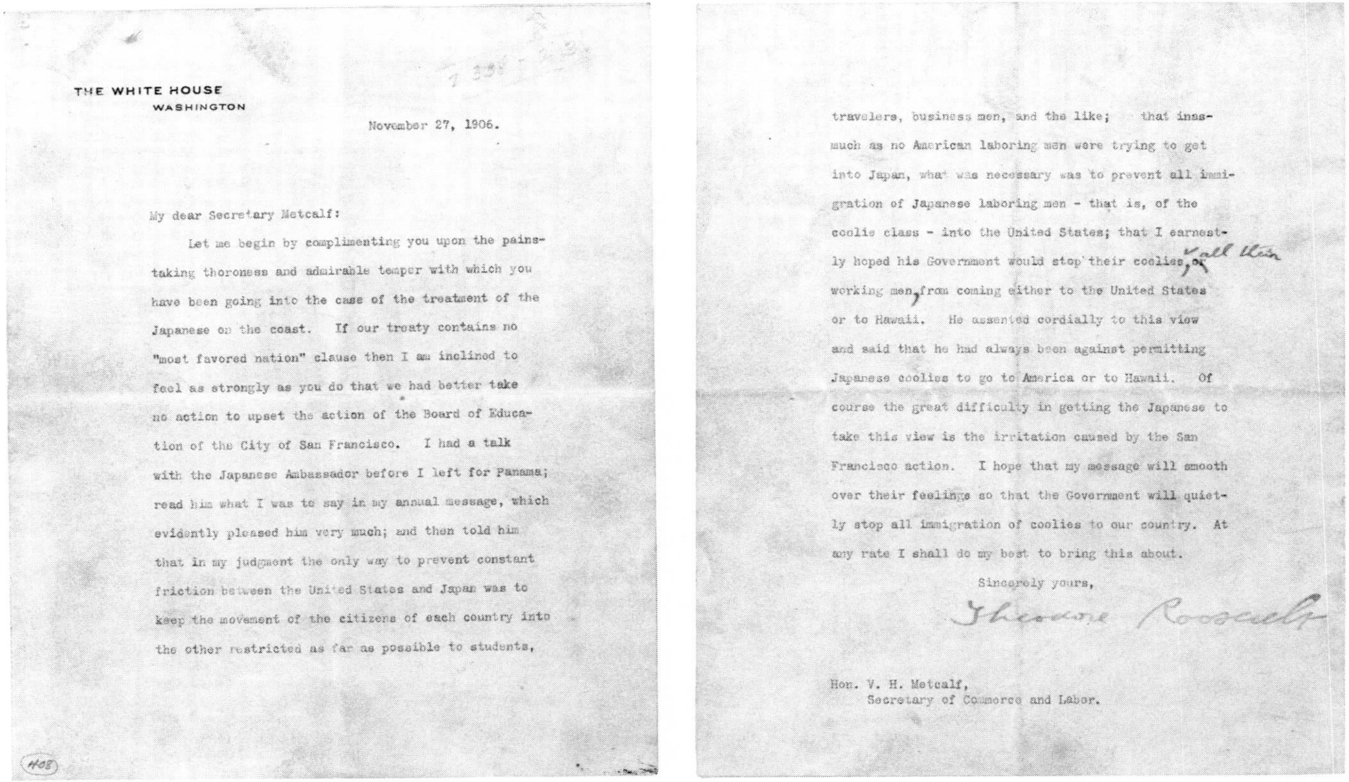

THE WHITE HOUSE
WASHINGTON

November 27, 1906.

My dear Secretary Metcalf:

Let me begin by complimenting you upon the painstaking thoroness and admirable temper with which you have been going into the case of the treatment of the Japanese on the coast. If our treaty contains no "most favored nation" clause then I am inclined to feel as strongly as you do that we had better take no action to upset the action of the Board of Education of the City of San Francisco. I had a talk with the Japanese Ambassador before I left for Panama; read him what I was to say in my annual message, which evidently pleased him very much; and then told him that in my judgment the only way to prevent constant friction between the United States and Japan was to keep the movement of the citizens of each country into the other restricted as far as possible to students, travelers, business men, and the like; that inasmuch as no American laboring men were trying to get into Japan, what was necessary was to prevent all immigration of Japanese laboring men - that is, of the coolie class - into the United States; that I earnestly hoped his Government would stop their coolies, all their working men, from coming either to the United States or to Hawaii. He assented cordially to this view and said that he had always been against permitting Japanese coolies to go to America or to Hawaii. Of course the great difficulty in getting the Japanese to take this view is the irritation caused by the San Francisco action. I hope that my message will smooth over their feelings so that the Government will quietly stop all immigration of coolies to our country. At any rate I shall do my best to bring this about.

Sincerely yours,

Theodore Roosevelt

Hon. V. H. Metcalf,
Secretary of Commerce and Labor.

Figure 1.2 Letter from Theodore Roosevelt to V. H. Metcalf, 27 Nov. 1906. National Archive and Records Administration, College Park, MD.

bassador before I left for Panama; read him what I was to say in my annual message, which evidently pleased him very much; and then told him that in my judgment the only way to prevent constant friction between the United States and Japan was to keep the movement of the citizens of each country into the other restricted as far as possible to students, travelers, business men, and the like; that inasmuch as no American laboring men were trying to get into Japan, what was necessary was to prevent all immigration of Japanese laboring men — that is, of the coolie class — into the United States; that I earnestly hoped his Government would stop their coolies, all their working men, from coming either to the United States or to Hawaii. He assented cordially to this view and said that he had always been against permitting Japanese coolies to go to America or to Hawaii. Of course the great difficulty in getting the Japanese to take this view is the irritation caused by the San Francisco action. I hope that my message will smooth over their feelings so that the Government will quietly stop all immigration of coolies to our country. At any rate I shall do my best to bring this about.

Sincerely yours,
THEODORE ROOSEVELT

Immigration Act of 1917 (Barred Zone Act)

The Immigration Act of 1917 (also known as the Asiatic Barred Zone Act) was passed by Congress on February 5, 1917, despite a previous veto by President Woodrow Wilson. The act extended immigration prohibition by detailing various "undesirable" groups and individuals; it also barred immigrants older than age sixteen who were illiterate. Last, but certainly not least, the act established an "Asiatic Barred Zone" that included many Asian countries and Pacific Island states; this provision extended exclusion to include not only Chinese immigrants, but also other Asian immigrant groups (particularly those from South Asia and Southeast Asia; fig. 1.3). (Immigration Act of 1917 [An Act to Regulate the Immigration of Aliens to, and the Residence of Aliens in, the United States]. Pub. L. 301; 39 Stat. 874. 5 Feb. 1917.)

Be it enacted by the Senate and the House of Representatives of the United States of America in Congress assembled, that the word "alien" wherever used in this Act shall include any person not a native-born or naturalized citizen of the United States; but this definition shall not be held to include Indians of the United States not taxed or citizens of the islands under the jurisdiction of the United States. That the term "United States" as used in the title as well as in the various sections of this Act shall be construed to mean the United States, and any waters, territory, or other place subject to the jurisdiction thereof, except the Isthmian Canal Zone; but if any alien shall leave the Canal Zone or any insular possession of the United States and attempt to enter any other place under the jurisdiction of the United States, nothing contained in this Act shall be construed as permitting him to enter under any other conditions than those applicable to all aliens. That the term "seaman" as used in this Act shall include every person signed on the ship's articles and employed in any capacity on board any vessel arriving in the United States from any foreign port or place.

That this Act shall be enforced in the Philippine Islands by officers of the general government thereof, unless and until it is superseded by an act passed by the Philippine Legislature and approved by the President of the United States to regulate immigration in the Philippine Islands as authorized in the Act entitled, "An Act to declare the purpose of the people of the United States as to the future political status of the people of the Philippine Islands, and to provide a more autonomous government for those islands," approved August twenty-ninth, nineteen hundred and sixteen. . . .

SEC. 3. That the following classes of aliens shall be excluded from admission into the United States: All idiots, imbeciles, feeble-minded persons, epileptics, insane persons; persons who have had one or more attacks of insanity at any time previously; persons of constitutional psychopathic inferiority; persons with chronic alcoholism; paupers; professional beggars; vagrants; persons afflicted with tuberculosis in any form or with a loathsome or dangerous disease; persons not comprehended within any of the foregoing excluded classes who are found to be and are certified by the examining surgeon as being mentally or physically defective, such physical defect being of a nature which may affect the ability of such alien to earn a living; persons who have been convicted of or admitted having committed a felony or other crime or misdemeanor involving moral turpitude; polygamists, or persons who practice polygamy or believe in or advocate the practice of polygamy; anarchists, or persons who believe in or advocate the overthrow by force or violence of the Government of the United States, or all forms of law, or who disbelieve in or are opposed to organized government, or who advocate the assassination of public officials, or who advocate or teach the unlawful destruction of property; . . . all children under sixteen years of age, unaccompanied by or not coming with one or both of their parents, except that any such children may, in the discretion of the Secretary of Labor, be admitted if in his opinion they are not likely to become a public charge and are otherwise eligible; unless otherwise provided for by existing treaties, persons who are natives of islands not possessed by the United States adjacent to the Continent of Asia, situate south of the twentieth parallel latitude north, west of the one hundred and sixtieth meridian of longitude east from Greenwich, and north of the tenth parallel of latitude south, who are natives of any country, province, or dependency situate on the continent of Asia west of the one hundred and tenth meridian of longitude east from Greenwich and east of the fiftieth meridian of longitude east from Greenwich and south of the fiftieth parallel of latitude north, except that portion of said territory situate between the fiftieth and sixty-forth meridians of longitude east from Greenwich and the twenty-fourth and thirty-eighth parallels of latitude north, and no alien now in any way excluded from, or prevented from entering, the United States shall be admitted to the United States. . . . [S]uch persons or their legal wives or foreign-born children who fail to maintain in the United States a status or occupation placing them within the excepted classes shall be deemed to be in the United States contrary to law, and shall be subject to deportation as provided in section nineteen of this Act.

That after three months from the passage of this Act, in addition to the aliens who are by law now excluded from admission to the United States, the following persons shall also be excluded from admission thereto, to wit:

All aliens over sixteen years of age, physically capable of reading, who cannot read the English language, or some other language or dialect, including Hebrew or Yiddish . . .

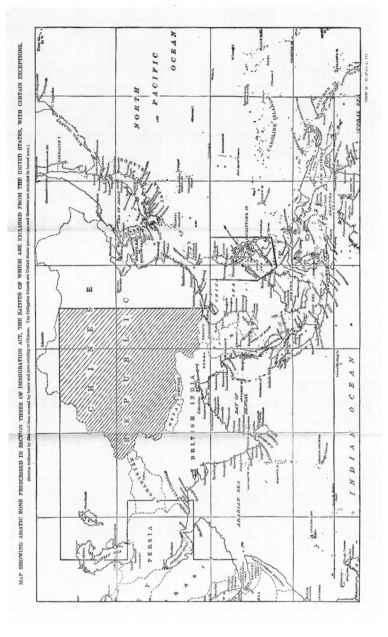

MAP SHOWING ASIATIC ZONE PRESCRIBED IN SECTION THREE OF IMMIGRATION ACT, THE NATIVES OF WHICH ARE EXCLUDED FROM THE UNITED STATES, WITH CERTAIN EXCEPTIONS.

(Section indicated by diagonal lines covered by treaty and laws relating to Chinese. The Philippine Islands are United States possessions and therefore not included in barred zone.)

Figure 1.3 Map that accompanied the Immigration Act of 1917 showing the "Asiatic Zone prescribed in Section Three of Immigration Act, the natives of which are excluded from the United States, with certain exceptions."

Takao Ozawa v. United States (1922)

Takao Ozawa, a first-generation Japanese immigrant, applied for natural-
ized U.S. citizenship in 1914. His petition, originally filed in California, was
rejected on the basis that he was neither "white" nor a person of "African
descent." Ozawa refiled his petition with the U.S. District Court in Hawai'i,
where his application was similarly denied. He then appealed the decision
on the grounds that he was in fact "white": in his legal brief, Ozawa empha-
sized his light complexion, the length of his U.S. residency, the fact that his
Japanese wife was educated in the United States, and his Christian faith.
While Justice George Sutherland of the U.S. Supreme Court admitted that
"the color test alone would result in a confused overlapping of races and a
gradual merging of one into the other," he nevertheless stressed that "white"
was synonymous with "what is popularly known as the Caucasian race."
The court subsequently ruled that Japanese immigrants were "clearly of a
race which is not Caucasian" and were thus aliens ineligible for citizenship.
(Takao Ozawa v. United States. 260 U.S. 178. Supreme Court of the United
States. 1922.)

Mr. Justice Sutherland delivered the opinion of the Court.

The appellant is a person of the Japanese race born in Japan. He applied, on October 16, 1914, to the United States District Court for the Territory of Hawai'i to be admitted as a citizen of the United States. His petition was opposed by the United States District Attorney for the District
of Hawai'i. Including the period of his residence in Hawai'i appellant had
continuously resided in the United States for 20 years. He was a graduate
of the Berkeley, Cal., high school, had been nearly three years a student
in the University of California, had educated his children in American
schools, his family had attended American churches and he had maintained the use of the English language in his home. That he was well qualified by character and education for citizenship is conceded.

The District Court of Hawai'i, however, held that, having been born in
Japan and being of the Japanese race, he was not eligible to naturalization
under section 2169 of the Revised Statutes (Comp. St. § 4358), and denied
the petition. Thereupon the appellant brought the cause to the Circuit
Court of Appeals for the Ninth Circuit and that court has certified the
following questions, upon which it desires to be instructed:

"1. Is the act of June 29, 1906 (34 Stats. at Large, pt. 1, p. 596), providing 'for a uniform rule for the naturalization of aliens' complete in itself, or is it limited by section 2169 of the Revised
   Statutes of the United States?
"2. Is one who is of the Japanese race and born in Japan eligible to
   citizenship under the naturalization laws?
"3. If said act of June 29, 1906, is limited by section 2169 and naturalization is limited to aliens being free white persons and to
   aliens of African nativity and to persons of African descent,
   is one of the Japanese race, born in Japan, under any circumstances eligible to naturalization?"

These questions for purposes of discussion may be briefly restated:

1. Is the Naturalization Act of June 29, 1906 (Comp. St. § 4351 et
   seq.), limited by the provisions of section 2169 of the Revised
   Statutes of the United States?
2. If so limited, is the appellant eligible to naturalization under
   that section?

First. Section 2169 is found in title XXX of the Revised Statutes, under
the heading "Naturalization," and reads as follows:
"The provisions of this title shall apply to aliens, being free white persons and to aliens of African nativity and to persons of African descent."
The act of June 29, 1906, entitled "An Act To establish a Bureau of Immigration and Naturalization, and to provide for a uniform rule for the
naturalization of aliens throughout the United States," consists of thirty-
one sections and deals primarily with the subject of procedure. There is
nothing in the circumstances leading up to or accompanying the passage
of the act which suggests that any modification of § 2169, or of its application, was contemplated.
The report of the House Committee on Naturalization and Immigration, recommending its passage, contains this statement:
"It is the opinion of your committee that the frauds and crimes which
have been committed in regard to naturalization have resulted more from
a lack of any uniform system of procedure in such matters than from any
radical defect in the fundamental principles of existing law governing in
such matters. The two changes which the committee has recommended
in the principles controlling in naturalization matters and which are em-
bodied in the bill submitted herewith are as follows: First. The require-

ment that before an alien can be naturalized he must be able to read, either in his own language or in the English language and to speak or understand the English language; and, Second, that the alien must intend to reside permanently in the United States before he shall be entitled to naturalization."

This seems to make it quite clear that no change of the fundamental character here involved was in mind.

Section 26 of the Act expressly repeals §§ 2165, 2167, 2168, 2173 of title XXX, the subject-matter thereof being covered by new provisions. The sections of title XXX remaining without repeal are: Section 2166, relating to honorably discharged soldiers; § 2169, now under consideration; § 2170, requiring five years' residence prior to admission; § 2171, forbidding the admission of alien enemies; § 2172, relating to the status of children of naturalized persons; and § 2174, making special provision in respect of the naturalization of seamen.

There is nothing in § 2169 which is repugnant to anything in the act of 1906. Both may stand and be given effect. It is clear, therefore, that there is no repeal by implication.

But it is insisted by appellant that § 2169, by its terms, is made applicable only to the provisions of Title XXX and that it will not admit of being construed as a restriction upon the act of 1906. Since § 2169, it is in effect argued, declares that "the provisions of this title shall apply to aliens being free white persons . . ." it should be confined to the classes provided for in the unrepealed sections of that title, leaving the Act of 1906 to govern in respect of all other aliens, without any restriction except such as may be imposed by that act itself.

It is contended that, thus construed, the act of 1906 confers the privilege of naturalization without limitation as to race, since the general introductory words of § 4 are: "That an alien may be admitted to become a citizen of the United States in the following manner, and not otherwise." But, obviously, this clause does not relate to the subject of eligibility but to the "manner," that is, the procedure, to be followed. Exactly the same words are used to introduce the similar provisions contained in § 2165 of the Revised Statutes. In 1790, the first naturalization act provided that, "Any alien, *being a free white person* . . . may be admitted to become a citizen . . ." C. 3, 1 Stat. 103. This was subsequently enlarged to include aliens of African nativity and persons of African descent. These provisions were restated in the Revised Statutes, so that § 2165 included only the procedural portion, while the substantive parts were carried into a separate section (2169) and the words "An alien" substituted for the words "Any alien."

In all of the Naturalization Acts from 1790 to 1906 the privilege of naturalization was confined to white persons (with the addition in 1870 of those of African nativity and descent), although the exact wording of the various statutes was not always the same. If Congress in 1906 desired to alter a rule so well and so long established it may be assumed that its purpose would have been definitely disclosed and its legislation to that end put in unmistakable terms.

The argument that, because § 2169 is in terms made applicable only to the title in which it is found, it should now be confined to the unrepealed sections of that title is not convincing. The persons entitled to naturalization under these unrepealed sections include only honorably discharged soldiers and seamen who have served three years on board an American vessel, both of whom were entitled from the beginning to admission on more generous terms than were accorded to other aliens. It is not conceivable that Congress would deliberately have allowed the racial limitation to continue as to soldiers and seamen to whom the statute had accorded an especially favored status, and have removed it as to all other aliens. Such a construction cannot be adopted unless it be unavoidable.

The division of the Revised Statutes into titles and chapters is chiefly a matter of convenience, and reference to a given title or chapter is simply a ready method of identifying the particular provisions which are meant. The provisions of Title XXX affected by the limitation of § 2169, originally embraced the whole subject of naturalization of aliens. The generality of the words in § 2165, "An alien may be admitted . . ." was restricted by § 2169 in common with the other provisions of the title. The words "this title" were used for the purpose of identifying that provision (and others), but it was the *provision* which was restricted. That provision having been amended and carried into the act of 1906, § 2169 being left intact and unrepealed, it will require something more persuasive than a narrowly literal reading of the identifying words "this title" to justify the conclusion that Congress intended the restriction to be no longer applicable to the provision.

It is the duty of this Court to give effect to the intent of Congress. Primarily this intent is ascertained by giving the words their natural significance, but if this leads to an unreasonable result plainly at variance with the policy of the legislation as a whole, we must examine the matter further. We may then look to the reason of the enactment and inquire into its antecedent history and give it effect in accordance with its design and purpose, sacrificing, if necessary, the literal meaning in order that the purpose may not fail. See *Holy Trinity Church v. United States,* 143 U.S. 457; *Heydenfeldt v. Daney Gold Mining Co.,* 93 U.S. 634, 638. We are asked to conclude that Congress, without the consideration or recommendation of any committee, without a suggestion as to the effect, or a word of debate as to the desirability, of so fundamental a change, nevertheless, by failing to alter the identifying words of § 2169, which section we may assume was continued for some serious purpose, has radically modified a statute always theretofore maintained and considered as of great importance. It is inconceivable that a rule in force from the beginning of the government, a part of our history as well as our law, welded into the structure of our national polity by a century of legislative and administrative acts and judicial decisions, would have been deprived of its force in such dubious and casual fashion. We are, therefore, constrained to hold that the Act of 1906 is limited by the provisions of § 2169 of the Revised Statutes.

Second. This brings us to inquire whether, under § 2169, the appellant is eligible to naturalization. The language of the naturalization laws from 1790 to 1870 had been uniformly such as to deny the privilege of naturalization to an alien unless he came within the description "free white person." By § 7 of the Act of July 14, 1870, c. 16 Stat. 254, 256, the naturalization laws were "extended to aliens of African nativity and to persons of African descent." Section 2169 of the Revised Statutes, as already pointed out, restricts the privilege to the same classes of persons, viz.: "to aliens [being free white persons, and to aliens] of African nativity and to persons of African descent." It is true that in the first edition of the Revised Statutes of 1873 the words in brackets, "being free white persons, and to aliens" were omitted, but this was clearly an error of the compilers and was corrected by the subsequent legislation of 1875 (c. 80, 18 Stat. 316, 318). Is appellant, therefore, a "free white person," within the meaning of that phrase as found in the statute?

On behalf of the appellant it is urged that we should give to this phrase the meaning which it had in the minds of its original framers in 1790 and that it was employed by them for the sole purpose of excluding the black or African race and the Indians then inhabiting this country. It may be true that those two races were alone thought of as being excluded, but to say that they were the only ones within the intent of the statute would be to ignore the affirmative form of the legislation. The provision is not that

Negroes and Indians shall be *excluded*, but it is, in effect, that only free white persons shall be *included*. The intention was to confer the privilege of citizenship upon that class of persons whom the fathers knew as white, and to deny it to all who could not be so classified. It is not enough to say that the framers did not have in mind the brown or yellow races of Asia. It is necessary to go farther and be able to say that had these particular races been suggested the language of the act would have been so varied as to include them within its privileges. As said by Chief Justice Marshall in *Dartmouth College v. Woodward*, 4 Wheat. 518, 644, in deciding a question of constitutional construction: "It is not enough to say that this particular case was not in the mind of the convention, when the article was framed, nor of the American people, when it was adopted. It is necessary to go farther, and to say that, had this particular case been suggested, the language would have been so varied, as to exclude it, or it would have been made a special exception. The case being within the words of the rule, must be within its operation likewise, unless there be something in the literal construction so obviously absurd, or mischievous, or repugnant to the general spirit of the instrument, as to justify those who expound the Constitution in making it an exception." If it be assumed that the opinion of the framers was that the only persons who would fall outside the designation "white" were Negroes and Indians, this would go no farther than to demonstrate their lack of sufficient information to enable them to foresee precisely who would be excluded by that term in the subsequent administration of the statute. It is not important in construing their words to consider the extent of their ethnological knowledge or whether they thought that under the statute the only persons who would be denied naturalization would be Negroes and Indians. It is sufficient to ascertain whom they intended to include and having ascertained that it follows, as a necessary corollary, that all others are to be excluded.

The question then is: Who are comprehended within the phrase "free white persons"? Undoubtedly the word "free" was originally used in recognition of the fact that slavery then existed and that some white persons occupied that status. The word, however, has long since ceased to have any practical significance and may now be disregarded.

We have been furnished with elaborate briefs in which the meaning of the words "white person" is discussed with ability and at length, both from the standpoint of judicial decision and from that of the science of ethnology. It does not seem to us necessary, however, to follow counsel in their extensive researches in these fields. It is sufficient to note the fact that these decisions are, in substance, to the effect that the words import a racial and not an individual test, and with this conclusion, fortified as it is by reason and authority, we entirely agree. Manifestly the test afforded by the mere color of the skin of each individual is impracticable, as that differs greatly among persons of the same race, even among Anglo-Saxons, ranging by imperceptible gradations from the fair blond to the swarthy brunette, the latter being darker than many of the lighter-hued persons of the brown or yellow races. Hence to adopt the color test alone would result in a confused overlapping of races and a gradual merging of one into the other, without any practical line of separation. Beginning with the decision of Circuit Judge Sawyer, in *In re Ah Yup,* 5 Sawy. 155 (1878), the federal and state courts, in an almost unbroken line, have held that the words "white person" were meant to indicate only a person of what is popularly known as the Caucasian race. Among these decisions, see for example: *In re Camille,* 6 Fed. 256; *In re Saito,* 62 Fed. 126; *In re Nian,* 6 Utah 259; *In re Kumagai,* 163 Fed. 922; *In re Yamashita,* 30 Wash. 234, 237; *In re Ellis,* 179 Fed. 1002; *In re Mozumdar,* 207 Fed. 115, 117; *In re Singh,* 257 Fed. 209, 211–212; and *Petition of Charr,* 273 Fed. 207. With the conclusion reached in these several decisions we see no reason to differ. Moreover, that conclusion has become so well established by judicial and executive concurrence and legislative acquiescence that we should not at this late day feel at liberty to disturb it, in the absence of reasons far more cogent than any that have been suggested. *United States v. Midwest Oil Co.,* 236 U.S. 459, 472.

The determination that the words "white person" are synonymous with the words "a person of the Caucasian race" simplifies the problem, although it does not entirely dispose of it. Controversies have arisen and will no doubt arise again in respect of the proper classification of individuals in borderline cases. The effect of the conclusion that the words "white person" means a Caucasian is not to establish a sharp line of demarcation between those who are entitled and those who are not entitled to naturalization, but rather a zone of more or less debatable ground outside of which, upon the one hand, are those clearly eligible, and outside of which, upon the other hand, are those clearly ineligible for citizenship. Individual cases falling within this zone must be determined as they arise from time to time by what this court has called, in another connection (*Davidson v. New Orleans,* 96 U.S. 97, 104), "the gradual process of judicial inclusion and exclusion."

The appellant, in the case now under consideration, however, is clearly of a race which is not Caucasian and therefore belongs entirely outside the zone on the negative side. A large number of the federal and state courts have so decided and we find no reported case definitely to the contrary. These decisions are sustained by numerous scientific authorities, which we do not deem it necessary to review. We think these decisions are right and so hold.

The briefs filed on behalf of appellant refer in complimentary terms to the culture and enlightenment of the Japanese people, and with this estimate we have no reason to disagree; but these are matters which cannot enter into our consideration of the questions here at issue. We have no function in the matter other than to ascertain the will of Congress and declare it. Of course there is not implied—either in the legislation or in our interpretation of it—any suggestion of individual unworthiness or racial inferiority. These considerations are in no manner involved.

The questions submitted are, therefore, answered as follows:

Question No. 1. The act of June 29, 1906, is not complete in itself, but is limited by § 2169 of the Revised Statutes of the United States.

Question No. 2. No.

Question No. 3. No.

It will be so certified.

United States v. Bhagat Singh Thind (1923)

Bhagat Singh Thind, a Punjabi Sikh, immigrated to the United States in 1913; when the nation entered World War I in 1917, Thind joined the U.S. Army and was honorably discharged in 1918. In 1920, Thind applied for naturalized U.S. citizenship. Initially, his application was approved by the district court; however, a naturalization examiner appealed the decision on the grounds that Thind was not white and therefore was ineligible for citizenship. Thind maintained that he was "Aryan" because of his high-caste Indian status; as such, he was, according to prevailing ethnology, "Caucasian" and thus white. The case soon went to the U.S. Supreme Court, which eventually ruled that the term "Aryan" was a linguistic, not a racially stable, classification; "common sense" dictated that Asian Indians were not white. As a nonwhite subject, Thind was deemed an alien ineligible for citizenship. (United States v. Bhagat Singh Thind. 261 U.S. 204. Supreme Court of the United States. 1923.)

Mr. Justice Sutherland delivered the opinion of the Court.

This cause is here upon a certificate from the Circuit Court of Appeals, requesting the instruction of this Court in respect of the following questions:

> "1. Is a high caste Hindu of full Indian blood, born at Amrit Sar, Punjab, India, a white person within the meaning of section 2169, Revised Statutes?
> "2. Does the act of February 5, 1917 (39 Stat. L. 875, section 3), disqualify from naturalization as citizens those Hindus, now barred by that act, who had lawfully entered the United States prior to the passage of said act?" . . .

Section 2169, Revised Statutes, provides that the provisions of the Naturalization Act "shall apply to aliens, being free white persons, and to aliens of African nativity and to persons of African descent."

If the applicant is a white person within the meaning of this section he is entitled to naturalization; otherwise not. . . . [T]he conclusion that the phrase "white persons" and the word "Caucasian" are synonymous does not end the matter. . . . Mere ability on the part of an applicant for naturalization to establish a line of descent from a Caucasian ancestor will not *ipso facto* and necessarily conclude the inquiry. "Caucasian" is a conventional word of much flexibility, as a study of the literature dealing with racial questions will disclose, and while it and the words "white persons" are treated as synonymous for the purposes of that case, they are not of identical meaning—*idem per idem.*

In the endeavor to ascertain the meaning of the statute we must not fail to keep in mind that it does not employ the word "Caucasian" but the words "white persons," and these are words of common speech and not of scientific origin. The word "Caucasian" not only was not employed in the law but was probably wholly unfamiliar to the original framers of the statute in 1790. . . . But in this country, during the last half century especially, the word by common usage has acquired a popular meaning, not clearly defined to be sure, but sufficiently so to enable us to say that its popular as distinguished from its scientific application is of appreciably narrower scope. It is in the popular sense of the word, therefore, that we employ it as an aid to the construction of the statute . . .

[The words of the statute] imply, as we have said, a racial test; but the term "race" is one which, for the practical purposes of the statute, must be applied to a group of living persons now possessing in common the requisite characteristics, not to groups of persons who are supposed to be or really are descended from some remote, common ancestor, but who, whether they both resemble him to a greater or less extent, have, at any rate, ceased altogether to resemble one another. It may be true that the blond Scandinavian and the brown Hindu have a common ancestor in the dim reaches of antiquity, but the average man knows perfectly well that there are unmistakable and profound differences between them today . . .

The term "Aryan" has to do with linguistic and not at all with physical characteristics, and it would seem reasonably clear that mere resemblance in language, indicating a common linguistic root buried in remotely ancient soil, is altogether inadequate to prove common racial origin. There is, and can be, no assurance that the so-called Aryan language was not spoken by a variety of races living in proximity to one another. Our own history has witnessed the adoption of the English tongue by millions of Negroes, whose descendants can never be classified racially with the descendants of white persons notwithstanding both may speak a common root language. . . .

What we now hold is that the words "free white persons" are words of common speech, to be interpreted in accordance with the understanding of the common man, synonymous with the word "Caucasian" only as that word is popularly understood. As so understood and used, whatever may be the speculations of the ethnologist, it does not include the body of people to whom the appellee belongs. It is a matter of familiar observation and knowledge that the physical group characteristics of the Hindus render them readily distinguishable from the various groups of persons in this country commonly recognized as white. The children of English, French, German, Italian, Scandinavian, and other European parentage, quickly merge into the mass of our population and lose the distinctive hallmarks of their European origin. On the other hand, it cannot be doubted that the children born in this country of Hindu parents would retain indefinitely the clear evidence of their ancestry. It is very far from our thought to suggest the slightest question of racial superiority or inferiority. What we suggest is merely racial difference, and it is of such character and extent that the great body of our people instinctively recognize it and reject the thought of assimilation.

It is not without significance in this connection that Congress, by the Act of February 5, 1917, c. 29, § 3, 39 Stat. 874, has now excluded from admission into this country all natives of Asia within designated limits of latitude and longitude, including the whole of India. This not only constitutes conclusive evidence of the congressional attitude of opposition to Asiatic immigration generally, but is persuasive of a similar attitude toward Asiatic naturalization as well, since it is not likely that Congress would be willing to accept as citizens a class of persons whom it rejects as immigrants.

It follows that a negative answer must be given to the first question, which disposes of the case and renders an answer to the second question unnecessary, and it will be so certified.

Answer to question No. 1, No.

The Johnson-Reed Immigration Act (1924)

Passed by Congress on May 26, 1924, and sponsored by Representative Albert Johnson (Republican–Washington) and Senator David Reed (Republican–Pennsylvania), the Johnson-Reed Act was intended to "preserve the ideal of American homogeneity" by stemming the "rising tide" of unwanted immigrants from Southern Europe, Eastern Europe, and Asia. Between 1880 and 1920, an estimated twenty-two million to twenty-four million immigrants (principally from Italy, Ireland, Eastern Europe, and Russia) entered the United States. The act, which contained as legislative corollaries the National Origins Act and the Asian Exclusion Act, severely curtailed migration through quota and state-specific prohibition.

As congressional precedent, the Johnson-Reed Act accessed the 1921 Immigration Act (also sponsored by Johnson and Reed), an "emergency" provision that established, for the first time in U.S. immigration history, a nation-based quota system. This quantification, based on previous census data, limited annual immigration from any country to at most 3 percent of the number of people of that nationality already in the United States in 1910. The 1921 law had a dramatic demographic effect: it cut immigration to the United States from eight hundred thousand to three hundred thousand in a single year; moreover, the quota system it established would persist until the midcentury passage of the 1965 Immigration and Nationality Act (Hart-Celler Act). Building on the "closed door" politics of the 1921 law, the Johnson-Reed Act banned immigration from Asia entirely; it also reduced the quota for Europeans from 3 percent to 2 percent. Last, but certainly not least, the Johnson-Reed Act extended the "Asiatic Barred Zone" to include the Far East (namely, Japan). (Immigration Act of 1924 [Johnson-Reed Act; An Act to Limit the Immigration of Aliens into the United States, and for Other Purposes]. Pub. L. 68-139; 43 Stat. 153. 26 May 1924.)

Be it enacted by the Senate and the House of Representatives of the United States of America in Congress assembled, That this Act may be cited as the "Immigration Act of 1924."

Immigration Visas

SEC. 2. (a) A consular officer upon the application of any immigrant . . . may (under the conditions hereinafter prescribed and subject to the limitations prescribed in this Act or regulations made thereunder as to the number of immigration visas which may be issued by each officer) issue to such immigrant an immigration visa which shall consist of one copy of the application provided for in section 7, visaed by such consular officer. Such visa shall specify (1) the nationality of the immigrant; (2) whether he is a quota immigrant (as defined in section 5) or non-quota immigrant (as defined in section 4); (3) the date on which the validity of the immigration visa shall expire; and (4) such additional information necessary to the proper enforcement of the immigration laws and the naturalization laws as may be by regulations prescribed.

(b) The immigrant shall furnish two copies of his photograph to the consular officer. One copy shall be permanently attached by the consular officer to the immigration visa and the other copy shall be disposed of as may be by regulations prescribed.

(c) The validity of an immigration visa shall expire at the end of such period, specified in the immigration visa, not exceeding four months, as shall be by regulations prescribed. In the case of an immigrant arriving in the United States by water, or arriving by water in foreign contiguous territory on a continuous voyage to the United States, if the vessel, before the expiration of the validity of his immigration visas, departed from the last port outside the United States and outside foreign contiguous territory at which the immigrant embarked, and if the immigrant proceeds on a continuous voyage to the United States, then, regardless of the time of his arrival in the United States, the validity of his immigration visa shall not be considered to have expired. . . .

Numerical Limitations

SEC. 11. (a) The annual quota of any nationality shall be 2 percentum of the number of foreign-born individuals of such nationality resident in continental United States as determined by the United States census of 1890, but the minimum quota of any nationality shall be 100.

(b) The annual quota of any nationality for the fiscal year beginning July 1, 1927, and for each fiscal year thereafter, shall be a number which bears the same ratio to 150,000 as the number of inhabitants in the continental United States in 1920 having that national origin (ascertained as hereinafter provided in this section) bears to the number of inhabitants in continental United States in 1920, but the minimum quota of any nationality shall be 100.

(c) For the purpose of subdivision (d) national origin shall be ascertained by determining as nearly as may be, in respect of each geographical area under which section 12 is to be treated as a separate country . . . the number of inhabitants in the continental United States in 1920 whose origin by birth or ancestry is attributable to such geographical area. Such determination shall not be made by tracing the ancestors or descendants of particular individuals, but shall be based upon statistics of immigration and emigration, together with rates of increase of population as shown by successive decennial United States censuses, and such other data as may be found to be reliable. . . .

Steamship Fines Under 1917 Act

SEC. 26. Section 9 of the Immigration Act of 1917 is amended to read as follows:

"SEC. 9. That it shall be unlawful for any person, including any transportation company other than railway lines entering the United States from foreign contiguous territory, or the owner, master, agent, or consignee of any vessel to bring to the United States either from a foreign country or any insular possession of the United States any alien afflicted with idiocy, insanity, imbecility, feeble-mindedness, epilepsy, constitutional psychopathic inferiority, chronic alcoholism, tuberculosis in any form, or a loathsome or dangerous contagious disease, and if it shall appear to the satisfaction of the Secretary of Labor that any alien so brought to the United States was afflicted with any of the said diseases or disabilities at the time of foreign embarkation, and that the existence of such disease or disability might have been detected by means of competent medical examination at such time, such person or transportation company, or the master, agent, owner, or consignee of any such vessel shall pay to the collector of customs of the customs district in which the port of arrival is located, the sum of $1,000, and in addition a sum equal to that paid by such alien for his transportation from the initial point of departure, indicated in his ticket, to the port of arrival for each and every violation of provisions of this section, such latter sum to be delivered by the collector of customs to the alien on whose account assessed. It shall also be unlawful for any such person to bring to any port of the United States any alien afflicted with any mental defect other than those above specifically named, or physical defect of a nature which may affect his ability to earn a living, as contemplated in section 3 of this Act. . . . It shall also be unlawful for any such person to bring to any port of the United States any alien who is excluded by the provisions of section 3 of this Act because unable to read, or who is excluded by the terms of section 3 of this Act as a native of that portion of the Continent of Asia and the islands adjacent thereto described in said section. . . ."

The Philippine Independence Act (Tydings-McDuffie Act) (1934)

Enacted on March 24, 1934, the Tydings-McDuffie Act (officially known as the Philippine Independence Act) was intended to provide a template for Filipino independence from the United States after a ten-year period. The act allowed the United States to maintain a military presence in the Philippines; it also reclassified Filipinos as "aliens" with regard to immigration policy. Previously, Filipinos were classified as U.S. nationals and fell outside the purview of immigration law; the act limited Filipino migration to the United States to fifty immigrants per year. (The Philippine Independence Act [An Act to Provide for the Complete Independence of the Philippine Islands, to Provide for the Adoption of a Constitution and a Form of Government for the Philippine Islands, and for Other Purposes]. Pub. L. 73-127; 48 Stat. 456. 24 Mar. 1934.)

Convention to Frame Constitution for Philippine Islands

SEC. 1. The Philippine Legislature is hereby authorized to provide for the election of delegates to a constitutional convention, which shall meet in the hall of the House of Representatives in the capital of the Philippine Islands at such time as the Philippine Legislature may fix, but not later than October 1, 1934, to formulate and draft a constitution for the government of the Commonwealth of the Philippine Islands, subject to the conditions and qualifications prescribed in this Act, which shall exercise jurisdiction over all the territory ceded to the United States by the treaty of peace concluded between the United States and Spain on the 10th day of December, 1898, the boundaries of which are set forth in Article III of said treaty, together with those islands embraced in the treaty between Spain and the United States concluded at Washington on the 7th day of November, 1900. The Philippine Legislature shall provide for the necessary expenses of such convention.

Character of Constitutions—Mandatory Provisions

SEC. 2. (a) The constitution formulated and drafted shall be republican in form, shall contain a bill of rights, and shall, either as a part thereof or in an ordinance appended thereto, contain provisions to the effect that, pending the final and complete withdrawal of the sovereignty of the United States over the Philippine Islands—

  (1) All citizens of the Philippine Islands shall owe allegiance to the United States.
  (2) Every officer of the government of the Commonwealth of the Philippine Islands shall, before entering upon the discharge of his duties, take and subscribe an oath of office, declaring, among other things, that he recognizes and accepts the supreme authority of and will maintain true faith and allegiance to the United States.
  (3) Absolute toleration of religious sentiment shall be secured and no inhabitant or religious organization shall be molested in person or property on account of religious belief or mode of worship.
  (4) Property owned by the United States, cemeteries, churches, and parsonages or convents appurtenant thereto, and all lands, buildings, and improvements used exclusively for reli-

gious, charitable, or educational purposes shall be exempt from taxation.

(5) Trade relations between the Philippine Islands and the United States shall be upon the basis prescribed in section 6.

(6) The public debt of the Philippine Islands and its subordinate branches shall not exceed limits now or hereafter fixed by the Congress of the United States; and no loans shall be contracted in foreign countries without the approval of the President of the United States.

(7) The debts, liabilities, and obligations of the present Philippine Government, its provinces, municipalities, and instrumentalities, valid and subsisting at the time of the adoption of the constitution, shall be assumed and paid by the new government.

(8) Provision shall be made for the establishment and maintenance of an adequate system of public schools, primarily conducted in the English language.

(9) Acts affecting currency, coinage, imports, exports, and immigration shall not become law until approved by the President of the United States.

(10) Foreign affairs shall be under the direct supervision and control of the United States.

(11) All acts passed by the Legislature of the Commonwealth of the Philippine Islands shall be reported to the Congress of the United States.

(12) The Philippine Islands recognizes the right of the United States to expropriate property for public uses, to maintain military and other reservations and armed forces in the Philippines, and, upon order of the President, to call into the service of such armed forces all military forces organized by the Philippine Government.

(13) The decisions of the courts of the Commonwealth of the Philippine Islands shall be subject to review by the Supreme Court of the United States as provided in paragraph 6 of section 7.

(14) The United States may, by Presidential proclamation, exercise the right to intervene for the preservation of the government of the Commonwealth of the Philippine Islands and for the maintenance of the government as provided in the con-

stitution thereof, and for the protection of life, property, and individual liberty and for the discharge of government obligations under and in accordance with the provisions of the constitution.

(15) The authority of the United States High Commissioner to the government of the Commonwealth of the Philippine Islands, as provided in this Act, shall be recognized.

(16) Citizens and corporations of the United States shall enjoy in the Commonwealth of the Philippine Islands all the civil rights of the citizens and corporations, respectively, thereof. . . .

SEC. 8. (a) Effective upon the acceptance of this Act by concurrent resolution of the Philippine Legislature or by a convention called for that purpose, as provided in section 17:

(1) For the purposes of the Immigration Act of 1917, the Immigration Act of 1924 (except section 13 [c]), this section, and all other laws of the United States relating to the immigration, exclusion, or expulsion of aliens, citizens of the Philippine Islands who are not citizens of the United States shall be considered as if they were aliens. For such purposes the Philippine Islands shall be considered as a separate country and shall have for each fiscal year a quota of fifty. This paragraph shall not apply to a person coming or seeking to come to the Territory of Hawaii who does not apply for and secure an immigration or passport visa, but such immigration shall be determined by the Department of the Interior on the basis of the needs of industries in the Territory of Hawaii.

(2) Citizens of the Philippine Islands who are not citizens of the United States shall not be admitted to the continental United States from the Territory of Hawaii (whether entering such territory before or after the effective date of this section) unless they belong to a class declared to be non-immigrants by section 3 of the Immigration Act of 1924 or to a class declared to be nonquota immigrants under the provisions of section 4 of such Act other than subdivision (c) thereof, or unless they were admitted to such territory under an immigration visa. The Secretary of Labor shall by regulations provide a method for such exclusion and for the admission of such excepted classes.

(3) Any Foreign Service officer may be assigned to duty in the Philippine Islands, under a commission as a consular officer, for such period as may be necessary and under such regulations as the Secretary of State may prescribe, during which assignment such officer shall be considered as stationed in a foreign country; but his powers and duties shall be confined to the performance of such of the official acts and notarial and other services, which such officer might properly perform in respect to the administration of the immigration laws if assigned to a foreign country as a consular officer, as may be authorized by the Secretary of State.

(4) For the purposes of sections 18 and 20 of the Immigration Act of 1917, as amended, the Philippine Islands shall be considered a foreign country.

(b) The provisions of this section are in addition to the provisions of the immigration laws now in force, and shall be enforced as part of such laws, and all the penal or other provisions of such laws not applicable, shall apply to and be enforced in connection with the provisions of this section. An alien, although admissible under the provisions of this section, shall not be admitted to the United States if he is excluded by any provision of the immigration laws other than this section, and an alien, although admissible under the provisions of the immigration laws other than this section, shall not be admitted to the United States if he is excluded by any provision of this section.

(c) Terms defined in the Immigration Act of 1924 shall, when used in this section, have the meaning assigned to such terms in the Act. . . .

The Magnuson Act (1943)

The Magnuson Act repealed the Chinese Exclusion Act of 1882 and all of the subsequent extensions of that act which followed. In addition, it allowed Chinese immigrants the right to apply for naturalized citizenship — the first time Asian immigrants were given that right. However, despite the lifting of exclusion and the right to naturalization, the act allowed for only 105 Chinese immigrants per year to enter the United States, regardless of their country of origin. (The Magnuson Act [An Act to Repeal the Chinese Exclusion

Act, to Establish Quotas, and for Other Purposes]. Pub. L. 78-199; 57 Stat. 600. 17 Dec. 1943.)

Be it enacted by the Senate and the House of Representatives of the United States of America in Congress assembled, That the following Acts or parts of Acts relating to the exclusion or deportation of persons of the Chinese race are hereby repealed: May 6, 1882 (22 Stat. L. 58); July 5, 1884 (23 Stat. L. 115); September 13, 1888 (25 Stat. L. 476); October 1, 1888 (25 Stat. L. 7); that portion of section 1 of the Act of July 7, 1898 (30 Stat. L. 750, 751), which reads as follows: "There shall be no further immigration of Chinese into the Hawaiian Islands except upon such conditions as are now or may hereafter be allowed by the laws of the United States; and no Chinese, by reason of anything herein contained, shall be allowed to enter the United States from the Hawaiian Islands."; section 101 of the Act of April 30, 1900 (31 Stat. L. 141, 161); those portions of section 1 of the Act of June 6, 1900 (31 Stat. L. 588, 611), which read as follows: "And nothing in section four of the Act of August fifth, eighteen hundred and eighty-two (Twenty-second Statutes at Large, page two hundred and twenty-five), shall be construed to prevent the Secretary of the Treasury from hereafter detailing one officer employed in the enforcement of the Chinese Exclusion Acts for duty at the Treasury Department at Washington . . . and hereafter the Commissioner-General of Immigration, in addition to his other duties, shall have charge of the administration of the Chinese exclusion law . . . , under the supervision and direction of the Secretary of the Treasury."; March 3, 1901 (31 Stat. L. 1093); April 29, 1902 (32 Stat. L. 176); April 27, 1904 (33 Stat. L. 428); section 25 of the Act of March 3, 1911 (36 Stat. L. 1087, 1094); that portion of the Act of August 24, 1912 (37 Stat. L. 417, 476), which reads as follows: "*Provided,* That all charges for maintenance or return of Chinese persons applying for admission to the United States shall hereafter be paid or reimbursed to the United States by the person, company, partnership, or corporation, bringing such Chinese to a port of the United Sates as applicants for admission."; that portion of the Act of June 23, 1913 (38 Stat. L. 4, 65), which reads as follows: "*Provided,* That from and after July first, nineteen hundred and thirteen, all Chinese persons ordered deported under judicial writs shall be delivered by the marshal of the district or his deputy into the custody of any officer designated for that purpose by the Secretary of Commerce and Labor, for conveyance to the frontier or seaboard for deportation in the same manner as aliens deported under the immigration laws."

SEC. 2. With the exception of those coming under subsections (b), (d), (e), and (f) of section 4, Immigration Act of 1924 (43 Stat. 155; 44 Stat. 812; 45 Stat. 1009; 46 Stat. 854; 47 Stat. 656; 8 U.S.C. 204), all Chinese persons entering the United States annually as immigrants shall be allocated to the quota for the Chinese computed under the provisions of section 11 of the said Act. A preference up to 75 per centum of the quota shall be given to Chinese born and residents in China.

SEC. 3. Section 303 of the Nationality Act of 1940, as amended (54 Stat. 1140; 8 U.S.C. 703), is hereby amended by striking out the word "and" before the word "descendants," changing the colon after the word "Hemisphere" to a comma, and adding the following: "and Chinese persons or persons of Chinese descent."

Approved December 17, 1943.

The 1945 War Brides Act

The War Brides Act, and subsequent amendments, allowed for the alien spouses and minor children of U.S. citizens who were members of the armed forces to enter the United States. This was especially beneficial for Chinese Americans as it allowed thousands of Chinese women to immigrate to the United States as new brides and many others to rejoin their husbands after years of separation. This increase in the population of Chinese women finally allowed for Chinese immigrants to establish families in ways that were impossible during the years of exclusion, which generally prohibited the immigration of Chinese women. (The War Brides Act [An Act to Expedite the Admission to the United States of Alien Spouses and Alien Minor Children of Citizen Members of the United States Armed Forces]. Pub. L. 79-271; 59 Stat. 659. 28 Dec. 1945.)

Be it enacted by the Senate and House of Representatives of the United States of America in Congress assembled, That notwithstanding any of the several clauses of section 3 of the Act of February 5, 1917, excluding physically and mentally defective aliens, and notwithstanding the documentary requirements of any of the immigration laws or regulations, Executive orders, or Presidential proclamations issued thereunder, alien spouses or alien children of United States citizens serving in, or having an honorable discharge certificate from the armed forces of the United States during the Second World War shall, if otherwise admissible under the immigration laws and if application for admission is made within three years of the effective date of this Act, be admitted to the United States: *Provided,* That every alien of the foregoing description shall be medically examined at the time of arrival in accordance with the provisions of section 16 of the Act of February 5, 1917, and if found suffering from any disability which would be the basis for a ground of exclusion except for the provision of this Act, the Immigration and Naturalization Service shall forthwith notify the appropriate public medical officer of the local community to which the alien is destined: *Provided further,* That the provisions of this Act shall not affect the duties of the United States Public Health Service so far as they relate to quarantinable diseases.

SEC. 2. Regardless of section 9 of the Immigration Act of 1924, any alien admitted under section 1 of this Act shall be deemed to be a non-quota immigrant as defined in section 4 (a) of the Immigration Act of 1924.

SEC. 3. Any alien admitted under section 1 of this Act who at any time returns to the United States after a temporary absence abroad shall not be excluded because of the disability or disabilities that existed at the time of that admission.

SEC. 4. No fine or penalty shall be imposed under the Act of February 5, 1917, except those arising under section 14, because of the transportation to the United States of any alien admitted under this Act.

SEC. 5. For the purpose of this Act, the Second World War shall be deemed to have commenced on December 7, 1941, and to have ceased upon the termination of hostilities as declared by the President or by a joint resolution of Congress.

Approved December 28, 1945.

The McCarran-Walter Act (1952)

The McCarran-Walter Act (also known as the Immigration and Nationality Act) was enacted on June 27, 1952. The provision was sponsored by Pat McCarran (Democrat–Nevada) and Francis Walter (Democrat–Pennsylvania). President Harry S. Truman originally vetoed the act because of its overt anti-Communist provisions. In particular, while the act abolished racial restrictions to naturalized citizenship (expressly those that had historically delimited first-generation Asian immigrants from obtaining U.S. citizenship), it also allowed the United States to deport immigrants and naturalized citizens who were suspected of Communist affiliation. It also restricted the number of immigrants who could enter the United States to 270,000. President Truman vetoed the law on the grounds that it was discriminatory, stating, "In no other realm of our national life are we so hampered and stultified by the dead hand of the past, as we are in the field of immigration"; however, Congress overrode the president's veto and passed the law. (Immigration and Nationality Act of 1952 [McCarran-Walter Act; An Act to Revise the Laws Relating to Immigration, Naturalization, and Nationality; and for Other Purposes]. Pub. L. 414; 66 Stat. 163. 27 June 1952.)

Be it enacted by the Senate and House of Representatives of the United States of America in Congress assembled, That this Act, divided into titles, chapters, and sections according to the following table of contents, may be cited as the "Immigration and Nationality Act." . . .

(17) The term "immigration laws" includes this Act and all laws, conventions, and treaties of the United States relating to the immigration, exclusion, deportation, or expulsion of aliens.

(18) The term "immigration officer" means any employee or class of employees of the Service or of the United States designated by the Attorney General, individually or by regulation, to perform the functions of an immigration officer specified by this Act or any section thereof.

(19) The term "ineligible to citizenship," when used in reference to any individual, means, notwithstanding the provisions of any treaty relating to military service, an individual who is, or was at any time, permanently debarred from becoming a citizen of the United States under section 3 (a) of the Selective Training and Service Act of 1940, as amended (54 Stat. 885; 55 Stat. 844), or under section 4 (a) of the Selective Service Act of 1948, as amended (62 Stat. 605; 65 Stat. 76), or under any section of this Act, or any other Act, or under any law amendatory of, supplementary to, or in substitution for, any of such sections or Acts.

(20) The term "lawfully admitted for permanent residence" means the status of having been lawfully accorded the privilege of residing permanently in the United States as an immigrant in accordance with the immigration laws, such status not having changed.

(21) The term "national" means a person owing permanent allegiance to a state.

(22) The term "national of the United States" means (A) a citizen of the United States, or (B) a person who, though not a citizen of the United States owes permanent allegiance to the United States.

(23) The term "naturalization" means the conferring of nationality of a state upon a person after birth, by any means whatsoever. . . .

(27) The term "nonquota immigrant" means—

(A) an immigrant who is the child or the spouse of a citizen of the United States;

(B) an immigrant, lawfully admitted for permanent residence, who is returning from a temporary visit abroad;

(C) an immigrant who was born in Canada, the Republic of Mexico, the Republic of Cuba, the Republic of Haiti, the Dominican Republic, the Canal Zone, or an independent country of Central or South America, and the spouse or the child of any such immigrant, if accompanying or following to join him;

(D) an immigrant who was a citizen of the United States and may, under section 324 (a) or 327 of title III, apply for reacquisition of citizenship;

(E) an immigrant included within the second proviso to section 349 (a) (1) of title III;

(F) (i) an immigrant who continuously for at least two years immediately preceding the time of his application for admission to the United States has been, and who seeks to enter the United States solely for the purpose of carrying on the vocation of minister of a religious denomination, and whose services are needed by such religious denomination having a bona fide organization in the United States; and (ii) the spouse or the child of any such immigrant, if accompanying or following to join him; or

(G) an immigrant who is an employee, or an honorably retired former employee, of the United States Government abroad, and who has performed faithful service for a total of fifteen years or more, and his accompanying spouse and children: *Provided,* That the principal officer of a Foreign Service establishment, in his discretion, shall have recommended the granting of nonquota status to such alien in exceptional circumstances and the Secretary of State approves such recommendation and finds that it is in the national interest to grant such status. . . .

(e) For the purposes of this Act—

(1) The giving, loaning, or promising of support or of money or any other thing of value to be used for advocating any doctrine shall constitute the advocating of such doctrine; but nothing in this paragraph shall be construed as an exclusive definition of advocating.

(2) The giving, loaning, or promising of support or of money or any other thing of value for any purpose to any organization shall be presumed to constitute affiliation therewith; but nothing in this paragraph shall be construed as an exclusive definition of affiliation.

(3) Advocating the economic, international, and governmental doctrines of world communism means advocating the establishment of a totalitarian Communist dictatorship in any or all of the countries of the world through the medium of an internationally coordinated Communist movement.

(f) For the purposes of this Act—

No person shall be regarded as, or found to be, a person of good moral character who, during the period for which good moral character is required to be established, is, or was—

(1) a habitual drunkard;

(2) one who during such period has committed adultery;

(3) a member of one or more of the classes of persons, whether excludable or not, described in paragraphs (11), (12), and (31) of section 212 (a) of this Act; or paragraphs (9), (10), and (23) of section 212 (a), if the offense described therein, for which such person was convicted or of which he admits the commission, was committed during such period;

(4) one whose income is derived principally from illegal gambling activities;

(5) one who has been convicted of two or more gambling offenses committed during such period;

(6) one who has given false testimony for the purpose of obtaining any benefits under this Act;

(7) one who during such period has been confined, as a result of conviction, to a penal institution for an aggregate period of one hundred and eighty days or more, regardless of whether the offense, or offenses, for which he has been confined were committed within or without such period;

(8) one who at any time has been convicted of the crime of murder.

The fact that any person is not within any of the foregoing classes shall not preclude a finding that for other reasons such person is or was not of good moral character.

(g) For the purposes of this Act any alien ordered deported (whether before or after the enactment of this Act) who has left the United States, shall be considered to have been deported in pursuance of law, irrespective of the source from which the expenses of his transportation were defrayed or of the place to which he departed. . . .

CHAPTER 1—Quota System
NUMERICAL LIMITATIONS; ANNUAL QUOTA BASED UPON NATIONAL ORIGIN; MINIMUM QUOTAS

SEC. 201. (a) The annual quota of any quota area shall be one-sixth of 1 per centum of the number of inhabitants in the continental United States in 1920, which number, except for the purpose of computing quotas for quota areas within the Asia-Pacific triangle, shall be the same number heretofore determined under the provisions of section 11 of the Immigration Act of 1924, attributable by national origin to such quota area: *Provided,* That the quota existing for Chinese persons prior to the date of enactment of this Act shall be continued, and, except as otherwise provided in section 202 (e), the minimum quota for any quota area shall be one hundred.

(b) The determination of the annual quota of any quota area shall be made by the Secretary of State, the Secretary of Commerce, and the Attorney General, jointly. Such officials shall, jointly, report to the President the quota of each quota area, and the President shall proclaim and make known the quotas so reported. Such determination and report shall be made and such proclamation shall be issued as soon as practicable after the date of enactment of this Act. Quotas proclaimed therein shall take effect on the first day of the fiscal year, or the next fiscal half year, next following the expiration of six months after the date of the proclamation, and until such date the existing quotas proclaimed under the Immigration Act of 1924 shall remain in effect. After the making of a proclamation under this subsection the quotas proclaimed therein shall continue with the same effect as if specifically stated herein and shall be final and conclusive for every purpose, except (1) insofar as it is made to appear to the satisfaction of such officials and proclaimed by the President, that an error of fact has occurred in such determination or in such proclamation, or (2) in the case provided for in section 202 (e).

(c) There shall be issued to quota immigrants chargeable to any quota (1) no more immigrant visas in any fiscal year than the quota for such year, and (2) in any calendar month of any fiscal year, no more immigrant visas than 10 per centum of the quota for such year; except that during the last two months of any fiscal year immigrant visas may be issued without regard to the 10 per centum limitation contained herein.

(d) Nothing in this Act shall prevent the issuance (without increasing the total number of quota immigrant visas which may be issued) of an immigrant visa to an immigrant as a quota immigrant even though he is a nonquota immigrant.

(e) The quota numbers available under the annual quotas of each quota area proclaimed under this Act shall be reduced by the number of quota numbers which have been ordered to be deducted from the annual quotas authorized prior to the effective date of the annual quotas proclaimed under this Act under—

(1) section 19 (c) of the Immigration Act of 1917, as amended;
(2) the Displaced Persons Act of 1948, as amended; and
(3) any other Act of Congress enacted prior to the effective date of the quotas proclaimed under this Act. . . .

Amendments to Other Laws

SEC. 402. (a) Section 1546 of title 18 of the United States Code is amended to read as follows:

"§ 1546. Fraud and misuse of visas, permits, and other entry documents

"Whoever, knowingly, forges, counterfeits, alters, or falsely makes any immigrant or nonimmigrant visa, permit, or other document required for entry into the United States, or utters, uses, attempts to use, possesses, obtains, accepts, or receives any such visa, permit, or document, knowing it to be forged, counterfeited, altered, or falsely made, or to have been procured by means of any false claim or statement, or to have been otherwise procured by fraud or unlawfully obtained; or

"Whoever, except under direction of the Attorney General or the Commissioner of the Immigration and Naturalization Service, or other proper officer, knowingly possesses any blank permit, or engraves, sells, brings into the United States, or has in his control or possession any plate in the likeness of a plate designed for the printing of permits, or makes any print, photograph, or impression in the likeness of any immigrant or nonimmigrant visa, permit, or other document required for entry into the United States, or has in his possession a distinctive paper which has been adopted by the Attorney General or the Commissioner of the Immigration and Naturalization Service for the printing of such visas, permits, or documents; or

"Whoever, when applying for an immigrant or nonimmigrant visa, permit, or other document required for entry into the United States, or for admission to the United States personates another, or falsely appears in the name of a deceased individual, or evades or attempts to evade the immigration laws by appearing under an assumed or fictitious name without disclosing his true identity, or sells or otherwise disposes of, or offers to sell or otherwise dispose of, or utters, such visa, permit, or other document, to any person not authorized by law to receive such document; or

"Whoever knowingly makes under oath any false statement with respect to a material fact in any application, affidavit, or other document required by the immigration laws or regulations prescribed thereunder, or knowingly presents any such application, affidavit, or other document containing any such false statement—

"Shall be fined not more than $2,000 or imprisoned not more than five years, or both."

(b) Chapter 69 of title 18, United States Codes, is amended by adding after section 1428 the following new section:

"SEC. 1429. Penalties for neglect or refusal to answer subpoena.

"Any person who has been subpoenaed under the provisions of subsection (e) of section 336 of the Immigration and Nationality Act to appear at the final hearing of a petition for naturalization, and who shall neglect or refuse to so appear and to testify, if in the power of such person to do so, shall be fined not more than $5,000 or imprisoned not more than five years, or both."

(c) Section 1114 of title 18, United States Code, is amended by deleting the language "any immigrant inspector or any immigration patrol inspector" and by substituting therefore the language "any immigration officer."

(d) Subsection (c) of section 8 of the Act of June 8, 1938 (52 Stat. 631; 22 U.S.C. 611–621), entitled "An Act to require the registration of certain persons employed by agencies to disseminate propaganda in the United States, and for other purposes," as amended, is hereby further amended by deleting the language "sections 19 and 20 of the Immigration Act of 1917 (39 Stat. 889, 890), as amended." and by substituting therefor the language "sections 241, 242, and 243 of the Immigration and Nationality Act."

(e) Section 4 of the Act of June 30, 1950 (Public Law 597, Eighty-first Congress, second session), entitled "An Act to provide for the enlistment of aliens in the regular Army" is amended to read as follows:

"SEC. 4. Notwithstanding the dates or periods of service specified and designated in section 329 of the Immigration and Nationality Act, the provisions of that section are applicable to aliens enlisted or reenlisted pursuant to the provisions of this Act and who have completed five or more years of military service, if honorably discharged therefrom. Any alien enlisted or reenlisted pursuant to the provisions of this Act who subsequently enters the United States, American Samoa, Swains Island, or the Canal Zone, pursuant to military orders shall, if otherwise qualified for citizenship, and after completion of five or more years of military service, if honorably discharged therefrom, be deemed to have been lawfully admitted to the United States for permanent residence within the meaning of such section 329 (a)."

(f) Section 201 of the Act of January 27, 1948 (Public Law 402, Eightieth Congress, second session, 62 Stat. 6), entitled "An Act to promote the better understanding of the United States among the peoples of the world and to strengthen cooperative international relations" is amended to read as follows:

"SEC. 201. The Secretary is authorized to provide for interchanges on a reciprocal basis between the United States and other countries of students, trainees, teachers, guest instructors, professors, and leaders in fields of specialized knowledge or skill and shall wherever possible provide these interchanges by using the services of existing reputable agencies which are successfully engaged in such activity. The Secretary may provide for orientation courses and other appropriate services for such persons from other countries upon their arrival in the United States, and for such persons going to other countries from the United States. When any country fails or refuses to cooperate in such program on a basis of reciprocity the Secretary shall terminate or limit such program, with respect to such country, to the extent he deems to be advisable in the interests of the United States. The persons specified in this section shall be admitted as nonimmigrants under section 101 (a) (15) of the Immigration and Nationality Act, for such time and under such conditions as may be prescribed by regulations promulgated by the Secretary of State and the Attorney General. A person admitted under this section who fails to maintain the status under which he was admitted or who fails to depart from the United States at the expiration of the time for which he was admitted, or who engages in activities of a political nature detrimental to the interest of the United States, or in activities not consistent with the security of the United States, shall, upon the warrant of the Attorney General, be taken into custody and promptly deported pursuant to sections 241, 242, and 243 of the Immigration and Nationality Act. Deportation proceedings under this section shall be summary and the findings of the Attorney General as to matters of fact shall be conclusive. Such persons shall not be eligible for suspension of deportation under section 244 of the Immigration and Nationality Act." . . .

Savings Clauses

SEC. 405. (a) Nothing contained in this Act, unless otherwise specifically provided therein, shall be construed to affect the validity of any declaration of intention, petition for naturalization, certificate of naturalization, certificate of citizenship, warrant of arrest, order or warrant of deportation, order of exclusion, or other document or proceeding which shall be valid at the time this Act shall take effect; or to affect any prosecution, suit, action, or proceedings, civil or criminal, brought, or any status, condition, right in process of acquisition, act, thing, liability, obligation, or matter, civil or criminal, done or existing, at the time this Act shall take effect; but as to all such prosecutions, suits, actions, proceedings, statutes, conditions, rights, acts, things, liabilities, obligations, or matters the statutes or parts of statutes repealed by this Act are, unless otherwise specifically provided therein, hereby continued in force and effect. When an immigrant, in possession of an unexpired immigrant visa issued prior to the effective date of this Act, makes application for admission, his admissibility shall be determined under the provisions of law in effect on the date of the issuance of such visa. An application of suspension of deportation under section 19 of the Immigration Act of 1917, as amended, or for adjustment of status under section 4 of the Displaced Persons Act of 1948, as amended, which is pending on the date of enactment of this Act, shall be regarded as a proceeding within the meaning of this subsection.

(b) Except as otherwise specifically provided in title III, any petition for naturalization heretofore filed which may be pending at the time this Act shall take effect shall be heard and determined in accordance with the requirements of law in effect when such petition was filed.

(c) Except as otherwise specifically provided in this Act, the repeal of any statute by this Act shall not terminate nationality heretofore lawfully acquired nor restore nationality heretofore lost under any law of the United States or any treaty to which the United States may have been a party.

(d) Except as otherwise specifically provided in this Act, or any amendment thereto, fees, charges and prices for purposes specified in title V of the Independent Offices Appropriation Act, 1952 (Public Law 137, Eighty-second Congress, approved August 31, 1951), may be fixed and established in the manner and by the head of any Federal Agency as specified in that Act.

(e) This Act shall not be construed to repeal, alter, or amend section 231 (a) of the Act of April 30, 1946 (60 Stat. 148; 22 U.S.C. 1281 (a)), the Act of June 20, 1949 (Public Law 110, section 8, Eighty-first Congress, first session; 63 Stat. 208), the Act of June 5, 1950 (Public Law 535, Eighty-first Congress, second session), nor title V of the Agricultural Act of 1949, as amended (Public Law 78, Eighty-second Congress, first session). . . .

The Hart-Celler Act (1965)

Signed into law by President Lyndon B. Johnson on October 3, 1965, the Immigration and Nationality Act of 1965, known as the Hart-Celler Act, was enacted on June 30, 1968. The act abolished nation-state quotas that had been in place since the passage of the 1921 Emergency Quota Act. The move away from quotas reflected the effect of both the civil rights movement and the Cold War engagements in Southeast Asia. The law was sponsored by Representative Emanuel Celler (Democrat–New York) and Senator Philip Hart (Democrat–Michigan) and established a system of seven preferences (including family reunification and professional skills) for determining who could immigrate to the United States. The elimination of quotas in favor of hemispheric designations (Eastern and Western) enabled the largest en masse migration of Asian and Latino immigrants to date. (Immigration and Nationality Act of 1965 [Hart-Celler Act; An Act to Amend the Immigration and Nationality Act, and for Other Purposes]. Pub. L. 89-236; 79 Stat. 911. 3 Oct. 1965.)

Be it enacted by the Senate and House of Representatives of the United States of America in Congress assembled, That section 201 of the Immigration and Nationality Act (66 Stat. 175; 8 U.S.C. 1151) be amended to read as follows:

"Sect. 201. (a) Exclusive of special immigrants defined in section 101 (a) (27), and of the immediate relatives of United States citizens specified in subsection (b) of this section, the number of aliens who may be issued immigrant visas or who may otherwise acquire the status of an alien lawfully admitted to the United States for permanent residence, or who may, pursuant to section 203 (a) (7) enter conditionally (i) shall not in any of the first three quarters of any fiscal year exceed a total of 45,000 and (ii) shall not in any fiscal year exceed a total of 170,000.

"(b) The 'immediate relatives' referred to in subsection (a) of this section shall mean the children, spouses, and parents of a citizen of the United States: *Provided,* That in the case of parents such citizens must be at least twenty-one years of age. The immediate relatives specified in this subsection who are otherwise qualified for admission as immigrants shall be admitted as such, without regard to the numerical limitations in this Act. . . .

"(e) The immigration pool and the quotas of quota areas shall terminate June 30, 1968. Thereafter immigrants admissible under the provisions of this Act who are subject to the numerical limitations of subsection (a) of this section shall be admitted in accordance with the percentage limitations and in the order of priority specified in section 203."

SEC. 2. Section 202 of the Immigration and Nationality Act (66 Stat. 175; 8 U.S.C. 1152) is amended to read as follows:

"(a) No person shall receive preference or priority or be discriminated against in the issuance of an immigrant visa because of his race, sex, nationality, place of birth, or place of residence except as specifically provided in section 101 (a) (27), section 201 (b), and section 203: *Provided,* That the total number of immigrant visas and the number of conditional entries made available to natives of any single foreign state under paragraphs (1) through (8) of section 203 (a) shall not exceed 20,000 in any fiscal year: *Provided further,* That the foregoing proviso shall not operate to reduce the number of immigrants who may be admitted under the quota of any quota area before June 30, 1968.

"(b) Each independent country, self-governing dominion, mandated territory, and territory under the international trusteeship system of the United Nations, other than the United States and its outlying possessions shall be treated as a separate foreign state for the purposes of the numerical limitation set forth in the proviso to subsection (a) of this section when approved by the Secretary of State. All other inhabited lands shall be attributed to a foreign state specified by the Secretary of State. For the purposes of this Act the foreign state to which an immigrant is chargeable shall be determined by birth within such foreign state except that (1) an alien child, when accompanied by his alien parent or parents, may be charged to the same foreign state as the accompanying parent or of either accompanying parent if such parent has received or would be qualified for an immigrant visa, if necessary to prevent the separation of the child from the accompanying parent or parents, and if the foreign state to which such parent has been or would be chargeable has not exceeded the numerical limitation set forth in the proviso to subsection (a) of this section for that fiscal year; (2) if an alien is chargeable to a different foreign state from that of his accompanying spouse, the foreign state to which such alien is chargeable may, if necessary to prevent the separation of husband and wife, be determined by the foreign state of the accompanying spouse, if such spouse has received or would be qualified for an immigrant visa and if the foreign state to which such spouse has been or would be chargeable has not exceeded the numerical limitation set forth in the proviso to subsection (a) of this section for that fiscal year; (3) an alien born in the United States shall be considered as having been born in the country of which he is a citizen or subject, or if he is not a citizen or subject of any country than in the last foreign country in which he had his residence as determined by the consular officer; (4) an alien born within any foreign state in which neither of his parents was born and in which neither of his parents had a residence at the time of such alien's birth may be charged to the foreign state of either parent. . . ."

Sec. 3. Section 203 of the Immigration and Nationality Act (66 Stat. 175; 8 U.S.C. 1153) is amended to read as follows:

"Sec. 203. (a) Aliens who are subject to the numerical limitations specified in section 201 (a) shall be allotted visas or their conditional entry authorized, as the case may be, as follows:

"(1) Visas shall be first made available, in a number not to exceed 20 per centum of the number specified in section 201 (a) (ii), to qualified immigrants who are the unmarried sons or daughters of citizens of the United States.

"(2) Visas shall next be made available, in a number not to exceed 2 per centum of the number specified in section 201 (a) (ii), plus any visas not required for the classes specified in paragraph (1), to qualified immigrants who are the spouses, unmarried sons or unmarried daughters of an alien lawfully admitted for permanent residence.

"(3) Visas shall next be made available, in a number not to exceed 10 per centum of the number specified in section 201 (a) (ii), to qualified immigrants who are members of the professions, or who because of their exceptional ability in the sciences or the arts will substantially benefit prospectively the national economy, cultural interests, or welfare of the United States.

"(4) Visas shall next be made available, in a number not to exceed 10 per centum of the number specified in section 201 (a) (ii), plus any visas not required for the classes specified in paragraphs (1) through (3), to qualified immigrants who are the married sons or the married daughters of citizens of the United States.

"(5) Visas shall next be made available in a number not to exceed 24 per centum of the number specified in section 201 (a) (ii), plus any visas not required for the classes specified in paragraphs (1) through (4), to qualified immigrants who are the brothers or sisters of citizens of the United States.

"(6) Visas shall next be made available, in a number not to exceed 10 per centum of the number specified in section 201 (a) (ii), to qualified immigrants who are capable of performing specified skilled or unskilled labor, not of a temporary or seasonal nature, for which a shortage of employable and willing persons exists in the United States.

"(7) Conditional entries shall next be made available by the Attorney General, pursuant to such regulations as he may prescribe and in a number not to exceed 6 per centum of the number specified in section 201 (a) (ii), to aliens who satisfy an Immigration and Naturalization Service officer at an examination in any non-Communist or non-Communist-dominated country, (A) that (i) because of persecution or fear of persecution on account of race, religion, or political opinion they have fled

(I) from any Communist or Communist-dominated country or area or (II) from any country within the general area of the Middle East, and (ii) are unable or unwilling to return to such country or area on account of race, religion, or political opinion, and (iii) are not nationals of the countries or areas in which their application for conditional entry is made; or (B) that they are persons uprooted by catastrophic natural calamity as defined by the President who are unable to return to their usual place of abode. For the purpose of the foregoing terms 'general area of the Middle East' means the area between and including (1) Libya on the west, (2) Turkey on the north, (3) Pakistan on the east and (4) Saudi Arabia and Ethiopia on the south: *Provided,* That immigrant visas in a number not exceeding one-half the number specified in this paragraph may be made available, in lieu of conditional entries of a like number, to such aliens who have been continuously physically present in the United States for a period of at least two years prior to application for adjustment of status.

"(8) Visas authorized in any fiscal year, less those required for issuance to the classes specified in paragraphs (1) through (6) and less the number of conditional entries and visas made available pursuant to paragraph (7), shall be made available to other qualified immigrants strictly in the chronological order in which they qualify. Waiting lists of applicants shall be maintained in accordance with regulations prescribed by the Secretary of State. No immigrant visa shall be issued to a nonpreference immigrant under this paragraph, or to an immigrant with a preference under paragraph (3) or (6) of this subsection, until the consular officer is in receipt of a determination made by the Secretary of Labor pursuant to the provisions of section 212 (1) (14). . . ."

Approved October 3, 1965, 3:25 p.m.

The Indochina Migration and Refugee Assistance Act (1975)

Signed into law on May 23, 1975, the Indochina Migration and Refugee Assistance Act was intended to deal with an impending refugee crisis developing in Southeast Asia after the so-called Fall of Saigon on April 30, 1975. In particular, the act granted asylum in the United States for former U.S. allies (specifically South Vietnamese, Laotians, and Cambodians). An estimated 130,000 Southeast Asian refugees gained admittance to the United States through the act. (The Indochina Migration and Refugee Assistance Act [An Act to Enable the United States to Render Assistance to, or in Behalf of, Certain Migrants and Refugees]. Pub. L. 94-23; 89 Stat. 87. 23 May 1975.)

Be it enacted by the Senate and House of Representatives of the United States of American Congress assembled. That this Act may be cited as "The Indochina Migration and Refugee Assistance Act of 1975."

SEC. 2. (a) Subject to the provisions of subsection (b) there are hereby authorized to be appropriated, in addition to amounts otherwise available for such purposes, $155,000,000 for the performance of functions put forth in the Migration and Refugee Assistance Act of 1962 (76 Stat. 121), as amended with respect to aliens who have fled from Cambodia or Vietnam, such sums to remain available in accordance with the provisions of subsection (b) of this section.

(b) None of the funds authorized to be appropriated by this Act shall be available for the performance of functions after June 30, 1976, other than for carrying out the provisions of clauses (3), (4), (5), and (6) of section 2 (b) of the Migration and Refugee Assistance Act of 1962, as amended. None of such funds shall be available for any purpose after September 30, 1977.

SEC. 3. In carrying out functions utilizing the funds made available under this Act, the term "refugee" as defined in section 2 (b) (3) of the Migration and Refugee Assistance Act of 1962, as amended, shall be deemed to include aliens who (A) because of persecution or fear of persecution on account of race, religion, or political opinion, fled from Cambodia or Vietnam; (B) cannot return there because of fear of persecution on account of race, religion, or political opinion; and (C) are in urgent need of assistance for the essentials of life.

SEC. 4. (a) The President shall consult with and keep the Committees on the Judiciary, Appropriations, and International Relations of the House of Representatives and the Committees on Foreign Relations, Appropriations and Judiciary of the Senate fully and currently informed of the use of funds and the exercise of functions authorized in this Act.

(b) Not more than thirty days after the date of enactment of this Act, the President shall transmit to such Committees a report describing fully and completely the status of refugees from Cambodia and South Vietnam. Such report shall set forth, in addition—

(1) a plan for the resettlement of those refugees remaining in receiving or staging centers;

(2) the number of refugees who have indicated an interest in returning to their homeland or being resettled in a third country, together with (A) a description of the plan for their return or resettlement and the steps taken to carry out such return or resettlement, and (B) any initiatives that have been made with respect to the Office of the High Commissioner for Refugees of the United Nations; and

(3) a full and complete description of the steps the President has taken to retrieve and deposit in the Treasury as miscellaneous receipts all amounts previously authorized and appropriated for assistance to South Vietnam and Cambodia but not expended for such purpose, exclusive of the $98,000,000 of Indochina Postwar Reconstruction funds allocated to the Department of State for movement and maintenance of refugees prior to the date of enactment of this Act.

(c) Supplementary reports setting forth recent information with respect to each of the items referred to in this section shall be transmitted not more than ninety days after the date of transmittal of the report referred to in subsection (b) of this section and not later than the end of each ninety-day period thereafter. Such reports shall continue until September 30, 1977, and a final report shall be submitted no later than December 31, 1977.

Approved May 23, 1975.

The Refugee Act of 1980

Signed into law by President Jimmy Carter on March 17, 1980, the Refugee Act revised the Indochina Refugee Migration and Assistance Act of 1975 to make more explicit and uniform a procedure of resettlement for those seeking asylum in the United States. The act also redefined the status of a "refugee" to cohere with the U.N. Convention and Protocol Relating to the Status of Refugees. (The Refugee Act [An Act to Amend the Immigration and Nationality Act to Revise the Procedures for the Admission of Refugees, to Amend the Migration and Refugee Assistance Act of 1962 to Establish a More Uniform Basis for the Provision of Assistance to Refugees, and for Other Purposes]. Pub. L. 96-212; 94 Stat. 102. 17 Mar. 1980.)

Be it enacted by the Senate and House of Representatives of the United States of America in Congress assembled, That this Act may be cited as the "Refugee Act of 1980."

Title I—Purpose

SEC. 101. (a) The Congress declares that it is the historic policy of the United States to respond to the urgent needs of persons subject to persecution in their homelands, including, where appropriate, humanitarian assistance for their care and maintenance in asylum areas, efforts to promote opportunities for resettlement or voluntary repatriation, aid for necessary transportation and processing, admission to this country of refugees of special humanitarian concern to the United States, and transitional assistance to refugees in the United States. The Congress further declares that it is the policy of the United States to encourage all nations to provide assistance and resettlement opportunities to refugees to the fullest extent possible.

(b) The objectives of this Act are to provide a permanent and systematic procedure for the admission to this country of refugees of special humanitarian concern to the United States, and to provide comprehensive and uniform provisions for the effective resettlement and absorption of those refugees who are admitted.

Title II—Admission of Refugees

SEC. 201. (a) Section 101 (a) of the Immigration and Nationality Act (8 U.S.C. 1101 (a)) is amended by adding after paragraph (41) the following new paragraph:

"(42) The term 'refugee' means (A) any person who is outside any country of such person's nationality or, in the case of a person having no nationality, is outside any country in which such person last habitually resided, and who is unable or unwilling to return to, and is unable or unwilling to avail himself or herself of the protection of, that country because of persecution or a well-founded fear of persecution on account of race, religion, nationality, membership in a particular social group, or political opinion, or (B) in such special circumstances that the President after appropriate consultation (as defined in section 207 (e) of this Act) may specify, any person who is within the country of such person's nationality or, in the case of a person having no nationality, within the country in which such person is habitually residing, and who is persecuted or who has a well-founded fear of persecution on account of race, religion, nationality, membership in a particular social group, or political opinion. The term 'refugee' does not include any person who ordered, incited, assisted, or otherwise participated in the persecution of any person on account of race, religion, nationality, membership in a particular social group, or political opinion." . . .

"(e) . . . the term 'appropriate consultation' means, with respect to the admission of refugees and the allocation of refugee admissions, discussions in person by designated Cabinet-level representatives of the President with members of the Committees on the Judiciary of the Senate and of the House of Representatives to review the refugee situation or emergency refugee situation, to project the extent of possible participation of the United States therein, to discuss the reasons for believing that the proposed admission of refugees is justified by humanitarian concerns or grave humanitarian concerns or is otherwise in the national interest, and to provide such members with the following information:

"(1) A description of the nature of the refugee situation.
"(2) A description of the number and allocation of refugees to be admitted and an analysis of conditions within the countries from which they came.
"(3) A description of the proposed plans for their movement and resettlement and the estimated cost of their movement and resettlement.
"(4) An analysis of the anticipated social, economic, and demographic impact of their admission to the United States.
"(5) A description of the extent to which other countries will admit and assist in the resettlement of other refugees.
"(6) An analysis of the impact of the participation of the United States in the resettlement of such refugees on the foreign policy interests of the United States.
"(7) Such additional information as may be appropriate or requested by such members.

To the extent possible, information described in this subsection shall be provided at least two weeks in advance of discussions in person by designated representatives of the President with such members. . . ."

Approved March 17, 1980.

Statement on Signing the American Competitiveness in the Twenty-First Century Act (2000)

A nonimmigrant visa, the H-1B visa, allows U.S. employers to temporarily employ foreign workers in specialty occupations for a limited time period. Such occupations include work in biotechnology, chemistry, architecture, engineering, mathematics, physical sciences, social sciences, medicine, education, law, accounting, business, and the arts. A holdover from the preferences listed in the 1965 Hart-Celler Act, the H-1B visa provision was responsible for bringing many workers from Asia (particularly India and China) to the United States. The temporary nature of the visa, coupled with disproportionate control that employers had over employees, led some to critique the program as a new form of indentured labor. In 1998 President Bill Clinton signed the American Competitiveness and Workforce Improvement Act, which expanded—via a temporary H-1B cap increase—the purview of the program to meet the needs of a growing information technology industry. What follows is a presidential statement about the American Competitiveness in the Twenty-First Century Act, which further increased the scope of the H-1B program. (Washington, DC, 17 Oct. 2000. American Presidency Project, University of California, Santa Barbara. Online at http://www .presidency.ucsb.edu/.)

I am pleased today to sign into law S. 2045, the "American Competitiveness in the Twenty-First Century Act," and H.R. 5362, an Act to increase the fees charged to employers who petition to employ H-1B nonimmigrant workers. Together, these laws increase the number of H-1B visas available to bring in highly skilled foreign temporary workers and double the fee charged to employers using the program to provide critical funding for training U.S. workers and students. The Acts recognize the importance of allowing additional skilled workers into the United States to work in the short-run, while supporting longer-term efforts to prepare American workers for the jobs of the new economy.

At the core of my economic strategy has been the belief that fiscal discipline and freeing up capital for private sector investment must be accompanied by a commitment to invest in human capital. The growing demand for workers with high-tech skills is a dramatic illustration of the need to "put people first" and increase our investments in education and training. Today, many companies are reporting that their number one constraint on growth is the inability to hire workers with the necessary skills. In today's knowledge-based economy, what you earn depends on what you learn. Jobs in the information technology sector, for example, pay 85 percent more than the private sector average.

My Administration has made clear that any increase in H-1B visas should be temporary and limited in number, that the fee charged to employers using the program should be increased significantly, and that the majority of the funds generated by the fee must go to the Department of Labor to fund training for U.S. workers seeking the necessary skills for these jobs. This legislation does those things. But the need to educate and train workers for these high-skilled jobs goes beyond what has been addressed here.

I want to challenge the high-tech companies to redouble their efforts to find long-term solutions to the rapidly growing demand for workers with technical skills. This will require doing more to improve K–12 science and math education, upgrading the skills of our existing workforce, and recruiting from underrepresented groups such as older workers, minorities, women, persons with disabilities, and residents of rural areas. Many companies have important initiatives in these areas, but we clearly need to be doing more.

This legislation contains a number of provisions that merit concern. For example, one provision allows an H-1B visa holder to work for an employer who has not yet been approved for participation in the H-1B program. In addition, there are provisions that could have the unintended consequence of allowing an H-1B visa holder who is applying for a permanent visa to remain in H-1B status well beyond the current 6-year limit. I am concerned that these provisions could weaken existing protections that ensure that the H-1B program does not undercut the wages and working conditions of U.S. workers, and could also increase the vulnerability of H-1B workers to any unscrupulous employers using the program. For example, one of the key requirements of the H-1B program is that the foreign worker is paid the same wage as U.S. workers doing the same job. This legislation, however, by allowing H-1B workers to change employers before a new employer's application has been approved, could result in an employer—knowingly or unknowingly—not paying the prevailing wage. For these reasons, I am directing the Immigration and Naturalization Service, in consultation with the Department of State and the Department of Labor, to closely monitor the impact of these provisions to determine whether the next congress should revisit these changes made to the H-1B program.

I had hoped that the Congress would take this opportunity to address important issues of fairness affecting many immigrants already in this country. We need to meet the needs of the high-tech industry by raising the number of visas for temporary high-tech workers. But we also must ensure fairness for immigrants who have been in this country for years, working hard and paying taxes. The Latino and Immigrant Fairness Act (LIFA) will allow people who have lived here for 15 years or more—and who have established families and strong ties to their communities—to become permanent residents. It will also amend the Nicaraguan Adjustment and Central American Relief Act (NACARA) to extend the same protections currently offered to people from Cuba and Nicaragua to immigrants from Honduras, Guatemala, El Salvador, Haiti, and Liberia who fled to this country to escape serious hardship. Finally, it will allow families to stay together while their applications for permanent resident status are being processed. These fundamental fairness provisions have been embraced by humanitarian groups, business groups, and Members of the Congress from both sides of the aisle. I will continue to insist strongly on passage of the Latino and Immigrant Fairness Act this year, before the Congress adjourns.

WILLIAM J. CLINTON
The White House,
October 17, 2000.

Cambodian-Americans Confronting Deportation
Olesia Plokhii and Tom Mashberg

In 1996, Congress (with the support of then-president Bill Clinton) signed into law the Illegal Immigration Reform and Immigrant Responsibility Act. Among its most significant provisions was the expanded use of deportation as a punishment for both undocumented immigrants and permanent residents. Before the act's passage, deportation was a possible sentence only in cases involving a crime that would lead to five or more years of impris-

onment; after 1996, deportable offenses included more serious felonies and relatively minor crimes such as shoplifting or check kiting. The number of deportations rose dramatically after the terrorist attacks of September 11, 2001; treaties were orchestrated with a number of countries post-9/11, including Cambodia. An estimated sixteen hundred Cambodian Americans have been slated for deportation; these individuals originally came to the United States as refugees who had survived the genocidal policies of the Khmer Rouge. Many had spent the majority of their lives in the United States and considered themselves Americans, as the following newspaper article from January 2013 brings to light. (Boston Globe, 27 Jan. 2013. Online at https://www .bostonglobe.com. Reprinted with permission from the authors.)

The number of "Khmericans" being sent back to their homeland is on the rise. Meet one young man yearning for the old days in Lowell, Massachusetts, but committed to starting over.

Sokha Chhim rarely heads to work without a black Red Sox cap propped on his head. He makes sure his Nikes stay flashy and white, that the legs of his baggy jeans drape at just the right angle. Sometimes he'll don a royal blue jersey featuring Tom Brady's No. 12. But in a concession to his new homeland, Chhim hangs a black and gray scarf called a *krama* around his neck instead of the gangster chain he wore on the streets of Lowell.

Chhim is an outcast, one of 30 or so Cambodian-American lawbreakers from Massachusetts sent back to Cambodia in the last 10 years. He was deported to Phnom Penh in May 2011 after violating probation in the shooting of a rival drug dealer, arriving penniless and unwanted. He speaks broken Khmer, has no family to lean on, and needs a map to navigate this zigzagging city of nearly 2 million. Yet he is putting down roots in native soil he never knew. And unlike most exiled "Khmericans," who seethe over their loss of American residency, he is finding his own redemption.

"When I first arrived, I was stunned," the 31-year-old Chhim says of life in Cambodia's capital, an enchanting but fractured city that teems with amputees, beggars, and mutts, yet features glorious French Colonial architecture, fine European restaurants, and fleets of Lexus SUVs. "America is all I knew. Everything about me was American."

But "Cambodia opened my eyes," he says. "I've found a reason to live."

As federal officials broaden efforts nationwide to seize and deport immigrants with criminal records, the streets of Phnom Penh will inevitably see more Massachusetts exiles like Chhim. Some 600 Cambodian-Americans, virtually all of them male and a majority convicted criminals, have been shipped to Asia's most traumatized nation since 2002, when Cambodia signed a repatriation agreement with the United States. Federal data show that deportations averaged 41 per year from 2001 through 2010, only to leap to 97 in 2011 and 93 last year. "People are getting picked up left and right," says June Beack, a lawyer at Neighborhood Legal Services in Lynn who has defended Cambodian-Americans facing deportation.

Cambodians have long posed a deportation dilemma for the United States. Brought here as victims of the Vietnam War and the Killing Fields of the Khmer Rouge, most were dropped into ghettos in Lowell, Lynn, and Long Beach, California, and left to overcome cultural and language barriers with little support from the government that took them in. While illiterate adults fell into low-pay work, their children stumbled through crowded public schools or took to the streets in violent gangs. Many of those eventually deported had become hardened felons, but others were exiled for first-time misdemeanors like shoplifting or check fraud. A major reason for their expulsion is that they never obtained citizenship, an option open to them as war refugees. Chhim was in that category, and the result of his blunder was a one-way trip to an unknown land.

"All of them want to become citizens," says Rasy Ross An, director of the Cambodian Mutual Assistance Association of Lowell, a nonprofit group. "But it's not easy to learn English, and it's expensive when you are struggling to survive."

Lowell's 13,300 Cambodians form the second-largest concentration in the nation, after Long Beach, with 50,000. (Lynn has 3,500.) They account for 13 percent of Lowell's population, according to city data. Since settling there in the 1980s, they have taken notable strides, owning dozens of small businesses and seating the City Council's second Cambodian-American member, Vesna Nuon, last year. But there are well-documented problems. For two decades, Southeast Asian gangs lured Khmerican teens living in Lowell by the hundreds, offering them a sense of belonging they could not find elsewhere. Jean Sherlock, a high school teacher in Chicopee who studied Lowell's Cambodian gangs in graduate school, was a mentor to Chhim. She recalls him as an "upbeat, gregarious" teenager. "I remember there is one photo of a birthday party at our house and there he is, at the back of the photo, holding up a peace sign," she says. Some of the fault for his fate, she says, belongs with the state's education and justice systems, which do too little to steer young people like Chhim and his peers away from gang life. "The system isn't set up to give these kids what they need. It's set up to lock them up."

Chhim started life as a lucky survivor of the murderous revolutionaries known as the Khmer Rouge. He was born in 1981 in a refugee camp on the Thai-Cambodian border, where he contracted a bacterial infection. Chhim's mother, who remained in Cambodia, asked his aunt and uncle to take the ailing baby to Western Massachusetts, where they were being sponsored by a local couple. "I guess I was a cute baby, but I was sickly," he says. As he came of age in Amherst, Chhim built up a resentment toward the endless list of responsibilities that came with being the sole English speaker in his home. "I felt like the whole world was on my back," he recalls. "I got tired of always waiting for the cable guy." He began skipping school, getting into fights, and smoking marijuana. His first run-in with the law was at age 14, when he spent a night in jail for driving a stolen vehicle. He soon quit school and moved to Lowell on his own to find work. "Lowell was just worse," he says. "Everybody around you was drug dealers, gangbangers." Chhim joined up, eager to make money for that "new pair of Jordans," he says.

After tapping into a drug network, he moved back to Amherst to take over a profitable piece of turf near the state university. Conflicts with other dealers flared, and in 1998 Chhim decided to make a statement by robbing a rival at gunpoint. During a standoff, he fired, striking his victim in the neck. "If I could take it all back, I would," Chhim says. "I have to live with that crime my whole life."

The rival dealer survived to testify, and Chhim received a 10-year sentence. In prison, remorse at disappointing his aunt ate at him. His worst day came in 2002, he says, when he learned she had died of a heart attack. (Chhim's uncle has suffered poor health since 2000.) Despite poverty, diabetes, and dialysis, his aunt had routinely visited him behind bars, Chhim says; she would travel for hours by bus and then weep softly as he rubbed her tired feet and work-worn hands. "I would usually cry after her visits," he recalls, tearing up. "That's when I really started to experience love."

It was also when he decided he could turn his life around. He obtained his GED in prison and took anger management and resume-writing courses. Prison "taught me how to grow up," he says. Still, after serving nine years and four months, Chhim failed to transition to the clean life he imagined and began violating probation. Fearing the inevitable deportation, he began a year underground. "It was just keep running and trying to survive," he says.

Chhim knew only horror stories of his homeland: a quarter of the population diseased, starved, or put to death by the Khmer Rouge; a life of tilling fields from dusk till dawn; a sweltering climate and authoritarian system in which the privileged crush and exploit the impoverished. And worse. "Everybody heard stories about Cambodian jails," he says.

Lowell police caught up with Chhim in 2010. He spent 15 months in jail and detention centers and in May 2011 was flown to Phnom Penh. There, he could have tumbled into a life of crime, substance abuse, and resentment, the fate of many returnees. But the affable, broad-shouldered Chhim does not believe in "thinking backwards." Sipping a Coke on a 99-degree day in Phnom Penh, he says: "A lot of deportees are bitter. We have to break that cycle."

Chhim works six days a week as a projectionist at a movie theater, husbanding his $300 or so in monthly income by sleeping in a cheap room provided by the theater owner. "I've never worked this hard in my life," he says. "I'm really proud of myself and wish my [aunt] could see my potential."

That potential is something the Rev. Bill Herod has been trying to unlock for years. An Indiana minister who has lived in Cambodia since 1994, he started the Returnee Integration Support Center in Phnom Penh in 2002 to help deportees like Chhim obtain documents, housing, jobs, and drug treatment. He knows of 12 returnees who have died, several from suicide or drug overdoses. Another 17 are in prison. Some arrive without the medical paperwork required under the US-Cambodia repatriation agreement, which Herod believes is crucial for their physical and emotional well-being. All are left to fend for themselves.

"Most do not transition easily into Cambodian life," says Herod. He lost an eye when drain cleaner splashed into his face as he tried to tear the poison from the hands of a suicidal returnee. "Most have strong resistance to the country, the people, the food, the society, the traditions, the language," he says. Those who succeed must choose not to give up.

"Virtually all of these individuals lived in the US during their formative years," says Herod, "and whatever trouble they got into was the result of their time in the United States, not Cambodia. It is unfair to penalize these people, and the people of Cambodia, for the failures of the US refugee resettlement program."

In Lowell, the effects of poor integration, lack of education, and bad decisions continue to plague the new generation of Cambodian-Americans. Gregg Croteau, executive director of the United Teen Equality Center in Lowell, which offers work and study opportunities for at-risk youths, has seen it firsthand. Many come from broken homes, have criminal records, and do drugs. His newly refurbished center is trying to battle this epidemic, Croteau says, by helping these kids "trade violence and poverty for social and economic success."

Opened in 1999 and serving 1,000 teens a year, a third of them Cambodian, the center is a haven from gang violence and life on the fringes. Located in an old Methodist church, it offers training in the building trades, culinary classes, counseling, and GED preparation. Cambodian youths stop by after work or school to learn carpentry, play foosball, shoot baskets, and hone their music skills in a new recording studio, part of a recent 8,000-square-foot addition inaugurated by Governor Deval Patrick in mid-November.

The center is a place of redemption for men like Sakieth "Sako" Long. A mentor and program leader at the center, the 33-year-old Long arrived in Lowell from Cambodia as a child and grew up with street gangsters for role models. He got into trouble with the law in the late 1990s, but a few years later connected with the center and got a job there. He has since focused on saving young Cambodian-Americans from crime, gangs, and a life of regret. "You can leave the gang life and be successful the hard blood-and-sweat way instead of hustling," he says.

But without people like Long to put them on the right path, many Cambodian-Americans lacking US citizenship end up back in a homeland they never knew. Nationwide, nearly 1,900 have final orders of removal, according to federal Immigration and Customs Enforcement officials, meaning they can be expelled at any time, while 669 are in deportation proceedings.

The ones facing exile can look to Chhim, whose odyssey from Massachusetts to the Mekong has led to a paycheck and a budding hip-hop career. He hopes to try out for Cambodia's national baseball team, and he released a mix tape titled "Take Over" in September. "It feels good to be appreciated for doing the right thing, and it took Cambodia to do that," Chhim says. Under his musical moniker, Dolla, he pens melancholy lyrics like these: *Can't go back, go back, to a place that I call home. Exiled American is who I am, a one-way flight wasn't part of the plan.*

It is a far from ideal fate, and Chhim rues the fact that he will never experience another live Patriots game or night of clubbing and fast food in Boston. Still, he has no choice but to call this troubled nation home. "I failed the test," Chhim says of his squandered American experience. "They didn't believe in me anymore, and now I get a chance to show them that I am somebody."

Recommended Resources

Chinese Immigration to the Americas

Chan, Sucheng. *Entry Denied: Exclusion and the Chinese Community in America, 1882–1943*. Philadelphia: Temple University Press, 1991.

———. *This Bittersweet Soil: The Chinese in California Agriculture, 1860–1910*. Berkeley: University of California Press, 1986.

Hsu, Madeline Y. *Dreaming of Gold, Dreaming of Home: Transnationalism and Migration Between the United States and South China, 1882–1943*. Stanford, CA: Stanford University Press, 2000.

———. *The Good Immigrants: How the Yellow Peril Became the Model Minority*. Princeton, NJ: Princeton University Press, 2015.

Lee, Erika. *At America's Gates: Chinese Immigration During the Exclusion Era, 1882–1943*. Chapel Hill: University of North Carolina Press, 2003.

Lui, Mary Ting Yi. *The Chinatown Trunk Mystery: Murder, Miscegenation, and Other Dangerous Encounters in Turn-of-the-Century New York City*. Princeton, NJ: Princeton University Press, 2005.

McKeown, Adam. *Chinese Migrant Networks and Cultural Change: Peru, Chicago, Hawaii, 1900–1936*. Chicago: University of Chicago Press, 2001.

Meagher, Arnold J. *The Coolie Trade: The Traffic in Chinese Laborers to Latin America, 1847–1874*. Philadelphia: Xlibris, 2008.

Peffer, George Anthony. *If They Don't Bring Their Women Here: Chinese Female Immigration Before Exclusion*. Champaign: University of Illinois Press, 1999.

Schiavone, Julia María Camacho. *Chinese Mexicans: Transpacific Migration and the Search for a Homeland, 1910–1960*. Chapel Hill: University of North Carolina Press, 2012.

Siu, Lok. *Memories of a Future Home: Diasporic Citizenship of Chinese in Panama*. Stanford, CA: Stanford University Press, 2005.

Tchen, John Kuo Wei. *New York Before Chinatown: Orientalism and the Shaping of American Culture, 1776–1882*. Baltimore: Johns Hopkins University Press, 1999.

Wong, K. Scott, and Sucheng Chan, eds. *Claiming America: Constructing Chinese American Identities During the Exclusion Era*. Philadelphia: Temple University Press, 1998.

Yun, Lisa. *The Coolie Speaks: Chinese Indentured Laborers and African Slaves in Cuba*. Philadelphia: Temple University Press, 2007.

Japanese Immigration to the Americas

Endō, Toake. *Exporting Japan: Politics of Emigration Toward Latin America*. Champaign: University of Illinois Press, 2009.

Geiger, Andrea A. E. *Subverting Exclusion: Transpacific Encounters with Race, Caste, and Borders, 1885–1928*. New Haven, CT: Yale University Press, 2011.

Lee, Shelley Sang-Hee. *Claiming the Oriental Gateway: Prewar Seattle and Japanese America*. Philadelphia: Temple University Press, 2012.

Masterson, Daniel M., and Sayaka Funada-Classen. *The Japanese in Latin America*. Champaign: University of Illinois Press, 2004.

Okihiro, Gary Y. *Cane Fires: The Anti-Japanese Movement in Hawaii, 1865–1945*. Philadelphia: Temple University Press, 1991.

Spickard, Paul R. *Japanese Americans: The Formation and Transformations of an Ethnic Group*. New York: Twayne, 1996.

Tsuda, Takeyuki. *Strangers in the Ethnic Homeland: Japanese Brazilian Return Migration in Transnational Perspective*. New York: Columbia University Press, 2003.

Korean Immigration to the United States

Chin, Soo-Young. *Doing What Had to Be Done: The Life Narrative of Dora Yum Kim*. Philadelphia: Temple University Press, 1999.

Cho, Grace M. *Haunting the Korean Diaspora: Shame, Secrecy, and the Forgotten War*. Minneapolis: University of Minnesota Press, 2008.

Kim, Eleana J. *Adopted Territory: Transnational Korean Adoptees and the Politics of Belonging*. Durham, NC: Duke University Press, 2010.

Kim, Richard S. *The Quest for Statehood: Korean Immigrant Nationalism and U.S. Sovereignty, 1905–1945*. New York: Oxford University Press, 2011.

Kwon, Victoria Hyonchu. *Entrepreneurship and Religion: Korean Immigrants in Houston, Texas*. New York: Routledge, 2014.

Park, Kyeyoung. *The Korean American Dream: Immigrants and Small Business in New York City*. Ithaca, NY: Cornell University Press, 1997.

Tuan, Mia, and Jiannbin Lee Shiao. *Choosing Ethnicity, Negotiating Race: Korean Adoptees in America*. New York: Russell Sage Foundation, 2011.

Yoo, David K. *Contentious Spirits: Religion in Korean American History, 1903–1945*. Stanford, CA: Stanford University Press, 2010.

Filipino Migration to the United States

Baldoz, Rick. *The Third Asiatic Invasion: Empire and Migration in Filipino America, 1898–1946*. New York: New York University Press, 2011.

Choy, Catherine Ceniza. *Empire of Care: Nursing and Migration in Filipino American History.* Durham, NC: Duke University Press, 2003.

Cruz, Denise. *Transpacific Femininities: The Making of the Modern Filipina.* Durham, NC: Duke University Press, 2012.

España-Maram, Linda. *Creating Masculinity in Los Angeles's Little Manila: Working-Class Filipinos and Popular Culture in the United States.* New York: Columbia University Press, 2006.

Espiritu, Augusto Fauni. *Five Faces of Exile: The Nation and Filipino American Intellectuals.* Stanford, CA: Stanford University Press, 2005.

Friday, Chris. *Organizing Asian American Labor: The Pacific Coast Canned-Salmon Industry, 1870–1942.* Philadelphia: Temple University Press, 1994.

Fujita-Rony, Dorothy B. *American Workers, Colonial Power: Philippine Seattle and the Transpacific West, 1919–1941.* Berkeley: University of California Press, 2003.

Guevarra, Rudy. *Becoming Mexipino: Multiethnic Identities and Communities in San Diego.* New Brunswick, NJ: Rutgers University Press, 2012.

Poblete, JoAnna. *Islanders in the Empire: Filipino and Puerto Rican Laborers in Hawai'i.* Champaign: University of Illinois Press, 2014.

Southeast Asian Migration and Immigration to the United States

Bao, Jiemin. *Creating a Buddhist Community: A Thai Temple in Silicon Valley.* Philadelphia: Temple University Press, 2014.

Chan, Sucheng, ed. *Hmong Means Free: Life in Laos and America.* Philadelphia: Temple University Press, 1994.

———. *Survivors: Cambodian Refugees in the United States.* Champaign: University of Illinois Press, 2004.

———, ed. *The Vietnamese American 1.5 Generation: Stories of War, Revolution, Flight, and New Beginnings.* Philadelphia: Temple University Press, 2006.

Espiritu, Yến Lê. *Body Counts: The Vietnam War and Militarized Refuge(es).* Berkeley: University of California Press, 2014.

Her, Vincent K., and Mary Louise Buley-Meissner, eds. *Hmong and American: From Refugees to Citizens.* Minneapolis: Minnesota Historical Society Press, 2012.

Ong, Aihwa. *Buddha Is Hiding: Refugees, Citizenship, the New America.* Berkeley: University of California Press, 2003.

Smith-Hefner, Nancy J. *Khmer Americans: Identity and Moral Education in a Diasporic Community.* Berkeley: University of California Press, 1999.

Võ, Linda Trinh. *Mobilizing an Asian American Community.* Philadelphia: Temple University Press, 2004.

South Asian Immigration to the Americas

Bahadur, Gaiutra. *Coolie Woman: The Odyssey of Indenture*. Chicago: University of Chicago Press, 2013.

Bald, Vivek. *Bengali Harlem and the Lost Histories of South Asian America*. Cambridge, MA: Harvard University Press, 2013.

Jensen, Joan. *Passage from India: Asian Indian Immigrants in North America*. New Haven, CT: Yale University Press, 1988.

Leonard, Karen. *Making Ethnic Choices: California's Punjabi Mexican Americans*. Philadelphia: Temple University Press, 2010.

Prashad, Vijay. *The Karma of Brown Folk*. Minneapolis: University of Minnesota Press, 2000.

Tatla, Darshan S. *The Sikh Diaspora: The Search for Statehood*. London: UCL, 1999.

Citizenship

Ancheta, Angelo N. *Race, Rights, and the Asian American Experience*. New Brunswick, NJ: Rutgers University Press, 1998.

Chang, Kornel S. *Pacific Connections: The Making of the Western U.S.-Canadian Borderlands*. Berkeley: University of California Press, 2012.

FitzGerald, David, and David Cook-Martín. *Culling the Masses: The Democratic Origins of Racist Immigration Policy in the Americas*. Cambridge, MA: Harvard University Press, 2014.

Hing, Bill Ong. *Making and Remaking Asian America Through Immigration Policy, 1850–1990*. Stanford, CA: Stanford University Press, 1993.

Jacobson, Matthew Frye. *Whiteness of a Different Color: European Immigrants and the Alchemy of Race*. Cambridge, MA: Harvard University Press, 1999.

Jun, Helen Heran. *Race for Citizenship: Black Orientalism and Asian Uplift from Pre-Emancipation to Neoliberal America*. New York: New York University Press, 2011.

Jung, Moon-Ho. *Coolies and Cane: Race, Labor, and Sugar in the Age of Emancipation*. Baltimore: Johns Hopkins University Press, 2008.

Jung, Moon-Kie. *Reworking Race: The Making of Hawai'i's Interracial Labor Movement*. New York: Columbia University Press, 2010.

Lee, Erika, and Judy Yung. *Angel Island: Immigrant Gateway to America*. New York: Oxford University Press, 2010.

Lien, Pei-Te. *The Making of Asian America Through Political Participation*. Philadelphia: Temple University Press, 2001.

Ling, Huping. *Chinese Chicago: Race, Transnational Migration, and Community Since 1870*. Stanford, CA: Stanford University Press, 2012.

———. *Chinese St. Louis: From Enclave to Cultural Community.* Philadelphia: Temple University Press, 2004.

López, Ian Haney. *White by Law: The Legal Construction of Race.* New York: New York University Press, 1997.

Motomura, Hiroshi. *Americans in Waiting: The Lost History of Immigration and Citizenship in the United States.* New York: Oxford University Press, 2006.

Ngai, Mae M. *Impossible Subjects: Illegal Aliens and the Making of Modern America.* Princeton, NJ: Princeton University Press, 2004.

Omi, Michael, and Howard Winant. *Racial Formation in the United States: From the 1960s to the 1990s.* 3rd ed. New York: Routledge, 2015.

Park, John S. W. *Elusive Citizenship: Immigration, Asian Americans, and the Paradox of Civil Rights.* New York: New York University Press, 2004.

Pegler-Gordon, Anna. *In Sight of America: Photography and the Development of U.S. Immigration Policy.* Berkeley: University of California Press, 2009.

Schlund-Vials, Cathy J. *Modeling Citizenship: Jewish and Asian American Writing.* Philadelphia: Temple University Press, 2011.

Shah, Nayan. *Contagious Divides: Epidemics and Race in San Francisco's Chinatown.* Berkeley: University of California Press, 2001.

———. *Stranger Intimacy: Contesting Race, Sexuality and the Law in the North American West.* Berkeley: University of California Press, 2011.

Takaki, Ronald T. *Pau Hana: Plantation Life and Labor in Hawaii, 1835–1920.* Honolulu: University of Hawaii Press, 1984.

PART II

War and Imperialism

"Benevolent Assimilation" Proclamation (1898)

One outcome of the Spanish-American War (1898) was the annexation of Spanish colonies (the Philippines, Cuba, Guam, Panama, and Puerto Rico) by the United States. The premise of liberating these colonies from Spanish rule at the outset of the war quickly shifted from support of colonial insurgents to ever-greater control over their affairs and governance. President William McKinley issued a proclamation of the guiding principles for the U.S. military administration of the Philippines. The proclamation illustrates the disavowal of Philippine independence and emphasized instead Philippine instability and vulnerability as justification for the protective oversight by the U.S. military and civil service. This discourse of "compassionate occupation"—visually evident in the accompanying cartoon titled "Holding His End Up" (fig. 2.1)—was used to justify the U.S. war against hundreds of thousands of Filipino independence fighters, the economic domination of the archipelago, and increased military and economic influence upon the Southeast and East Asian regions. (William McKinley. Benevolent Assimilation Proclamation. Washington, DC, 21 Dec. 1898.)

The destruction of the Spanish fleet in the harbor of Manila by the United States naval squadron commanded by Rear-Admiral Dewey, followed by the reduction of the city and the surrender of the Spanish forces, practically effected the conquest of the Philippine Islands and the suspension of the Spanish sovereignty therein. With the signature of the treaty of peace between the United States and Spain by their respective plenipotentiaries at Paris on the 10th instant, and as a result of the victories of American arms, *the future control, disposition, and government of the Philippine Islands are ceded to the United States.* In the fulfillment of the *rights of sovereignty* thus acquired and the responsible obligations of government thus assumed, the actual occupation and administration of the entire group of the Philippine Islands becomes immediately necessary, and the *military government* heretofore maintained by the United States in the city, harbor, and bay of Manila *is to be extended* with all possible dispatch *to the whole of the ceded territory.*

In performing this duty the military commander of the United States is enjoined to make known to the inhabitants of the Philippine Islands that in *succeeding to the sovereignty of Spain,* in severing the former political relations, and in establishing a new political power, the authority of the United States is to be exerted for the securing of the persons and property of the people of the islands and for the confirmation of all their private rights and relations. It will be the duty of the commander of the forces of occupation to announce and proclaim in the most public manner that *we come,* not as invaders or conquerors, but as friends, *to protect* the natives in their homes, in their employments, and in their personal and religious rights. All persons who, either by active aid or by honest submission, co-operate with the Government of the United States to give effect to these beneficent purposes will receive the reward of its support and *protection.* All others will be brought within the lawful rule we have assumed, with firmness if need be, but without severity, so far as possible. Within the absolute domain of *military authority,* which necessarily is and *must remain supreme* in the ceded territory until the legislation of the United States shall otherwise provide, the municipal laws of the territory in respect to private rights and property and the repression of crime are to be considered as continuing in force, and to be administered by the ordinary tribunals, so far as practicable. The operations of civil and municipal government are to be performed by such officers as may accept *the supremacy of the United States* by taking the oath of allegiance, or by officers chosen, as far as practicable, from the inhabitants of the islands. While the control of all the public property and the revenues of the state passes with the cession, and while the use and management of all public means of transportation are necessarily reserved to the authority of the United States, private property, whether belonging to individuals or corporations, is to be respected except for cause duly established. The taxes and duties heretofore payable by the inhabitants to the late government become payable to the authorities of the United States unless it be seen fit to substitute for them other reasonable rates or modes of contribution to the expenses of government, whether general or local. If private property be taken for military use, it shall be paid for when possible in cash, at a fair valuation, and when payment in cash is not practicable, receipts are to be given. All ports and places in the Philippine Islands in the actual possession of the land and naval forces of the United States will be opened to the commerce of all friendly nations. All goods and wares not prohibited for military reasons by due announcement of the military authority will be admitted upon payment of such duties and other charges as shall be in force at the time of their importation. Finally, it should be the earnest wish and paramount aim of the military administration to win the confidence, respect, and affection of the inhabitants of the Philippines by as-

HOLDING HIS END UP.

JOHN BULL—"It's really most extraordinary what training will do. Why, only the other day I thought that man unable to support himself."—Philadelphia Inquirer.

Figure 2.1 Fred Morgan, "Holding His End Up," *Philadelphia Inquirer* (1899). Caption: "JOHN BULL — 'It's really most extraordinary what training will do. Why, only the other day I thought that man unable to support himself.'"

suring them in every possible way that full measure of individual rights and liberties which is the heritage of free peoples, and by proving to them that the mission of the United States is one of

BENEVOLENT ASSIMILATION

substituting the mild sway of justice and right for arbitrary rule. In the fulfillment of this high mission, supporting the temperate administration of affairs for the greatest good of the governed, there must be sedulously maintained the strong arm of authority, to repress disturbance and to overcome all obstacles to the bestowal of the blessings of good and stable government upon the people of the Philippine Islands under the free flag of the United States.

WILLIAM MCKINLEY.

Queen Liliuokalani's Letter of Protest

Incremental U.S. encroachment upon the Hawaiian Kingdom since the 1880s culminated in a staged military assault in 1893 after a failed attempt to pass a treaty of annexation. The threat of a violent and lethal overthrow by U.S. forces led Queen Liliuokalani to cede her sovereign authority to the Provisional Government formed by U.S. expansionists. Disagreement within the U.S. government concerning Hawai'i's annexation left the Hawaiian Kingdom in an uncertain state, during which time the Hawaiian people unequivocally expressed their opposition to annexation. Protests, petitions, and the formation of an armed Hawaiian counterinsurgency document a clear refutation of the Provisional Government and resistance to U.S. incorporation. Similar opposition to U.S. occupation arose in the Philippines during this period. The status of the Hawaiian Islands was transformed under the 1898 Newlands Resolution to annex the territory for military purposes. What follows is Queen Liliuokalani's letter of protest to this act of Congress. (Liliuokalani of Hawai'i. Letter to William McKinley. 17 June 1897.)

The House of Representatives of the United States:

I, Liliuokalani of Hawaii, named heir apparent on the 10th day of April, 1877, and proclaimed queen of the Hawaiian Islands on the 29th day of January, 1891, do hereby earnestly and respectfully protest against the assertion of ownership by the United States of America of the so-called Hawaiian Crown Lands amounting to about one million acres and which are my property, and I especially protest against such assertion of ownership as a taking of property without due process of law and without just or other compensation.

Therefore, supplementing my protest of June 17, 1897, I call upon the President and the National Legislature and the People of the United States to do justice in this matter and to restore to me this property, the enjoyment of which is being withheld from me by your Government under what must be a misapprehension of my right and title.

Done at Washington, District of Columbia, United States of America, this nineteenth day of December, in the year one thousand eight hundred and ninety-eight.

LILIUOKALANI

Japanese on the West Coast

C. B. Munson

The "Report on Japanese on the West Coast," known more colloquially as the "Munson Report," was authored by Curtis B. Munson, a businessman from Detroit who was commissioned as a special representative of the State Department. The report was intended to clarify the loyalties of Japanese Americans living on the West Coast. It was submitted to the White House on October 7, 1941 (exactly two months before the Japanese attack on Pearl Harbor). The report circulated among several cabinet officials, including Secretary of War Henry L. Stimson, who gave it to President Franklin D. Roosevelt on January 9, 1942. However, journalist John Franklin Carter, a close friend to the president, incompletely summarized the report in an earlier presidential memo of November 7, 1941 (included below); this truncated report emphasized Japanese American disloyalty. (Los Angeles, 7 Oct. 1941.)

Ground Covered

In reporting on the Japanese "problem" on the West Coast the facts are, on the whole, fairly clear and opinion toward the problem exceedingly uniform. In reporting, the main difficulty is to know where to leave off and what to leave out. One could gather data for fifteen years with fifteen men and still be in the position of the Walrus and the Carpenter:

> If seven maids with seven mops
> Swept it for half a year—
> Do you suppose, the Walrus said,
> That they could get it clear?

Whisking up the grains of sand is the wrong approach, yet when your reporter declares there is a sea and a shore and some sand, and that he has sampled the general quality of sand in many varying beaches, do not be too hard in your judgment for him if he has stopped far short of sorting out each layer or tint or even each beach. You have to feel this problem—not figure it out with your pencil. We only cite the sand that our reader may never forget the complexities of even a shovel full of sand.

Your reporter spent about a week each in the 11th, 12th, and 13th Naval Districts with the full cooperation of the Naval and Army intelligences and the F.B.I. Some mention should also be made of the assistance rendered from time to time by the British Intelligence. Our Navy has done by far the most work on this problem, having given it intense consideration for the last ten or fifteen years. Your reporter commenced in the 12th Naval District, which covers Northern California, from thence to the 13th, covering Washington and Oregon, winding up his observations in the 11th Naval District, covering Southern California, where to his mind the whole "problem" finally focuses. Your reporter also turned the corner into British Columbia through a member of the R.C.M.P. and the corner into Mexico through a conference with our Consul at Tijuana.

Opinions of the various services were obtained, also of business, employees, universities, fellow white workers, students, fish packers, lettuce packers, farmers, religious groups, etc., etc. The opinion expressed with minor differences was uniform. Select Japanese in all groups were sampled. To mix indiscriminately with the Japanese was not considered advisable chiefly because the opinions of many loyal white Americans who made this their life work for the last fifteen years were available and it was foolish to suppose your reporter could add to the sum of knowledge in three weeks by running through the topmost twigs of a forest.

Background

Unless familiar with the religious and family background of the Japanese, this rough background summary should be skimmed over as it has a bearing on the Japanese question. If the reader is familiar with the Japanese background, it may be omitted.

An American wit once said, "You cannot tell the truth about Japan without lying." This same witticism might be made with reference to the Japanese people, but, like all generalizations, it needs corrective explanation. A study of Japan is a study in the category of social fully as much as of political science. The study of Japanese people is one of absorbing interest.

Who are the Japanese people? From whence did they come and what emotional concepts did they bring with them? While there might not be unanimity of opinion as to the various strains that go to make up the Japanese of today, one leading anthropologist, Dr. Frederick Star of the University of Chicago, a number of years ago said to the writer, "the Japanese are the most mixed race of people that I have ever studied." The Malay strain is pronounced in the Japanese, especially in the Province of Kumamoto. The Mongol is very pronounced in the upper middle as well as in the so-called higher brackets of society. Then there is the Aryan strain still to be seen in its unmixed form in the 17,000 and more Ainu who inhabit portions of Hokkaido and the Kurile Islands. These latter are related to the Aryan group in physiognomy and in language. These three strains have produced the Japanese of today. . . .

Associations

The Japanese is the greatest joiner in the world. To take care of this passion he has furnished himself with ample associations to join. There are around 1,563 of these in the United States. Your reporter has before him a Japanese publication entitled "The Japanese-American Directory of 1941" at least two inches thick listing the Japanese associations in fine print. Your reporter also has before him lists furnished him in various Naval Districts of some of the leading associations considered the most important, with full descriptions of their activities as far as known. It is endless to clutter up this report with them.

Family Set-Up in United States

In the United States there are four divisions of Japanese to be considered:

1) The *ISSEI*—First generation Japanese. Entire cultural background Japanese. Probably loyal romantically to Japan. They must be considered, however, as other races. They have made this their home. They have brought up children here, and many would have become American citizens had they been allowed to do so. They are for the most part simple people. Their age group is largely 55 to 65, fairly old for a hard-working Japanese.

2) The *NISEI*—Second generation who have received their whole education in the United States and usually, in spite of discrimination against them and a certain amount of insults accumulated through the years from irresponsible elements, have a pathetic eagerness to be Americans. They are in constant conflict with the orthodox, well-disciplined family life of their elders. Age group—1 to 30 years.

3) The *KIBEI*—This is an important division of the NISEI. This is the term used by the Japanese to signify those American-born Japanese who received part or all of their education in Japan. In any consideration of the KIBEI they should be again divided into two classes, i.e. THOSE WHO RECEIVED THEIR EDUCATION IN JAPAN FROM CHILDHOOD TO ABOUT 17 YEARS OF AGE and THOSE WHO RETURNED TO JAPAN FOR FOUR OR FIVE YEARS OF JAPANESE EDUCATION. The Kibei are considered the most dangerous element and closer to the Issei with especial reference to those who received their early education in Japan. It must be noted, however, that many of those who visited Japan subsequent to their early American education come back with an added loyalty to the United States. In fact it is a saying that all a Nisei needs is a trip to Japan to make a loyal American out of him. The American-educated Japanese is a boor in Japan and treated as a foreigner and with a certain amount of contempt there. His trip is usually a painful experience.

4) The *SANSEI*—The third generation Japanese is a baby and may be disregarded for the purposes of our survey.

We must now think back to the paragraph entitled BACKGROUND. This is tied into the family of which the Issei is the head with more authority and hold over his family than an old New England Bible-thumping pioneer. Their family life is disciplined and honorable. The children are obedient and the girls virtuous. We must also think of the Associations, some sinister, some emanating from Imperial Japan, some with Japanese Consular contacts. It all weaves up into a sinister pattern on paper. This pattern has been set up in a secret document entitled, "Japanese Organizations and Activities in the 11th Naval District," and may be scrutinized with proper authorization in the Navy Department in Washington. We only suggest this to our reader in case our words have not built up the proper Hallowe'en atmosphere. It is like looking at the "punkin" itself. There is real fire in it, yet in many ways it is hollow and dusty. However, your reporter desires to have you know that all this exists before he goes on to the main body of his report on how the Japanese in the United States are liable to react in case of war with Japan.

The Tokio-Sun God-Religious-Family-Association Plus Oriental Mind Set-Up Shows Signs of the Honorable Passage of Time

There are still Japanese in the United States who will tie dynamite around their waist and make a human bomb out of themselves. We grant this but today they are few. Many things indicate that very many joints in the Japanese set-up show age and many elements are not what they used to be. The weakest from a Japanese standpoint are the Nisei. They are universally estimated from 90 to 98% loyal to the United States if the Japanese-educated element of the Kibei is excluded. The Nisei are pathetically eager to show this loyalty. They are not Japanese in culture. They are foreigners to Japan. Though American citizens they are not accepted by Americans, largely because they look differently and can be easily recognized. The Japanese American Citizens League should be encouraged, that while an eye is kept open, to see that Tokio does not get its finger in this pie— which it has in a few cases attempted to do. The loyal Nisei hardly know where to turn. Some gesture of protection or wholehearted acceptance of this group would go a long way to swinging them away from any last romantic hankering after old Japan. They are not oriental or mysterious, they are very American and are of a proud, self-respecting race suffering from a little inferiority complex and a lack of contact with the white boys they went to school with. They are eager for this contact and to work alongside them.

The Issei or first generation is considerably weakened in their loyalty to Japan by the fact that they have chosen to make this their home and have brought up their children here. They expect to die here. They are quite fearful of being put in a concentration camp. Many would take out American citizenship if allowed to do so. The haste of this report does not allow us to go into this more fully. The Issei have to break with their religion, their god and Emperor, their family, their ancestors and their after-life in order to be loyal to the United States. They are also still legally Japanese. Yet they do break, and send their boys off to the Army with pride and tears. They are good neighbors. They are old men fifty-five to sixty-five, for the most part simple and dignified. Roughly they were Japanese lower-middle-class about analogous to the pilgrim fathers. They are largely farmers and fishermen. Today the Japanese is farmer, fisherman, and businessman. They get very attached to the land they work or own (through the second generation), they like their own business, they do not work at industrial jobs nor for others except as a stepping stone to becoming independent.

The Kibei, educated from childhood to seventeen, are still the element most to be watched.

What Will the Japanese Do

. . .

ESPIONAGE

The Japanese, if undisturbed and disloyal, should be well equipped for obvious physical espionage. A great part of this work was probably completed and forwarded to Tokio years ago, such as soundings and photography of every inch of the Coast. They are probably familiar with the location of every large building and garage including Mike O'Flaerty's out-house in the Siskiyous with all trails leading thereto. An experienced Captain in Navy Intelligence, who has from time to time and over a period of years intercepted information Tokio bound, said he would certainly hate to be a Japanese coordinator of information in Tokio. He stated that the mass of useless information was unbelievable. This would be fine for a fifth column in Belgium or Holland with the German army ready to march in over the border, but though the local Japanese could spare a man who intimately knew the country for each Japanese invasion squad, there would at least have to be a terrific American Naval disaster before his brown brothers would need his services. The dangerous part of their espionage is that they would be very effective as far as movement of supplies, movement of troops and movement of ships out of harbor mouths and over railroads is concerned. They occupy only rarely positions where they can get to confidential papers or in plants. They are usually, when rarely so placed, a subject of perpetual watch and suspicion by their fellow workers. They would have to buy most of this type of information from white people.

PROPAGANDA

Their direct propaganda is poor and rather ineffective on the whole. Their indirect is more successful. By indirect we mean propaganda preaching the beauties of Japan and the sweet innocence of the Japanese race to susceptible Americans.

Summary

Japan will commit some sabotage largely depending on imported Japanese as they are afraid of and do not trust the Nisei. There will be no wholehearted response from Japanese in the United States. They may get some helpers from certain Kibei. They will be in a position to pick up information on troop, supply and ship movements from local Japanese.

For the most part the local Japanese are loyal to the United States or, at worst, hope that by remaining quiet they can avoid concentration camps or irresponsible mobs. We do not believe that they would be at least any more disloyal than any other racial group in the United States with whom we went to war. Those being here are on a spot and they *know it.* . . .

We will re-work this report for final submittal later. We have missed a great deal through haste. We believe we have given the high points to the best of our ability. The Japanese are loyal on the whole, but we are wide open to sabotage on this Coast and as far inland as the mountains, and while this one fact goes unrectified I cannot unqualifiedly state that there is no danger from the Japanese living in the United States which I otherwise would be willing to state.

Memorandum on C. B. Munson's Report "Japanese on the West Coast"

John Franklin Carter

Although the "Munson Report" (above) was meant to clarify the loyalties of Japanese Americans living on the West Coast, John Franklin Carter's summary of that report instead emphasized their disloyalty. Carter's memo of November 7, 1941, reached President Roosevelt's desk before the "Munson Report" did in January 1942. (Washington, DC, 7 Nov. 1941.)

Attached herewith is the report [Munson's report], with supplementary reports on Lower California and British Columbia. The report, though lengthy, is worth reading in its entirety. Salient passages are:

1) "There are still Japanese in the United States who will tie dynamite around their waist and make a human bomb out of themselves . . . but today they are few."

2) "There is no Japanese 'problem' on the coast. There will be no armed uprising of Japanese. There will be undoubtedly some sabotage financed by Japan and executed largely by imported agents. There will be the odd case of fanatical sabotage by some Japanese 'crackpot.'"

3) "The dangerous part of their espionage is that they would be very effective as far as movement of supplies, movement of troops and movement of ships . . . is concerned."

4) "For the most part the local Japanese are loyal to the United States or, at worst, hope that by remaining quiet they can avoid concentration camps or irresponsible mobs."

5) "Your reporter . . . is horrified to note that dams, bridges, harbors, power stations etc. are wholly unguarded everywhere. The harbor of San Pedro could be razed by fire completely by four men with hand grenades and a little study in one night. Dams could be blown and half of lower California might actually die of thirst . . . One railway bridge at the exit from the mountains in some cases could tie up three or four main railroads."

How to Spot a Jap

Department of the U.S. Army

This cartoon excerpt was part of A Pocket Guide to China *(1942) issued to U.S. soldiers as they entered the Pacific Theater (specifically China, which was a wartime ally). Drawn by American cartoonist Milton Caniff (of* Terry and the Pirates *and* Steve Canyon *comic strip fame), "How to Spot a Jap" was intended to familiarize troops to alleged racial and phenotypical differences between Japanese and Chinese (fig. 2.2). Such guides were by no means limited to the military; indeed, this reading of racial difference was evident in a December 22, 1941,* Life *magazine article titled "How to Tell Japs from the Chinese." Read in certain ways, this document can reveal how the Chinese became the "good Asian in the good war" and laid the foundation of the "model minority" image of Chinese Americans.*

Anti-Japan War Posters

The anti-Japan war posters are an interesting mix of wartime propaganda (figs. 2.3 and 2.4). While the "Japanese enemy" is depicted as a racialized caricature, the real target of the posters are American workers in the defense industries. Although Americans produced an enormous amount of war-related products during the 1940s, these posters remind us that there was a high rate of worker absenteeism in the factories and waste of war material. It was believed that American workers would perform at a higher level of productivity if they were being admonished by Japanese.

Such anti-Japanese sentiments were by no means limited to wartime posters, as evidenced by the political cartoon "Waiting for the Signal from Home" (fig. 2.5). Created by Theodor Seuss Geisel (better known as the children's literature author "Dr. Seuss") for the leftist magazine PM, *this cartoon conflates imperial Japanese forces with individuals of Japanese descent on the West Coast. The cartoon's antifascist focus (via the Japanese enemy) was consistent with his other wartime cartoons, which denounced Adolf Hitler and Benito Mussolini. However, it was not consistent with Geisel's progressive racial politics: while he decried the treatment of African Americans and*

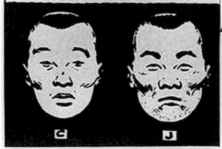

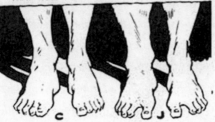

Figure 2.2 Milton Caniff, "How to Spot a Jap," in *A Pocket Guide to China.* U.S. Army Special Service Division. Washington, D.C.: War and Navy Departments, 1942. Courtesy of the American Social History Project, CUNY.

Figure 2.3 U.S. Office for Emergency Management, Office of War Information, ca. 1943. National Archives and Records Administration, College Park, MD.

Figure 2.4 Douglas Aircraft Company, 1941–1945. Bancroft Library, University of California, Berkeley.

Figure 2.5 Theodor Seuss Geisel (Dr. Seuss), 1942. Mandeville Special Collections, University of California, San Diego.

critiqued the pervasiveness of anti-Semitism at home, he did not extend such progressive politics to Japanese Americans.

Executive Order No. 9066 (1942)

On February 19, 1942, President Franklin D. Roosevelt authorized the secretary of war to establish military areas in which the military could restrict the movement of all people within those areas in order to control the actions of those considered enemy aliens, especially Japanese nationals and Japanese Americans. This order laid the foundation for the construction of the internment camps into which more than 110,000 Japanese and Japanese Americans were placed, most for the duration of World War II. The accompanying figure is based on the order: it is a poster that was hung in various public places that instructed those of Japanese descent what they must do in order to prepare for relocation and to be compliant with the order (fig. 2.6). (Franklin Delano Roosevelt. Executive Order No. 9066. Washington, DC, 19 Feb. 1942.)

Executive Order Authorizing the Secretary of War to Prescribe Military Areas

Whereas the successful prosecution of the war requires every possible protection against espionage and against sabotage to national-defense material, national-defense premises, and national-defense utilities as defined in Section 4, Act of April 20, 1918, 40 Stat. 533, as amended by the Act of November 30, 1940, 54 Stat. 1220, and the Act of August 21, 1941, 55 Stat. 655 (U.S.C., Title 50, Sec. 104):

NOW, THEREFORE, by virtue of the authority vested in me as President of the United States, and Commander in Chief of the Army and Navy, I hereby authorize and direct the Secretary of War, and the Military Commanders whom he may from time to time designate, whenever he or any designated Commander deems such action necessary or desirable, to prescribe military areas in such places and of such extent as he or the appropriate Military Commander may determine, from which any or all persons may be excluded, and with respect to which, the right of any person to enter, remain in, or leave shall be subject to whatever restrictions

WESTERN DEFENSE COMMAND AND FOURTH ARMY
WARTIME CIVIL CONTROL ADMINISTRATION
Presidio of San Francisco, California
May 3, 1942

INSTRUCTIONS
TO ALL PERSONS OF

JAPANESE

ANCESTRY

Living in the Following Area:

All of that portion of the City of Los Angeles, State of California, within that boundary beginning at the point at which North Figueroa Street meets a line following the middle of the Los Angeles River; thence southerly and following the said line to East First Street; thence westerly on East First Street to Alameda Street; thence southerly on Alameda Street to East Third Street; thence northwesterly on East Third Street to Main Street; thence northerly on Main Street to First Street; thence northwesterly on First Street to Figueroa Street; thence northeasterly on Figueroa Street to the point of beginning.

Pursuant to the provisions of Civilian Exclusion Order No. 33, this Headquarters, dated May 3, 1942, all persons of Japanese ancestry, both alien and non-alien, will be evacuated from the above area by 12 o'clock noon, P. W. T., Saturday, May 9, 1942.

No Japanese person living in the above area will be permitted to change residence after 12 o'clock noon, P. W. T., Sunday, May 3, 1942, without obtaining special permission from the representative of the Commanding General, Southern California Sector, at the Civil Control Station located at:

Japanese Union Church,
120 North San Pedro Street,
Los Angeles, California.

Such permits will only be granted for the purpose of uniting members of a family, or in cases of grave emergency.

The Civil Control Station is equipped to assist the Japanese population affected by this evacuation in the following ways:

1. Give advice and instructions on the evacuation.
2. Provide services with respect to the management, leasing, sale, storage or other disposition of most kinds of property, such as real estate, business and professional equipment, household goods, boats, automobiles and livestock.
3. Provide temporary residence elsewhere for all Japanese in family groups.
4. Transport persons and a limited amount of clothing and equipment to their new residence.

The Following Instructions Must Be Observed:

1. A responsible member of each family, preferably the head of the family, or the person in whose name most of the property is held, and each individual living alone, will report to the Civil Control Station to receive further instructions. This must be done between 8:00 A. M. and 5:00 P. M. on Monday, May 4, 1942, or between 8:00 A. M. and 5:00 P. M. on Tuesday, May 5, 1942.
2. Evacuees must carry with them on departure for the Assembly Center, the following property:
   (a) Bedding and linens (no mattress) for each member of the family;
   (b) Toilet articles for each member of the family;
   (c) Extra clothing for each member of the family;
   (d) Sufficient knives, forks, spoons, plates, bowls and cups for each member of the family;
   (e) Essential personal effects for each member of the family.

All items carried will be securely packaged, tied and plainly marked with the name of the owner and numbered in accordance with instructions obtained at the Civil Control Station. The size and number of packages is limited to that which can be carried by the individual or family group.

3. No pets of any kind will be permitted.
4. No personal items and no household goods will be shipped to the Assembly Center.
5. The United States Government through its agencies will provide for the storage, at the sole risk of the owner, of the more substantial household items, such as iceboxes, washing machines, pianos and other heavy furniture. Cooking utensils and other small items will be accepted for storage if crated, packed and plainly marked with the name and address of the owner. Only one name and address will be used by a given family.
6. Each family, and individual living alone, will be furnished transportation to the Assembly Center or will be authorized to travel by private automobile in a supervised group. All instructions pertaining to the movement will be obtained at the Civil Control Station.

Go to the Civil Control Station between the hours of 8:00 A. M. and 5:00 P. M.,
Monday, May 4, 1942, or between the hours of 8:00 A. M. and 5:00 P. M.,
Tuesday, May 5, 1942, to receive further instructions.

J. L. DeWITT
Lieutenant General, U. S. Army
Commanding

SEE CIVILIAN EXCLUSION ORDER NO. 33.

Figure 2.6 "Instructions to All Persons of Japanese Ancestry." Western Defense Command and Fourth Army Wartime Civil Control Administration, 1942. Facsimile poster. Cathy J. Schlund-Vials, personal collection.

the Secretary of War or the appropriate Military Commander may impose in his discretion. The Secretary of War is hereby authorized to provide for residents of any such area who are excluded therefrom, such transportation, food, shelter, and other accommodations as may be necessary, in the judgment of the Secretary of War or the said Military Commander, and until other arrangements are made, to accomplish the purpose of this order. The designation of military areas in any region or locality shall supersede designations of prohibited and restricted areas by the Attorney General under the Proclamations of December 7 and 8, 1941, and shall supersede the responsibility and authority of the Attorney General under the said Proclamations in respect of such prohibited and restricted areas.

I hereby further authorize and direct the Secretary of War and the said Military Commanders to take such other steps as he or the appropriate Military Commander may deem advisable to enforce compliance with the restrictions applicable to each Military area hereinabove authorized to be designated, including the use of Federal troops and other Federal Agencies, with authority to accept assistance of state and local agencies.

I hereby further authorize and direct all Executive Departments, independent establishments and other Federal Agencies, to assist the Secretary of War or the said Military Commanders in carrying out this Executive Order, including the furnishing of medical aid, hospitalization, food, clothing, transportation, use of land, shelter, and other supplies, equipment, utilities, facilities, and services.

This order shall not be construed as modifying or limiting in any way the authority heretofore granted under Executive Order No. 8972, dated December 12, 1941, nor shall it be construed as limiting or modifying the duty and responsibility of the Federal Bureau of Investigation, with respect to the investigation of alleged acts of sabotage or the duty and responsibility of the Attorney General and the Department of Justice under the Proclamations of December 7 and 8, 1941, prescribing regulations for the conduct and control of alien enemies, except as such duty and responsibility is superseded by the designation of military areas hereunder.

FRANKLIN D. ROOSEVELT
The White House,
February 19, 1942.

A Declaration of Policy of the Japanese American Citizens League (1942)

Founded in 1929, the Japanese Americans Citizens League (JACL), composed solely of American-born Japanese Americans, became the major political organization advocating for the Japanese American community. This "Declaration of Policy," issued after the attack on Pearl Harbor, set out both to assure the federal government of Japanese American loyalty to the United States and to encourage Japanese Americans to cooperate with the authorities as the United States entered the war. Seen by some as too accommodating to the internment of Japanese during the war, the JACL would survive the criticisms of its wartime positions to continue to be a major voice for Japanese Americans. (Japanese American Citizens League. "Declaration of Policy." 1942. Courtesy of the Japanese American Citizens League.)

In these critical days when the policies of many organizations representing various nationality groups may be viewed with suspicion and even alarm by certain individuals who are not intimately acquainted with the aims, ideals, and leadership of such associations, it becomes necessary and proper, in the public interest, that such fraternal and educational orders as the Japanese American Citizens League do unequivocally and sincerely announce their policies and objectives.

Now, therefore, in order to clear up any misconceptions, misunderstandings, and misapprehensions concerning the functions and activities of the body, the National Board of the Japanese American Citizens League issues the following statement and declaration of policy:

We, the members of the National Board of the Japanese American Citizens League of the United States of America, believe that the policies which govern this organization and our activities as their official representatives are fourfold in nature and are best illustrated by an explanation of the alphabetical sequence of the letters J-A-C-L.

"J" stands for justice. We believe that all peoples, regardless of race, color, or creed, are entitled to enjoy those principles of "life, liberty, and the pursuit of happiness" which are presumed to be the birthright of every individual; to the fair and equal treatment of all, socially, legislatively, judicially, and economically[; and] to the rights, privileges, and obligations of citizenship. To this end, this organization is dedicated.

"A" stands for Americanism. We believe that in order to prove ourselves worthy of the justice which we seek, we must prove ourselves to be, first of all, good Americans—in thought, in words, in deeds. We believe that we must acquaint ourselves with those traditions, ideals, and institutions which made and kept this Nation the foremost in the world. We believe that we must live for America—and, if need be, to die for America. To this end, this organization is consecrated.

"C" stands for citizenship. We believe that we must be exemplary citizens in addition to being good Americans for, as in the case of our parents, one may be a good American and yet be denied the privilege of citizenship. We believe that we must accept and even seek out opportunities in which to serve our country and to assume the obligations and duties as well as the rights and privileges of citizenship. To this end, this organization is committed.

"L" stands for leadership. We believe that the Japanese American Citizens League, as the only national organization established to serve the American citizens of Japanese ancestry, is in a position to actively lead the Japanese people and membership necessary to carry into living effect the principles of justice, Americanism, and citizenship for which our league was founded. We offer cooperation and support to all groups and individuals sincerely and legitimately interested in these same aims, but we propose to retain our independent and separate status as the Japanese American Citizens League. To this end, this organization is pledged.

Summed up briefly, the Japanese American Citizens League is devoted to those tasks which are calculated to win for ourselves and our posterity the status outlined by our two national slogans: "For Better Americans in a Greater America" and "Security through Unity."

Internment Photographs

Dorothea Lange

Known most for her work as a documentary photographer and photojournalist during the Depression era (as per her position with the Farm Security Administration), Dorothea Lange (1895–1965) was hired by the War Relocation Authority (WRA) to document the 1942 forced evacuation and relocation of Japanese Americans from the West Coast. The sympathetic portrayal of internees, which emphasized their "American-ness" and stressed the fact

Figure 2.7 "First-graders, some of Japanese ancestry, at the Weill Public School pledging allegiance to the United States flag. The evacuees of Japanese ancestry will be housed in war relocation authority centers for the duration of the war." April 1942. Library of Congress, Washington, DC.

that entire families were affected, caused the army to suppress Lange's photographs (figs. 2.7, 2.8, and 2.9). Many of her images were not released until almost fifty years after the Second World War ended.

Leave Clearance Interview Questions (1943)

In order to receive permission to seek residence and work outside of the internment camps, excluding the West Coast, Japanese internees had to first answer a series of questions. Aside from eliciting some general factual information, a number of questions sought to determine how knowledgeable of, and by inference, how attached the internees were to Japanese history and culture. In addition, there were a number of questions or conditions that if answered in the affirmative would lead to the eventual dismantling of the Japanese Ameri-

Figure 2.8 "Members of the Mochida family awaiting evacuation bus. Identification tags were used to aid in keeping a family unit intact during all phases of evacuation. Mochida operated a nursery and five greenhouses on a two-acre site in Eden Township." 8 May 1942. National Archives and Records Administration, College Park, MD.

Figure 2.9 "Grandfather and grandson of Japanese ancestry at this war relocation authority center." 2 July 1942. National Archives and Records Administration, College Park, MD.

can community, as the released internees would have had to agree to not live near other Japanese nor to speak the Japanese language. The questions involved assessing one's life before, during, and after incarceration; they also included queries concerning cultural affiliations and political allegiances: for instance, a question concerning the "Ise Shrine," one of the holiest Shinto sites in Japan, was intended to uncover the internee's proclivities via Japanese culture. Arizona, Nevada, and Utah are notably singled out: Arizona and Utah were home to two sizable internment camps (Poston and Topaz, respectively); then-governor Edward P. Carville of Nevada refused to allow the federal government to use his state as a "dumping ground" for "enemy aliens." (United States War Relocation Authority [W.R.A.]. 25 Aug. 1943.)

The purpose of this interview is to provide the W.R.A [War Relocation Authority] with the assurance that in permitting your leave from this center, it is doing the best thing for the United States as a whole and for you as an individual.

Before questioning you any further, we would like to ask if you have any objection to signing a Pledge of Allegiance to the United States.

1. Do you object to taking an oath that you will tell the truth and nothing but the truth in this interview?
2. What is your name?
3. Address?
4. Business, occupation, or profession before evacuation?
5. Did you belong to any Japanese organizations?
6. Did you attend a Japanese Language School?
7. Where did you get your education?
8. Have you at any time been a resident [of] or visitor to Japan? If so, give inclusive dates.
9. Have you ever asked for repatriation?
10. Give the names of your parents.
11. Where did they immigrate to the United States?
12. What was their occupation before evacuation?
13. How many people are there in your family?
14. Do you have any relatives in Japan?
15. Are any relatives serving in the Japanese Army?
16. Are any relatives serving in the Armed Forces of the United States?

17. Where are you planning to resettle?
18. Will you voluntarily remain out of the States of Arizona, Nevada, [and] Utah until such time that public opinion makes you more welcome?
19. What is your plan for mixing into the community to which you will resettle?
20. Do you know what clubs and organizations would welcome you?
21. Will you assist in the general resettlement program by staying away from large groups of Japanese?
22. Will you avoid the use of the Japanese language except when necessary?
23. Will you for the duration of the war avoid the organization of any typically Japanese clubs, associations, etc.?
24. Will you try to develop such American habits which will cause you to be accepted readily into American social groups?
25. Are you willing to serve in the Armed Forces of the United States if called upon by Selective Service to do so?
26. Are you willing to serve in war production?
27. Are you willing to give information to the proper authorities regarding any subversive activity which you might note or which you might be informed about directly or indirectly, both in the relocation center and in the communities in which you are resettled?
28. To whom would you report such information?
29. Would you consider an informer of this nature an "Inu" (Stoolpigeon)?
30. How long do you plan to stay on this job?
31. If you find a better job, how much notice will you give your employer?
32. Will you accept a position at a lower than standard wage? How will you find out what standard wages are?
33. Will you conform to the customs and dress of your new home?
34. Will you make every effort to represent all that is good, reliable, and honest in the Japanese Americans?
35. Will you report any change of residence or employment to the W.R.A. office?
36. What is your plan for your family?

37. What were your average expenses before evacuation for:
    a) Rent or housing? b) Food? c) Clothing? d) Misc. expenses?
38. What was your income?
39. Do you have any of your household equipment here [in the camp]?
40. Have you planned for what you need?
41. Have you contacted the Supervisor of Evacuee Property?
42. What do you consider the necessary items which you will have to purchase before you can resettle with your family?
43. Do you plan to take your family with you?
44. How many dependents do you have? Give names and ages.
45. Do you have any automotive equipment?
46. What has been your work while at the relocation center?
47. What part did you play in the development of any constructive organization or development at the center?
48. To what clubs do you belong?
49. Have you ever been accused [of] and pleaded guilty to any crime of any kind within the center?
50. Have you ever been associated with any radical groups, clubs, or gangs which have been accused of anti-social conduct within the center?
51. Have you ever participated in any stealing, destruction, or illegal use of government property?
52. Give 5 references of people who can vouch for your conduct in the center other than members of your family. Include at least 2 representatives of the administration. Can you furnish any proof that you have always been loyal to the United States?
53. What do you think of the United States in general?
54. What effect has the report of any Japanese *victory* in the Pacific and in the Far East [had] upon your thinking?
55. Why are you requesting leave?
56. What would you do if you found a shortwave set, both sending and receiving or either, in your neighbor's apartment?
57. What is the difference between the present Japanese government and that of 10 years ago?
58. Does the Japanese government have a parliamentary government at the present time?
59. Do you think you are "losing face" by cooperating with the United States?

60. What does the Samurai tradition mean to you?
61. Do you think that American people are generally soft and easy, both physically and mentally?
62. Do you believe in the divine origin of the Japanese race?
63. Have you ever celebrated February 11 [National Foundation Day]?
64. For what is the Ise Shrine famous?
65. What does "kigensetsu" [National Foundation Day] mean to you?
66. What would you consider a disloyal act to the United States?
67. What do you think loyalty to Japan would demand of a person in the centers under the present conditions?
68. What is your opinion of dual citizenship?
69. Would you, under any circumstances act contrary to the dictates of your parents?
70. Have you ever been associated with any groups whose membership is made up of those who have the majority of "No" answers on the Army Questionnaire? [This is a reference to questions 27 and 28 on the Loyalty Questionnaire, which concern one's willingness to join the military and denounce any allegiance to the Japanese emperor.]
71. What, in your opinion, did the "Yes" answer imply?
72. Do results at any time justify the means?
73. In your opinion, does the "population pressure" justify the Japanese expansion program?

Statement of United States Citizen of Japanese Ancestry (1943)

Also referred to as the "Loyalty Questionnaire," this form was distributed in the internment camps by camp officials to gather personal information about the internees, some of it similar to the information elicited in the previous "Leave Clearance" questions (fig. 2.10). This questionnaire is most well known for questions 27 and 28, which asked whether respondents would serve in the U.S. military "wherever ordered" and whether they would foreswear any allegiance to the Japanese emperor, implying that they might indeed harbor such an allegiance. An answer of "no" to these two questions resulted in the respondent being classified as a "no-no boy."

(LOCAL BOARD DATE STAMP WITH CODE)

STATEMENT OF UNITED STATES CITIZEN OF JAPANESE ANCESTRY

1. _____ _____ _____
   (Surname)   (English given name)   (Japanese given name)

   (a) Alias _____

2. Local selective service board _____
                                              (Number)

   _____ _____ _____
   (City)   (County)   (State)

3. Date of birth _____ Place of birth _____

4. Present address _____
                        (Street)   (City)   (State)

5. Last two addresses at which you lived 3 months or more (exclude residence at relocation center and at assembly center):

   _____ From _____ To _____

   _____ From _____ To _____

6. Sex _____ Height _____ Weight _____

7. Are you a registered voter? _____ Year first registered _____

   Where? _____ Party _____

8. Marital status _____ Citizenship of wife _____ Race of wife _____

9. _____ _____ _____ _____
   (Father's Name)   (Town or Ken) (State or Country)   (Occupation)
                                         (Birthplace)

10. _____ _____ _____ _____
    (Mother's Name)   (Town or Ken) (State or Country)   (Occupation)
                                          (Birthplace)

In items 11 and 12, you need not list relatives other than your parents, your children, your brothers and sisters.
For each person give name; relationship to you (such as father); citizenship; complete address; occupation.

11. Relatives in the United States (if in military service, indicate whether a selectee or volunteer):

   (a) _____ _____ _____
       (Name)   (Relationship to you)   (Citizenship)

   _____ _____ _____
   (Complete address)   (Occupation)   (Volunteer or selectee)

   (b) _____ _____ _____
       (Name)   (Relationship to you)   (Citizenship)

   _____ _____ _____
   (Complete address)   (Occupation)   (Volunteer or selectee)

   (c) _____ _____ _____
       (Name)   (Relationship to you)   (Citizenship)

   _____ _____ _____
   (Complete address)   (Occupation)   (Volunteer or selectee)

DSS Form 304A
(1-23-43)   (If additional space is necessary, attach sheets)   16—32565-1

Figure 2.10 United States Department of Selective Service, "Statement of United States Citizen of Japanese Ancestry" [facsimile], Form 304A, "The 'Loyalty Questionnaire,' 1943." Densho Encyclopedia, online at http://encyclopedia.densho.org/sources/en -denshopd-p72-00004-1/.

12. Relatives in Japan (see instruction above item 11):

....
(Name)   (Relationship to you)   (Citizenship)

....
(Complete address)   (Occupation)

....
(Name)   (Relationship to you)   (Citizenship)

....
(Complete address)   (Occupation)

13. Education:

Name	Place	Years of attendance
(Kindergarten)		From .... to ....
(Grade school)		From .... to ....
(Japanese language school)		From .... to ....
(High school)		From .... to ....
(Junior college, college, or university)		From .... to ....

....
(Type of military training, such as R. O. T. C. or Gunji Kyoren)   (Where and when)

....
(Other schooling)   (Years of attendance)

14. Foreign travel (give dates, where, how, for whom, with whom, and reasons therefor):

....

....

....

15. Employment (give employers' names and kind of business, addresses, and dates from 1935 to date):

....

....

....

....

16. Religion ....   Membership in religious groups ....

....

17. Membership in organizations (clubs, societies, associations, etc.).   Give name, kind of organization, and dates of membership.

....

....

16—22565-1

Figure 2.10 *Continued.*

18. Knowledge of foreign languages (put check mark (√) in proper squares):

(a) Japanese	Good	Fair	Poor	(b) Other............ (Specify)	Good	Fair	Poor
Reading	☐	☐	☐	Reading	☐	☐	☐
Writing	☐	☐	☐	Writing	☐	☐	☐
Speaking	☐	☐	☐	Speaking	☐	☐	☐

19. Sports and hobbies ....

....

....

20. List five references, other than relatives or former employers, giving address, occupation, and number of years known:

.... (Name)	.... (Complete address)	.... (Occupation)	.... (Years known)

21. Have you ever been convicted by a court of a criminal offense (other than a minor traffic violation)? ....

Offense	When	What court	Sentence

22. Give details on any foreign investments.

(a) Accounts in foreign banks.   Amount, $............................

Bank ....   Date account opened ....

(b) Investments in foreign companies.   Amount, $............................

Company............................   Date acquired ....

(c) Do you have a safe-deposit box in a foreign country?

What country? ....   Date acquired ....

Contents ....

16—32588-1

Figure 2.10 *Continued.*

23. List contributions you have made to any society, organization, or club:

Organization	Place	Amount	Date

24. List magazines and newspapers to which you have subscribed or have customarily read:

25. To the best of your knowledge, was your birth ever registered with any Japanese governmental agency for the purpose of establishing a claim to Japanese citizenship? _____

   (a) If so registered, have you applied for cancelation of such registration? _____ (Yes or no).

      When? _____ Where? _____

26. Have you ever applied for repatriation to Japan? _____

27. Are you willing to serve in the armed forces of the United States on combat duty, wherever ordered? _____

28. Will you swear unqualified allegiance to the United States of America and faithfully defend the United States from any or all attack by foreign or domestic forces, and forswear any form of allegiance or obedience to the Japanese emperor, or any other foreign government, power, or organization? _____

_____ (Date)   _____ (Signature)

NOTE.—Any person who knowingly and wilfully falsifies or conceals a material fact or makes a false or fraudulent statement or representation in any matter within the jurisdiction of any department or agency of the United States is liable to a fine of not more than $10,000 or 10 years' imprisonment, or both.

U. S. GOVERNMENT PRINTING OFFICE   16—32565-1

Figure 2.10 *Continued.*

Korematsu v. United States (1944)

This is one of the four major court cases brought before the U.S. Supreme Court by Japanese Americans challenging the legality of being interned during World War II. Fred Korematsu was arrested and convicted after he refused to report to a relocation camp. He argued that it was unconstitutional to incarcerate Japanese Americans based solely on their race. The Supreme Court, however, argued (in its majority opinion) that because the United States was at war with Japan, it was justifiable to remove those of Japanese ancestry from the West Coast. Korematsu's conviction was overturned in 1983 as part of the efforts of those involved in the redress and reparations movement. (Toyosaburo [Fred] Korematsu v. United States. 323 U.S. 214. Supreme Court of the United States. 1944.)

Certiorari to the Circuit Court of Appeals for the Ninth Circuit

No. 22. Argued October 11, 12, 1944. Decided December 18, 1944.

1. Civilian Exclusion Order No. 34 which, during a state of war with Japan and as a protection against espionage and sabotage, was promulgated by the Commanding General of the Western Defense Command under authority of Executive Order No. 9066 and the Act of March 21, 1942, and which directed the exclusion after May 9, 1942, from a described West Coast military area of all persons of Japanese ancestry, *held* constitutional as of the time it was made and when the petitioner—an American citizen of Japanese descent whose home was in the described area—violated it . . .

2. The provisions of other orders requiring persons of Japanese ancestry to report to assembly centers and providing for the detention of such persons in assembly and relocation centers were separate, and their validity is not in issue in this proceeding . . .

3. Even though evacuation and detention in the assembly center were inseparable, the order under which the petitioner was convicted was nevertheless valid . . .

CERTIORARI, 321 U.S. 760, to review the affirmance of a judgment of conviction.

Opinion of the Court

Mr. Justice Black delivered the opinion of the Court.

The petitioner, an American citizen of Japanese descent, was convicted in a federal district court for remaining in San Leandro, California, a "Military Area," contrary to Civilian Exclusion Order No. 34 of the Commanding General of the Western Command, U.S. Army, which directed that after May 9, 1942, all persons of Japanese ancestry should be excluded from that area. No question was raised as to petitioner's loyalty to the United States. The Circuit Court of Appeals affirmed, and the importance of the constitutional question involved caused us to grant certiorari.

It should be noted, to begin with, that all legal restrictions which curtail the civil rights of a single racial group are immediately suspect. That is not to say that all such restrictions are unconstitutional. It is to say that courts must subject them to the most rigid scrutiny. Pressing public necessity may sometimes justify the existence of such restrictions; racial antagonism never can. In the instant case prosecution of the petitioner was begun by information charging violation of an Act of Congress, of March 21, 1942, 56 Stat. 173, which provides that:

"... whoever shall enter, remain in, leave, or commit any act in any military area or military zone prescribed, under the authority of an Executive order of the President, by the Secretary of War, or by any military commander designated by the Secretary of War, contrary to the restrictions applicable to any such area or zone or contrary to the order of the Secretary of War or any such military commander, shall, if it appears that he knew or should have known of the existence and extent of the restrictions or order and that his act was in violation thereof, be guilty of a misdemeanor and upon conviction shall be liable to a fine of not to exceed $5,000 or to imprisonment for not more than one year, or both, for each offense."

Exclusion Order No. 34, which the petitioner knowingly and admittedly violated, was one of a number of military orders and proclamations, all of which were substantially based upon Executive Order No. 9066, 7 Fed. Reg. 1407. That order, issued after we were at war with Japan, declared that "the successful prosecution of the war requires every possible protection against espionage and against sabotage to national-defense material, national defense premises, and national-defense utilities . . ."

One of the series of orders and proclamations, a curfew order, which like the exclusion order here was promulgated pursuant to Executive Order 9066, subjected all persons of Japanese ancestry in prescribed

West Coast military areas to remain in their residences from 8 p.m. to 6 a.m. As is the case with the exclusion order here, that prior curfew order was designed as a "protection against espionage and against sabotage." In *Hirabayashi v. United States,* 320 U.S. 81, we sustained a conviction obtained for violation of the curfew order. The Hirabayashi conviction and this one thus rest on the same 1942 Congressional Act and the same basic executive and military orders, all of which were aimed at the twin dangers of espionage and sabotage.

The 1942 Act was attacked in the *Hirabayashi* case as an unconstitutional delegation of power; it was contended that the curfew order and other orders on which it rested were beyond the war powers of the Congress, the military authorities and of the President, as Commander in Chief of the Army; and finally that to apply the curfew order against none but citizens of Japanese ancestry amounted to a constitutionally prohibited discrimination solely on account of race. To these questions, we gave the serious consideration which their importance justified. We upheld the curfew order as an exercise of the power of the government to take steps necessary to prevent espionage and sabotage in an area threatened by Japanese attack.

In the light of the principles we announced in the *Hirabayashi* case, we are unable to conclude that it was beyond the war power of Congress and the Executive to exclude those of Japanese ancestry from the West Coast war area at the time they did. True, exclusion from the area in which one's home is located is a far greater deprivation than constant confinement to the home from 8 p.m. to 6 a.m. Nothing short of apprehension by the proper military authorities of the gravest imminent danger to the public safety can constitutionally justify either. But exclusion from a threatened area, no less than curfew, has a definite and close relationship to the prevention of espionage and sabotage. The military authorities, charged with the primary responsibility of defending our shores, concluded that curfew provided inadequate protection and ordered exclusion. They did so, as pointed out in our *Hirabayashi* opinion, in accordance with Congressional authority to the military to say who should, and who should not, remain in the threatened areas.

In this case the petitioner challenges the assumptions upon which we rested our conclusions in the *Hirabayashi* case. He also urges that by May 1942, when Order No. 34 was promulgated, all danger of Japanese invasion of the West Coast had disappeared. After careful consideration of these contentions we are compelled to reject them.

Here, as in the *Hirabayashi* case, *supra,* at p. 99, ". . . we cannot reject as unfounded the judgment of the military authorities and of Congress that there were disloyal members of that population, whose number and strength could not be precisely and quickly ascertained. We cannot say that the war-making branches of the Government did not have ground for believing that in a critical hour such persons could not readily be isolated and separately dealt with, and constituted a menace to the national defense and safety, which demanded that prompt and adequate measures be taken to guard against it."

Like curfew, exclusion of those of Japanese origin was deemed necessary because of the presence of an unascertained number of disloyal members of the group, most of whom we have no doubt were loyal to this country. It was because we could not reject the finding of the military authorities that it was impossible to bring about an immediate segregation of the disloyal from the loyal that we sustained the validity of the curfew order as applying to the whole group. In the instant case, temporary exclusion of the entire group was rested by the military on the same ground. The judgment that exclusion of the whole group was for the same reason a military imperative answers the contention that the exclusion was in the nature of group punishment based on antagonism to those of Japanese origin. That there were members of the group who retained loyalties to Japan has been confirmed by investigations made subsequent to the exclusion. Approximately five thousand American citizens of Japanese ancestry refused to swear unqualified allegiance to the United States and to renounce allegiance to the Japanese Emperor, and several thousand evacuees requested repatriation to Japan.

We uphold the exclusion order as of the time it was made and when the petitioner violated it. Cf. *Chastleton Corporation v. Sinclair,* 264 U.S. 543, 547; *Block v. Hirsh,* 256 U.S. 135, 154–5. In doing so, we are not unmindful of the hardships imposed by it upon a large group of American citizens. Cf. *Ex parte Kawato,* 317 U.S. 69, 73. But hardships are part of war, and war is an aggregation of hardships. All citizens alike, both in and out of uniform, feel the impact of war in greater or lesser measure. Citizenship has its responsibilities as well as its privileges, and in time of war the burden is always heavier. Compulsory exclusion of large groups of citizens from their homes, except under circumstances of direst emergency and peril, is inconsistent with our basic governmental institutions. But when under conditions of modern warfare our shores are threatened by hostile forces, the power to protect must be commensurate with the threatened danger. . . .

It is said that we are dealing here with the case of imprisonment of a citizen in a concentration camp solely because of his ancestry, without evidence or inquiry concerning his loyalty and good disposition towards the United States. Our task would be simple, our duty clear, were this a case involving the imprisonment of a loyal citizen in a concentration camp because of racial prejudice. Regardless of the true nature of the assembly and relocation centers—and we deem it unjustifiable to call them concentration camps with all the ugly connotations that term implies—we are dealing specifically with nothing but an exclusion order. To cast this case into outlines of racial prejudice, without reference to the real military dangers which were presented, merely confuses the issue. Korematsu was not excluded from the Military Area because of hostility to him or his race. He *was* excluded because we are at war with the Japanese Empire, because the properly constituted military authorities feared an invasion of our West Coast and felt constrained to take proper security measures, because they decided that the military urgency of the situation demanded that all citizens of Japanese ancestry be segregated from the West Coast temporarily, and finally, because Congress, reposing its confidence in this time of war in our military leaders—as inevitably it must—determined that they should have the power to do just this. There was evidence of disloyalty on the part of some, the military authorities considered that the need for action was great, and time was short. We cannot—by availing ourselves of the calm perspective of hindsight—now say that at that time these actions were unjustified.

Affirmed.

Dissenting Opinion, Mr. Justice Roberts

I dissent, because I think the indisputable facts exhibit a clear violation of Constitutional rights. This is not a case of keeping people off the streets at night as was *Hirabayashi v. United States*, 320 U.S. 81, nor a case of temporary exclusion of a citizen from an area for his own safety or that of the community, nor a case of offering him an opportunity to go temporarily out of an area where his presence might cause danger to himself or to his fellows. On the contrary, it is the case of convicting a citizen as a punishment for not submitting to imprisonment in a concentration camp, based on his ancestry, and solely because of his ancestry, without evidence or inquiry concerning his loyalty and good disposition towards the United States. If this be a correct statement of the facts disclosed by this record,

and facts of which we take judicial notice, I need hardly labor the conclusion that Constitutional rights have been violated. . . .

Dissenting Opinion, Mr. Justice Murphy

This exclusion of "all persons of Japanese ancestry, both alien and non-
alien," from the Pacific Coast area on a plea of military necessity in the
absence of martial law ought not to be approved. Such exclusion goes over
"the very brink of constitutional power" and falls into the ugly abyss of
racism.

In dealing with matters relating to the prosecution and progress of a
war, we must accord great respect and consideration to the judgments of
the military authorities who are on the scene and who have full knowledge of the military facts. The scope of their discretion must, as a matter
of necessity and common sense, be wide. And their judgments ought not
to be overruled lightly by those whose training and duties ill-equip them
to deal intelligently with matters so vital to the physical security of the
nation.

At the same time, however, it is essential that there be definite limits to
military discretion, especially where martial law has not been declared.
Individuals must not be left impoverished of their constitutional rights on
a plea of military necessity that has neither substance nor support. Thus,
like other claims conflicting with the asserted constitutional rights of the
individual, the military claim must subject itself to the judicial process of
having its reasonableness determined and its conflicts with other interests reconciled. "What are the allowable limits of military discretion, and
whether or not they have been overstepped in a particular case, are judicial questions." *Sterling v. Constantin,* 287 U.S. 378, 401.

The judicial test of whether the Government, on a plea of military necessity, can validly deprive an individual of any of his constitutional rights
is whether the deprivation is reasonably related to a public danger that is
so "immediate, imminent, and impending" as not to admit of delay and
not to permit the intervention of ordinary constitutional processes to alle-
viate the danger. *United States v. Russell,* 13 Wall. 623, 627–8; *Mitchell v.
Harmony,* 13 How. 115, 134–5; *Raymond v. Thomas,* 91 U.S. 712, 716. Civilian
Exclusion Order No. 34, banishing from a prescribed area of the Pacific
Coast "all persons of Japanese ancestry, both alien and non-alien," clearly
does not meet that test. Being an obvious racial discrimination, the order
deprives all those within its scope of the equal protection of the laws as

guaranteed by the Fifth Amendment. It further deprives these individuals of their constitutional rights to live and work where they will, to establish a home where they choose, and to move about freely. In excommunicating them without benefit of hearings, this order also deprives them of all their constitutional rights to procedural due process. Yet no reasonable relation to an "immediate, imminent, and impending" public danger is evident to support this racial restriction which is one of the most sweeping and complete deprivations of constitutional rights in the history of this nation in the absence of martial law.

It must be conceded that the military and naval situation in the spring of 1942 was such as to generate a very real fear of invasion of the Pacific Coast, accompanied by fears of sabotage and espionage in that area. The military command was therefore justified in adopting all reasonable means necessary to combat these dangers. In adjudging the military action taken in light of the then apparent dangers, we must not erect too high or too meticulous standards; it is necessary only that the action have some reasonable relation to the removal of the dangers of invasion, sabotage and espionage. But the exclusion, either temporarily or permanently, of all persons with Japanese blood in their veins has no such reasonable relation. And that relation is lacking because the exclusion order necessarily must rely for its reasonableness upon the assumption that *all* persons of Japanese ancestry may have a dangerous tendency to commit sabotage and espionage and to aid our Japanese enemy in other ways. It is difficult to believe that reason, logic or experience could be marshalled in support of such an assumption. . . .

No-No Boy (1957)

John Okada

No-No Boy (1957) was the first novel published by a Japanese American after World War II that grappled with both the effect of the internment experience and those Japanese men who chose not to serve in the armed forces—called "no-no boys" if they answered "no" to questions 27 and 28 of the "Loyalty Questionnaire." This scene depicts Ichiro, a no-no boy, just arriving in Seattle after serving time in prison for not complying with the draft. He is confronted by Eto, a childhood friend who had served in the army.

When Eto realizes that Ichiro had not served, he treats him with contempt, setting the stage for the novel's themes of guilt, the meaning of citizenship, and redemption. (From John Okada. Foreword by Ruth Ozeki. Introduction by Lawson Fusao Inada and Frank Chin. No-No Boy. pp. 2-4. © 1978. Reprinted with permission of the University of Washington Press.)

The fellow wore green, army-fatigue trousers and an Eisenhower jacket—Eto Minato. The name came to him [Ichiro] at the same time as did the horrible significance of the army clothes. In panic, he started to step off the curb. It was too late. He had been seen.

"Itchy!" That was his nickname.

Trying to escape, Ichiro urged his legs frenziedly across the street.

"Hey Itchy!" The caller's footsteps ran toward him.

An arm was placed across his back. Ichiro stopped and faced the other Japanese. He tried to smile, but could not. There was no way out now.

"I'm Eto. Remember?" . . .

The round face with the round eyes peered at him through silver-rimmed spectacles. "What the hell! It's been a long time, but not that long. How've you been? What's doing?"

"Well . . . that is, I'm . . ."

"Last time must have been before Pearl Harbor. God, it's been quite a while, hasn't it? Three, no closer to four years, I guess. Lotsa Japs coming back to the Coast. Lotsa Japs in Seattle. You'll see 'em around. Japs are funny that way. Gotta have their rice and saké [rice wine] and other Japs. Stupid, I say. The smart ones went to Chicago and New York and lotsa places back east, but there's still plenty coming back out this way. How long you been around?"

Ichiro touched his toe to the suitcase. "Just got in. Haven't been home yet."

"When'd you get discharged?"

A car grinding its gears started down the street. He wished he were in it. "I . . . that is . . . I never was in."

Eto slapped him good-naturedly on the arm. "No need to look so sour. So you weren't in. So what? Been in camp all this time?"

"No." He made an effort to be free of Eto with his questions. He felt as if he were in a small room whose walls were slowly closing in on him. "It's been a long time, I know, but I'm really anxious to see the folks."

"What the hell. Let's have a drink. One. I don't give a damn if I'm late to work. As for your folks, you'll see them soon enough. You drink, don't you?"

"Yeah, but not now."

"Ahh." Eto was disappointed. He shifted his lunch box from one arm to the other.

"I've really got to be going."

The round face wasn't smiling any more. It was thoughtful. The eyes confronted Ichiro with indecision which changed slowly to enlightenment and then suspicion. He remembered. He knew.

The friendliness was gone as he said: "No-no boy, huh?"

Ichiro wanted to say yes. He wanted simply to return the look of despising hatred and say yes, but it was too much to say. The walls had closed in and were crushing all the unspoken words back down into his stomach. He shook his head once, not wanting to evade the eyes but finding it impossible to meet them . . .

"Rotten bastard. Shit on you." Eto coughed up a mouthful of sputum and rolled his words around it: "Rotten, no-good bastard." . . .

"I'll piss on you next time," said Eto vehemently.

He turned as he lifted his suitcase off the ground and hurried away from the legs and the eyes from which no escape was possible.

Speech on the Far East (1950)

Dean Acheson

Dean Acheson (1893-1971) served as the U.S. secretary of state during the administration of President Harry S. Truman (1949-1953). He is credited as one of the chief influences on early Cold War policy; in particular, he was influential in the codification of the so-called Truman Doctrine of containment. This speech, delivered soon after the Communist takeover of mainland China in 1949, emphasizes the need to foster allies in the region as a means of developing and maintaining a "defensive perimeter." Such containment considerations became emblematic of the Cold War, wherein policymakers repeatedly stressed the importance of maintaining influence in the region in order to militate against the spread of Communism (via the "domino theory"). ("Speech on the Far East." National Press Club, Washington, DC. 12 Jan. 1950.)

I am frequently asked: Has the State Department got an Asian policy? And it seems to me that that discloses such a depth of ignorance that it is very hard to begin to deal with it. The peoples of Asia are so incredibly diverse and their problems are so incredibly diverse that how could anyone, even the most utter charlatan, believe that he had a uniform policy which would deal with all of them. On the other hand, there are very important similarities in ideas and in problems among the peoples of Asia and so what we come to, after we understand these diversities and these common attitudes of mind, is the fact that there must be certain similarities of approach, and there must be very great dissimilarities in action.

There is in this vast area what we might call a developing Asian consciousness, and a developing pattern, and this, I think, is based upon two factors.

One of these factors is a revulsion against the acceptance of misery and poverty as the normal condition of life. Throughout all of this vast area, you have that fundamental revolutionary aspect in mind and belief. The other common aspect that they have is the revulsion against foreign domination. Whether that foreign domination takes the form of colonialism or whether it takes the form of imperialism, they are through with it. They have had enough of it, and they want no more.

Now, may I suggest to you that much of the bewilderment which has seized the minds of many of us about recent developments in China comes from a failure to understand this basic revolutionary force which is loose in Asia. The reasons for the fall of the Nationalist Government in China are preoccupying many people. All sorts of reasons have been attributed to it. Most commonly, it is said in various speeches and publications that it is the result of American bungling, that we are incompetent, that we did not understand, that American aid was too little, that we did the wrong things at the wrong time. Now, what I ask you to do is to stop looking for a moment under the bed and under the chair and under the rug to find out these reasons, but rather to look at the broad picture and see whether something doesn't suggest itself.

What has happened in my judgment is that the almost inexhaustible patience of the Chinese people in their misery ended. They did not bother to overthrow this government. There was really nothing to overthrow. They simply ignored it. They completely withdrew their support from this government, and when that support was withdrawn, the whole military establishment disintegrated. Added to the grossest incompetence ever experienced by any military command was this total lack of support both in the armies and in the country, and so the whole matter just simply disintegrated.

The Communists did not create this. The Communists did not create this condition. They did not create this revolutionary spirit. They did not create a great force which moved out from under Chiang Kai-shek. But they were shrewd and cunning to mount it, to ride this thing into victory and into power.

Now, let me come to another underlying and important factor which determines our relations and, in turn, our policy with the peoples of Asia. That is the attitude of the Soviet Union toward Asia, and particularly towards those parts of Asia which are contiguous to the Soviet Union, and with great particularity this afternoon, to north China.

The attitude and interest of the Russians in north China, and in these other areas as well, long antedates communism. This is not something that has come out of communism at all. It long antedates it. But the Communist regime has added new methods, new skills, and new concepts to the thrust of Russian imperialism. This Communistic concept and techniques have armed Russian imperialism with a new and most insidious weapon of penetration. Armed with these new powers, what is happening in China is that the Soviet Union is detaching the northern provinces of China from China and is attaching them to the Soviet Union. This process is complete in outer Mongolia. It is nearly complete in Manchuria, and I am sure that in inner Mongolia and in Sinkiang there are very happy reports coming from Soviet agents to Moscow. This is what is going on. It is the detachment of these whole areas, vast areas—populated by Chinese—the detachment of these areas from China and their attachment to the Soviet Union.

I wish to state this and perhaps sin against my doctrine of non-dogmatism, but I should like to suggest at any rate that this fact that the Soviet Union is taking the four northern provinces of China is the single most significant, most important fact, in the relation of any foreign power with Asia.

What does that mean for us? It means something very, very significant. It means that nothing that we do and nothing that we say must be allowed to obscure the reality of this fact. All the efforts of propaganda will not be able to obscure it. The only thing that can obscure it is the folly of ill-conceived adventures on our part which easily could do so, and I urge all who are thinking about these foolish adventures to remember that we must not seize the unenviable position which the Russians have carved out for themselves. We must not undertake to deflect from the Russians to ourselves the righteous anger, and the wrath, and the hatred of the Chinese people which must develop. It would be folly to deflect it to ourselves. We must take the position we have always taken—that anyone who violates the integrity of China is the enemy of China and is acting contrary to our own interest. That, I suggest to you this afternoon, is the first and the great rule in regard to the formulation of American policy toward Asia.

I suggest that the second rule is very like the first. That is to keep our own purposes perfectly straight, perfectly pure, and perfectly aboveboard and do not get them mixed-up with legal quibbles or the attempt to do one thing and really achieve another . . .

What is the situation in regard to the military security of the Pacific area, and what is our policy in regard to it?

In the first place, the defeat and the disarmament of Japan has placed upon the United States the necessity of assuming the military defense of Japan so long as that is required, both in the interest of our security and in the interests of the security of the entire Pacific area and, in all honor, in the interest of Japanese security. We have American—and there are Australian—troops in Japan. I am not in a position to speak for the Australians, but I can assure you that there is no intention of any sort of abandoning or weakening the defenses of Japan and that whatever arrangements are to be made either through permanent settlement or otherwise, that defense must and shall be maintained.

The defensive perimeter runs along the Aleutians to Japan and then goes to the Ryukyus. We hold important defense positions in the Ryukyu Islands, and those we will continue to hold. In the interest of the population of the Ryukyu Islands, we will at an appropriate time offer to hold these islands under trusteeship of the United Nations. But they are essential parts of the defensive perimeter of the Pacific, and they must and will be held.

The defensive perimeter runs from the Ryukyus to the Philippine Islands. Our relations, our defensive relations with the Philippines are contained in agreements between us. Those agreements are being loyally carried out and will be loyally carried out. Both peoples have learned by bitter experience the vital connections between our mutual defense requirements. We are in no doubt about that, and it is hardly necessary for me to say an attack on the Philippines could not and would not be tolerated by the United States. But I hasten to add that no one perceives the imminence of any such attack.

So far as the military security of other areas in the Pacific is concerned, it must be clear that no person can guarantee these areas against military attack. But it must also be clear that such a guarantee is hardly sensible or necessary within the realm of practical relationship. Should such an attack occur—one hesitates to say where such an armed attack could come from—the initial reliance must be on the people attacked to resist it and then upon the commitments of the entire civilized world under the Charter of the United Nations which so far has not proved a weak reed to lean on by any people who are determined to protect their independence against outside aggression. But it is a mistake, I think, in considering Pacific and Far Eastern problems to become obsessed with military considerations. Important as they are, there are other problems that press, and these other problems are not capable of solution through military means. These other problems arise out of the susceptibility of many areas, and many countries in the Pacific area, to subversion and penetration. That cannot be stopped by military means.

The susceptibility to penetration arises because in many areas there are new governments which have little experience in governmental administration and have not become firmly established or perhaps firmly accepted in their countries. They grow, in part, from very serious economic problems. In part this susceptibility to penetration comes from the great social upheaval about which I have been speaking.

So after this survey, what we conclude, I believe, is that there is a new day which has dawned in Asia. It is a day in which the Asian peoples are on their own, and know it, and intend to continue on their own. It is a day in which the old relationships between East and West are gone, relationships which at their worst were exploitations, and which at their best were paternalism. That relationship is over, and the relationship of East and West must now be in the Far East one of mutual respect and mutual helpfulness. We are their friends. Others are their friends. We and those others are willing to help, but we can help only where we are wanted and only where the conditions of help are really sensible and possible. So what we can see is that this new day in Asia, this new day which is dawning, may go on to a glorious noon or it may darken and it may drizzle out. But that decision lies within the countries of Asia and within the power of the Asian people. It is not a decision which a friend or even an enemy from the outside can decide for them.

Harry S. Truman's Address on the Situation in Korea (1950)

The Korean War (June 25, 1950–July 27, 1953) was a conflict between North and South Korea that was originally termed a "police action" by then-president Harry S. Truman. The United States was the primary ally of South Korea. The war ostensibly began when the Communist Korean People's Army (KPA) crossed the 38th parallel into South Korea. However, the KPA claimed that Republic of Korea (ROK) troops attacked first. What follows is a radio and television address that President Truman delivered on July 19, 1950, roughly one month after the war started. (Harry S. Truman. "Radio and Television Address to the American People on the Situation in Korea." Washington, DC, 19 July 1950.)

My fellow citizens:

At noon today I sent a message to the Congress about the situation in Korea. I want to talk to you tonight about that situation, and about what it means to the security of the United States and to our hopes for peace in the world.

Korea is a small country, thousands of miles away, but what is happening there is important to every American.

On Sunday, June 25th, Communist forces attacked the Republic of Korea.

This attack has made it clear, beyond all doubt, that the international Communist movement is willing to use armed invasion to conquer independent nations. An act of aggression such as this creates a very real danger to the security of all free nations.

The attack upon Korea was an outright breach of the peace and a violation of the Charter of the United Nations. By their actions in Korea, Communist leaders have demonstrated their contempt for the basic moral principles on which the United Nations is founded. This is a direct challenge to the efforts of the free nations to build the kind of world in which men can live in freedom and peace.

This challenge has been presented squarely. We must meet it squarely....

The Communist invasion was launched in great force, with planes, tanks, and artillery. The size of the attack, and the speed with which it was followed up, make it perfectly plain that it had been plotted long in advance.

As soon as word of the attack was received, Secretary of State [Dean] Acheson called me at Independence, Mo., and informed me that, with my approval, he would ask for an immediate meeting of the United Nations Security Council. The Security Council met just 24 hours after the Communist invasion began.

One of the main reasons the Security Council was set up was to act in such cases as this—to stop outbreaks of aggression in a hurry before they develop into general conflicts. In this case the Council passed a resolution which called for the invaders of Korea to stop fighting, and to withdraw. The Council called on all members of the United Nations to help carry out this resolution. The Communist invaders ignored the action of the Security Council and kept right on with their attack.

The Security Council then met again. It recommended that members of the United Nations help the Republic of Korea repel the attack and help restore peace and security in that area.

Fifty-two of the 59 countries which are members of the United Nations have given their support to the action taken by the Security Council to restore peace in Korea.

These actions by the United Nations and its members are of great importance. The free nations have now made it clear that lawless aggression will be met with force. The free nations have learned the fateful lesson of the 1930s. That lesson is that aggression must be met firmly. Appeasement leads only to further aggression and ultimately to war.

The principal effort to help the Koreans preserve their independence, and to help the United Nations restore peace, has been made by the United States. We have sent land, sea, and air forces to assist in these operations. We have done this because we know that what is at stake here is nothing less than our own national security and the peace of the world.

So far, two other nations—Australia and Great Britain—have sent planes to Korea; and six other nations—Australia, Canada, France, Great Britain, the Netherlands, and New Zealand—have made naval forces available.

Under the flag of the United Nations a unified command has been established for all forces of the members of the United Nations fighting in Korea. Gen. Douglas MacArthur is the commander of this combined force.

The prompt action of the United Nations to put down lawless aggression, and the prompt response to this action by free peoples all over the world, will stand as a landmark in mankind's long search for a rule of law among nations.

Only a few countries have failed to endorse the efforts of the United Nations to stop the fighting in Korea. The most important of these is the Soviet Union. The Soviet Union has boycotted the meetings of the United Nations Security Council. It has refused to support the actions of the United Nations with respect to Korea.

The United States requested the Soviet Government, two days after the fighting started, to use its influence with the North Koreans to have them withdraw. The Soviet Government refused.

The Soviet Government has said many times that it wants peace in the world, but its attitude toward this act of aggression against the Republic of Korea is in direct contradiction of its statements.

For our part, we shall continue to support the United Nations action to restore peace in the world.

We know that it will take a hard, tough fight to halt the invasion, and to drive the Communists back. The invaders have been provided with enough equipment and supplies for a long campaign. They overwhelmed the lightly armed defense forces of the Korean Republic in the first few days and drove southward.

Now, however, the Korean defenders have reorganized and are making a brave fight for their liberty, and an increasing number of American troops have joined them. Our forces have fought a skillful, rearguard delaying action, pending the arrival of reinforcements. Some of these reinforcements are now arriving; others are on the way from the United States. . . .

Furthermore, the fact that Communist forces have invaded Korea is a warning that there may be similar acts of aggression in other parts of the world. The free nations must be on their guard, more than ever before, against this kind of sneak attack. . . .

When we have worked out with other free countries an increased program for our common defense, I shall recommend to the Congress that additional funds be provided for this purpose. This is of great importance. The free nations face a worldwide threat. It must be met with a worldwide defense. The United States and other free nations can multiply their strength by joining with one another in a common effort to provide this defense. This is our best hope for peace.

The things we need to do to build up our military defense will require considerable adjustment in our domestic economy. We have a tremendously rich and productive economy, and it is expanding every year.

Our job now is to divert to defense purposes more of that tremendous productive capacity—more steel, more aluminum, more of a good many things.

Some of the additional production for military purposes can come from making fuller use of plants which are not operating at capacity. But many of our industries are already going full tilt, and until we can add new capacity, some of the resources we need for the national defense will have to be taken from civilian uses.

This requires us to take certain steps to make sure that we obtain the things we need for national defense, and at the same time guard against inflationary price rises.

The steps that are needed now must be taken promptly.

In the message which I sent to the Congress today, I described the economic measures which are required at this time.

First, we need laws which will insure prompt and adequate supplies for military and essential civilian use. I have therefore recommended that the Congress give the Government power to guide the flow of materials into essential uses, to restrict their use for nonessential purposes, and to prevent the accumulation of unnecessary inventories.

Second, we must adopt measures to prevent inflation and to keep our Government in a sound financial condition. One of the major causes of inflation is the excessive use of credit. I have recommended that the Congress authorize the Government to set limits on installment buying and to curb speculation in agricultural commodities. In the housing field, where Government credit is an important factor, I have already directed that credit restraints be applied, and I have recommended that the Congress authorize further controls.

As an additional safeguard against inflation, and to help finance our defense needs, it will be necessary to make substantial increases in taxes. This is a contribution to our national security that every one of us should stand ready to make. As soon as a balanced and fair tax program can be worked out, I shall lay it before the Congress. This tax program will have as a major aim the elimination of profiteering.

Third, we should increase the production of goods needed for national defense. We must plan to enlarge our defense production, not just for the immediate future, but for the next several years. This will be primarily a task for our businessmen and workers. However, to help obtain the necessary increases, the Government should be authorized to provide certain types of financial assistance to private industry to increase defense production.

Our military needs are large, and to meet them will require hard work and steady effort. I know that we can produce what we need if each of us does his part—each man, each woman, each soldier, each civilian. This is a time for all of us to pitch in and work together. . . .

We have the resources to meet our needs. Far more important, the American people are unified in their belief in democratic freedom. We are united in detesting Communist slavery.

We know that the cost of freedom is high. But we are determined to preserve our freedom—no matter what the cost.

I know that our people are willing to do their part to support our soldiers and sailors and airmen who are fighting in Korea. I know that our fighting men can count on each and every one of you.

Our country stands before the world as an example of how free men, under God, can build a community of neighbors, working together for the good of all.

That is the goal we seek not only for ourselves, but for all people. We believe that freedom and peace are essential if men are to live as our Creator intended us to live. It is this faith that has guided us in the past, and it is this faith that will fortify us in the stern days ahead.

Gulf of Tonkin Resolution (1964)

On August 2, 1964, the USS Maddox *and three North Vietnamese torpedo boats skirmished in the Gulf of Tonkin, a body of water located off the northern coast of Vietnam, south of China. Eight days later, on August 10, 1964, Congress passed a joint resolution that authorized President Lyndon B. Johnson to call for the use of conventional military force without an overt declaration of war. The conflict would eventually witness the deployment of 2.15 million U.S. soldiers and lead to 58,220 American deaths; the number of Vietnamese casualties (both North and South Vietnam) is estimated at 1.1. million. (Joint Resolution to Promote the Maintenance of International Peace and Security in Southeast Asia. Pub. L. 88-408; 78 Stat. 384. 10 Aug. 1964.)*

Whereas naval units of the Communist regime in Vietnam, in violation of the principles of the Charter of the United Nations and of international law, have deliberately and repeatedly attacked United States naval vessels lawfully present in international waters, and have thereby created a serious threat to international peace; and

Whereas these attacks are part of a deliberate and systematic campaign of aggression that the Communist regime in North Vietnam has been waging against its neighbors and the nations joined with them in the collective defense of their freedom; and

Whereas the United States is assisting the peoples of southeast Asia to protect their freedom and has no territorial, military or political ambitions in that area, but desires only that these peoples should be left in peace to work out their own destinies in their own way: Now, therefore, be it

Resolved by the Senate and House of Representatives of the United States of America in Congress assembled, That the Congress approves and supports the determination of the President, as Commander in Chief, to take all necessary measures to repel any armed attack against the forces of the United States and to prevent further aggression.

SEC. 2. The United States regards as vital to its national interest and to world peace the maintenance of international peace and security in southeast Asia. Consonant with the Constitution of the United States and the Charter of the United Nations and in accordance with its obligations under the Southeast Asia Collective Defense Treaty, the United States is, therefore, prepared, as the President determines, to take all necessary steps, including the use of armed force, to assist any member or protocol state of the Southeast Asia Collective Defense Treaty requesting assistance in defense of its freedom.

SEC. 3. This resolution shall expire when the President shall determine that the peace and security of the area is reasonably assured by international conditions created by action of the United Nations or otherwise, except that it may be terminated earlier by concurrent resolution of the Congress.

My Lai Massacre: Court Testimony

The My Lai Massacre refers to the mass killing of an estimated 347 to 504 unarmed Vietnamese civilians by U.S. Army soldiers from Company C of the 1st Battalion, 20th Infantry Regiment, 11th Brigade of the 23rd Infantry Division on March 16, 1968. While twenty-six soldiers were originally charged with criminal offenses, only Lieutenant William Calley Jr., the troop's platoon leader, was convicted of killing twenty-two villagers. Calley was handed a life sentence, but he served only three and a half years under house arrest. What follows are excerpted transcripts from the November 1970 court-martial of Lt. Calley, including Lt. Calley's testimony and the testimony of Ronald L. Haeberle, the U.S. Army photographer who took photos of the massacre. (William L. Calley General Court-Martial Transcript. U.S. Army Judiciary. 1971. National Archives and Records Administration, College Park, MD.)

Direct Examination by George Latimer of Lt. Calley

Q: Now, during the course of your movement through the village, had you seen any Vietnamese dead, or dead bodies?

A: Yes, sir.

Q: And how would you classify it as to whether it was a few, many . . . what descriptive phrase would you use for your own impression?

A: Many.

Q: Now, did you see some live Vietnamese while you were going through the village?

A: I saw two, sir.

Q: All right. Now, tell us, was there an incident concerning those two?

A: Yes, sir. I shot and killed both of them.

Q: Under what circumstances?

A: There was a large concrete house and I kind of stepped up on the porch and looked in the window. There was about six to eight individuals laying on the floor, apparently dead. And one man was going for the window. I shot him. There was another man standing in a fireplace. He looked like he had just come out of the fireplace, or out of the chimney. And I shot him, sir. He was in a bright green uniform . . .

Q: All right. Now . . . did you see any other live individuals who were in the village itself as you made through the sweep?

A: Well, when I got to the eastern edge of the village, I saw a group of Vietnamese just standing right outside the eastern edge of the village, sir, the southeastern edge.

Q: All right. Was there anybody there with that group of individuals that you saw at that time?

A: I recollect that there were GIs there with them . . .

A: I heard a considerable volume of firing to my north, and I moved along the edge of the ditch and around a hootch [hut] and I broke into the clearing, and my men had a number of Vietnamese in the ditch and were firing upon them.

Q: When you say your men, can you identify any of the men?

A: I spoke to Dursi and I spoke to Meadlo, sir.

Q: Was there anybody else there that you can identify by name?

A: No, sir. There was a few other troops, but it was insignificant to me at the time and I didn't—

Q: What was your best impression of how many were there at the ditch?

A: Four to five, sir.

Q: Two of whom you can specifically identify, Meadlo and Dursi?

A: Yes, sir. I spoke to those two.

Q: What did you do after you saw them shooting in the ditch?

A: Well, I fired into the ditch also sir . . .

Q: Now, did you have a chance to look and observe what was in the ditch?

A: Yes, sir.

Q: And what did you see?

A: Dead people, sir.

Q: Let me ask you, at any time that you were alone and near the ditch, did you push or help push people into the ditch?

A: Yes and no, sir.

Q: Give us the yes part first.

A: Well, when I came out of this hedgerow, I came right up [to] . . . the last man to go into the ditch. I didn't physically touch him, but if he would have stopped, I guess I would have.

Q: Well, did he—was somebody there with him to order him in or push him in?

A: They had been ordered in—to go to the ditch, sir.

Q: Do you know who gave them that information?

A: Well, indirectly, I did, sir.

Q: And indirectly, what do you mean by that, was it through somebody?

A: I had told Meadlo to get them on the other side of the ditch, sir . . .

Q: All right. Then what did you do?

A: I butt-stroked him in the mouth, sir.

Q: With what effect?

A: It knocked him down.

Q: Did you shoot him?

A: No, sir, I did not . . .

Q: Let me ask you another—your impressions of another incident. There has been some testimony in the record to the effect that there was a child running from the ditch, that you threw him back into the ditch and you shot him. Did you participate in any such event?

A: No, sir, I did not.

Q: Did you see a boy or a child running from the ditch?

A: Wait, let me backtrack. Now this child that I supposedly said I shot, now, was running away from the ditch, but it is not in the same location. It is east of the ditch, but he was running away from the ditch. Now, I don't—

Q: To the extent that you shot and it turned out ultimately to be a child, is that the only impression you have of any incident which involved a child?

A: Yes, sir, I do.

Q: There has been some information disclosed that you heard before the court that you stood there at the ditch for a considerable period of time; that you waited and had your troops organized, groups of Vietnamese thrown in the ditch and knocked them down in the ditch or pushed them in the ditch and that you fired there for approximately an hour and a half as those groups were marched up. Did you participate in any such shooting or any such event?

A: No, sir, I did not.

Q: Did you at any time direct anybody to push people in the ditch?

A: Like I said, I gave the order to take those people through the ditch and had also told Meadlo if he couldn't move them, to waste them [kill them], and I directly—other than that, there was only that one incident. I never stood up there for any period of time. The main mission was to get my men on the other side of the ditch and get in that defensive position, and that is what I did, sir.

Q: Now, why did you give Meadlo a message or the order that if he couldn't get rid of them to waste them?

A: Because that was my order, sir. That was the order of the day, sir.

Q: Who gave you that order?

A: My commanding officer, sir.

Q: I am going to ask you this: During this operation, May Lai Four, did you intend specifically to kill Vietnamese — man, woman, or child?

A: No, sir, I did not.

Q: Did you ever form any intent, specifically or generally, in connection with that My Lai operation to waste any Vietnamese — man, woman, or child?

A: No sir, I did not.

Q: Now, did you on that occasion intend to waste something?

A: To waste or destroy the enemy, sir.

Q: All right. Now, what was your intention in connection with the carrying out of that operation as far as any premeditation or intent was concerned?

A: To go into the area and destroy the enemy that were designated there, and this is it. I went into the area to destroy the enemy, sir.

Q: Did you form any impression as to whether or not there were children, women, or men, or what did you see in front of you as you were going on?

A: I never sat down to analyze it, men, women, and children. They were enemy and just people.

Q: Did you consciously discriminate as you were operating through there insofar as sex or age is concerned?

A: The only time I denoted sex was when I stopped Conti from molesting a girl. That was the only time sex ever entered the — my whole scope of thinking.

Q: In this instance, you saw a group being supervised or guarded by Meadlo, how did you visualize that group? Did you go in the specifics in any way?

A: No, sir. It was a group of people that were the enemy, sir.

Q: And were you motivated by other things besides the fact that those were the enemy? Did you have some other reason for treating them that way altogether? I am talking now about your briefings [from your superiors]. Did you get any information out of that?

A: Well, I was ordered to go in there and destroy the enemy. That was my job on that day. That was the mission I was given. I did not sit down and think in terms of men, women, and children. They were all classified the same, and that was the classification that we dealt with, just as enemy soldiers.

Q: Who gave you that classification the last time you got it?

A: Captain Medina, sir . . .

Q: Now, I will ask you this, Lieutenant Calley: Whatever you did at My Lai on that occasion, I will ask you whether in your opinion you were acting rightly and according to your understanding of your directions and orders?

A: I felt then and I still do that I acted as I was directed, and I carried out the orders that I was given, and I do not feel wrong in doing so, sir . . .

Q: In connection with this operation, were you asked by Captain Medina to give a body count?

A: Yes, sir.

Direct Examination by Prosecutor Aubrey Daniels of Ronald Haeberle

A: They [the Vietnamese] were sitting in their kind of squat. First there were five soldiers standing in front of the group. The people were all sitting there facing north. Then three of the GIs walked off into the distance. Then I heard automatic fire. I looked back. The automatic fire was coming from one of the two soldiers. He was firing toward the people. Some of the people were trying to get up and run. They couldn't and fell down. This one woman, I remember, she stood up and tried to make it—tried to run—with a small child in her arms. But she didn't make it.

Q: Were any of the people standing when it was over?

A: No. I didn't see anyone.

Cross-Examination by George Latimer
of Ronald Haeberle

Q: Did you not testify that you never saw a lieutenant?

A: Yes sir.

Q: When did you first see a lieutenant?

A: I did not see a lieutenant all that day.

Q: Then you did not see Lieutenant Calley?

A: I did not see Lieutenant Calley.

Q: Do you not have a definite interest in the outcome of the suit?

A: Yes, sir, I do have an interest in it.

Q: And isn't that interest in selling books and magazine articles?

A: No, sir.

Q: Then what is your interest?

A: In seeing a fair trial.

Q: Did you have an interview with Captain Doyle in May?

A: Yes.

Q: Did you not make the following statement to him: that you wished you'd waited until after the court-martial to sell the pictures [of the massacre] because you would have made more money?

A: No, sir, I did not.

Q: From the time you took those pictures until after you got back to the United States, no one had been told of the color film, is that right? Did you ever tell any officer about what you'd seen?

A: I can't specifically recall. Jay [Roberts, the army journalist] and I talked about it. But I can't specifically recall.

Q: You never told anyone in the chain of command about the atrocity and massacre?

A: No, sir.

Q: Weren't you shocked at what you'd seen? Weren't you upset by what you'd seen? Why didn't you report it?

A: I felt it was unusual but I wasn't the one to bring it up. We decided to keep quiet until someone came to us and not to start the ball rolling . . .

Q: Have you never heard of a MAC-V [Military Assistance Command, Vietnam] order of 1967 that says it is the responsibility of all military personnel to report to their commanding officer any war crime they know of, that they should make every effort to discover war crimes, report them and preserve the physical evidence?

A: I never heard of that regulation before.

Q: Do you know that it is a serious offense not to comply with a regulation, known or unknown?

A: No.

Q: Did you ever consider the impact of your failure to disclose that you had these pictures or information to your commander or senior commanders?

A: No, sir, I did not.

Q: You had no feeling that failure to disclose that information was a dereliction of duty?

A: I've heard that.

Q: Is that the best excuse you can give us, that you didn't want to start the ball rolling?

A: That's what Jay Roberts and I talked about.

Vietnam War Images

As the first truly televised war, the Vietnam War was also among the most photographed. The following images highlight the costs of that war.

General Nguyen Ngoc Loan Executing a Viet Cong Prisoner in Saigon (1968)

Eddie Adams

On February 1, 1968, in the immediate aftermath of the Tet Offensive, when North Vietnamese troops overwhelmed U.S. fronts in and around Saigon (including the American Embassy), photographer Eddie Adams captured on film the South Vietnamese chief of the National Police executing suspected Viet Cong officer Nguyen Van Lem (also known as Bay Lop; fig. 2.11). Adams received the Pulitzer Prize for this photograph.

Figure 2.11 "General Nguyen Ngoc Loan Executing a Viet Cong Prisoner in Saigon" (1968). AP Photo/Eddie Adams. Reprinted with permission from the Associated Press.

The Terror of War (1972)

Nick Ut (Huynh Cong Ut)

Photographer Nick Ut also won a Pulitzer Prize for this photograph, "The Terror of War," also known as "Napalm Girl" (fig. 2.12). The photo features nine-year-old Kim Phuc, a napalm victim running naked from her village after it was bombed by a misdirected South Vietnamese plane on June 8, 1972.

Figure 2.12 "The Terror of War" (1972). AP Photo/Nick Ut. Reprinted with permission from the Associated Press.

Fall of Saigon (1975)

Hubert Van Es

An iconic image, Hubert Van Es's photograph has often been misidentified as detailing the evacuation of the U.S. Embassy in Saigon; however, the image actually captures the evacuation of CIA station personnel on April 29, 1975 (fig. 2.13). Nevertheless, the image is emblematic of what has come to be known as the "Fall of Saigon," which refers to the April 30, 1975, takeover of the city by North Vietnamese forces. This "fall" signaled the end of the Vietnam War.

Figure 2.13 Untitled photograph of the Fall of Saigon. United Press International. Copyright Hugh Van Es/Corbis. Courtesy of Corbis Images.

Vietnamese Refugees Arrive at
Camp Pendleton (1975)

Don Bartletti

In the days, weeks, and months that followed the April 30, 1975, "Fall of Saigon," thousands of Vietnamese refugees arrived in the United States; many had been connected with the previous South Vietnamese regime and were in search of asylum. This represented the first major wave of Southeast Asian refugees to arrive in the United States. Camp Pendleton in Southern California was one of four Southeast Asian resettlement camps in the United States (fig. 2.14); other sites were at Fort Chaffee in Arkansas, Eglin Air Force Base in Florida, and Fort Indiantown Gap in Pennsylvania. A total of 50,418 Southeast Asian refugees passed through Camp Pendleton, which was a major resettlement site. At its peak, Camp Pendleton was home to 18,500 refugees.

Figure 2.14 "Vietnamese Refugees Arrive at Camp Pendleton" (1975). Vista Press. Courtesy of Don Bartletti.

1.5-Generation Southeast Asian American Writers

The "1.5 generation" is marked by the fact that individuals spent their early childhoods or young adulthoods outside the United States. The artistic work of Bryan Thao Worra (b. 1973), Bao Phi (b. 1975), and Anida Yoeu Ali (b. 1974) engages an identifiable 1.5-generation sensibility. The work of Worra, a Laotian American writer born Thao Somnouk Silosoth, intimately negotiates a transnationalism that addresses the role of the United States in the making of Southeast Asian American refugees. Analogously, Bao Phi, a Vietnamese poet/spoken word artist living in Minnesota, considers the ways in which being Vietnamese American (as a subject of war) defines his relationship to the United States. Anida Yoeu Ali, a Muslim Cambodian performance poet/performance artist/activist, draws on her return to Cambodia as a way of translating an exilic sense of loss and dislocation.

Bryan Thao Worra

("E Pluribus Unum" and "Golden Triangle, Holy Mountain." Online at PoemHunter.com, 13 July 2012. Reprinted with permission from the author.)

E Pluribus Unum

Youa tells me a story over the hot hibachi:
How she went to Laos
To see her lucky sisters

For the first time in two decades,
Since the country has loosened up enough
To let tourists like us in.

"Isn't it beautiful?" she asks me,
Then says she gave her sister Mayli $50
To help her family.

When Youa returned to the Twin Cities,
She learned her sister had been murdered
For the money

By Mayli's ex-husband, who'd heard
Of their family reunion
And thought the cash rightfully belonged to him.

"Did you give your relatives anything?"
She asks.

"Yes," I reply. "$500. But they say they need more
To get to America."

Golden Triangle, Holy Mountain

Will I ever see poppies
In their natural habitat?
How red they appear in
All of these pictures beside
Mountain women with their
Dark turbans

Dour and thin
Up to their waists in grass.
Leftover bombs loiter
At their cautious feet
Who have no time for
Strangers pleading with
Them to say cheese

Gone with a flash of light
Before the harvest is done

Bao Phi

You Bring Out the Vietnamese in Me

You
bring out the Vietnamese in me

The waiting fireball.
The suntanned angel on a rice terrace.
The black haired miracle.

You
bring out the Vietnamese in me,
the salted yellow boat child and military brat on airplane in me,
the tracer-bullet eyed buddhist who gets presents on Christmas in
    me,

the nuoc mam, ca phe sua da, mangoes and mang cut,
mit and coconut, sugar dried strawberries in Da Lat
and sweet xa xui stains Asian/American in me,

the dry-season-heat hearted and black-eyebrow-as-floodgate
for monsoon eyes in me,

the three stripes of Song Huong blood
under yellow flag skin and Song Me Kong spine in me,

the phillips to cedar square projects to frogtown
in a powderblue used Datsun blaring Depeche Mode in me,
the aquanet mane and switchblade, razor boxcutter in left pocket
baseball bat in the backseat
gun in the glove compartment refugee in me,
You, yes you,
whiplash of black hair
and your heart a rose of flame,

You bring out the Vietnamese in me,

The dragon and phoenix cuz though I tell everybody
I'm Vietnamese I'm half Chinese in me,

The agent orange kool aid drinker and burner of government cheese
    in me,

The sharpener and painter of fingernails
sipping ginger ale in plastic snap champagne glasses
at Prom center while twisting tornado tango fandangoes
in mango colored suits and white ruffled shirts in me,

the I'm not gonna talk about love
I'm gonna be it in me,

the college degree prodigy thug in me,
the communist/republican/I wish there were more
Vietnamese progressives in me,
the I'll change the oil filter my goddamn self and
spend the money I saved on lottery tickets in me,
the incense and cigarettes and white clothes at the funeral in me,
the hip hop tennis captain kung fu expert don't fuck with me
the thinking snow is beautiful and keeping it to myself in me,

I am the most realistic dream you ever had,
the dream you had to fight for to love,

I am the one you stay up too late for,
I am the one that tells his heart and soul to you
after all the other stories have died,

You bring out the Vietnamese in me,
circling on the Le Loi boulevard loop
with a thousand other young Saigon Viets,
blinking tail lights of Honda Dream II mopeds like flicked
cigarette butts and laughter like wind in the face,

the firefly in a lee kum kee jar
the terraced voice
the sugarcane chunks in plastic bags
the weak beer and strong cigarettes
the fanta cola
the toothpick slinger
the sudden death syndrome
the Linda Trang Dai Dustin Nguyen Shortround Data kid in Goonies
the Hai Ba Trung Nguyen Du Thich Nhat Hanh

You bring out the Vietnamese in me
tell my life by reading my palm
and you'll find callouses
that's why love is at home
in my tired muscles
and burns under my eyelids while I sleep,

men, women, soldiers of every color
have walked into my life,
left burning flag shaped scars,
left ghosts shaped like my family,
left me
for dead,

I was the one who survived to love you.

That's why my love is like
rice growing from flooded bomb craters,

I love to save myself from myself,
I love so these things become me without ruling me,
I love
the way only a Vietnamese man can.

Anida Yoeu Ali

([RE]Visions. Chicago: Atomic Shogun, 2004. Reprinted with permission from the author.)

Visiting Loss

GIVEN: 20 million refugees
GIVEN: individuals who return home are not
the same people they were when they left
GIVEN: nearly every single family in Cambodia suffered
losses during the time of the Khmer Rouge
PROVE: the journey never ends for the refugee
PROVE: survivors must learn to live with the absence of 2 million
PROVE: it is absence that propels the living to remember

I will return to a country I have never known
that burns a hole inside my heart the size of home
when I arrive,
will I recognize Loss if she came to greet me at the airport
will she help me with my bags
usher me through customs
will she take me to my birth village
point me to the graves of ancestors
will she share silence with me
will she embrace me
will I ask these same questions
or will I be asked to prove my belonging

do I begin by pulling out remnants of my broken tongue
hunt for similarities in a sea of strangers
spot the same cheekbones on a little girl as she smiles selling trinkets

find a boy with a thick unmanageable wave of hair that kinks near his
    ears
focus in on an old man with a nose broadened brown and rounded
    soft
catch a familiar scowl from an ashy haired woman who sees me first

will I need to look deeper
scan for eyes gouged with the same obsidian tint of regret as mine
consider textures on dry flesh that flinch in a forest of touch
watch for veins beneath wrists that have stared down the teeth of
    razors
trace cracked lines on callous open palms
do I stitch a patchwork of borrowed resemblances to justify my
    birthright

will I be at a loss for words
or will I speak to Loss with what few memories I have kept secret
stowed away in a glass jar like inescapable fireflies
these memories flicker randomly
a dirty-face girl whimpers
one hand desperately balances a dripping wooden bowl
as her other scrapes her spilt ration off the floor,
then wipes her tears, runny nose, and a trail of porridge off her face.

a child's throat slices dry on piggyback rides
her tiny fingers slip,
grip the back of her father's wet neck

this same child's body still remembers
the tangling of flesh against jungle leaves,
clothes against barbed wires,
the night crickets lulling her to sleep,

these memories flicker randomly
they slide in and out of living thoughts
they are all I have left of this old home
Loss is the only proof of our surviving.

yet, I never chose to leave.
but there were those who understood things that I could not yet
    fathom
like the smell of a pogrom disguised as knuckles knocking at the door
faces of death angels sporting shoes made from old worn tires
maniacal laughter of gunfire mocking the unsuspecting
sound emptiness makes inside a newborn's belly
color of red pulled slowly to close off the sky

I often think about our leaving and all we left behind
imagined our lives without this exodus
dreamt of days when I could speak to Loss
to tell her we didn't choose to leave
leaving chose us.

I wonder, once I have visited Loss,
will she stamp my exit visa?

Brief of *Amicus Curiae* Fred Korematsu (2003)

Written in response to the denial of civil liberties and the indefinite deten-
tion of those classified as "enemy combatants" after the terrorist attacks of
September 11, 2001, Fred Korematsu's amicus brief was written in October
2003 in conjunction with two Supreme Court case appeals by individuals
held at Guantánamo Bay: Shafiq Rasul v. George W. Bush *and* Khaled A. F.
Al Odah v. United States of America. *Korematsu's brief, which recounts*
moments in U.S. history when civil liberties were suspended ostensibly in
the interest of national security and "military necessity," critiques the Bush
administration's policies vis-à-vis enemy combatants. Of particular note is
Korematsu's personal history with regard to the forced relocation and incar-
ceration of people of Japanese descent during World War II. (Brief of Amicus Curiae *Fred Korematsu in Support of Petitioners.* Rasul v. Bush. *542*
U.S. 466. Supreme Court of the United States, 2003.)

Argument

Since September 11th, the United States has taken significant steps to ensure the nation's safety. It is only natural that in times of crisis our government should tighten the measures it ordinarily takes to preserve our security. But we know from long experience that we often react too harshly
in circumstances of felt necessity and underestimate the damage to civil
liberties. Typically, we come later to regret our excesses, but for many that
recognition comes too late. The challenge is to identify excess when it
occurs and to protect constitutional rights before they are compromised
unnecessarily. These cases provide the Court with the opportunity to protect constitutional liberties when they matter most, rather than belatedly,
years after the fact.

As Fred Korematsu's life story demonstrates, our history merits attention. Only by understanding the errors of the past can we do better
in the present. Six examples illustrate the nature and magnitude of the
challenge: the Alien and Sedition Acts of 1798, the suspension of *habeas*
corpus during the Civil War, the prosecution of dissenters during World
War I, the Red Scare of 1919–1920, the internment of 120,000 individuals
of Japanese descent during World War II, and the era of loyalty oaths and
McCarthyism during the Cold War.

I.

Time and again, in periods of real or perceived crisis, the United States has unnecessarily restricted civil liberties.

History teaches that, in time of war, we have often sacrificed fundamental freedoms *unnecessarily*. The Executive and Legislative Branches, reflecting public opinion formed in the heat of the moment, frequently have overestimated the need to restrict civil liberties and failed to consider alternative ways to protect the national security. Courts, which are not immune to the demands of public opinion, have too often deferred to exaggerated claims of military necessity and failed to insist that measures curtailing constitutional rights be carefully justified and narrowly tailored. In retrospect, it is clear that judges and justices should have scrutinized these claims more closely and done more to ensure that essential security measures did not unnecessarily impair individual freedoms and the traditional separation of powers.

A. THE ALIEN AND SEDITION ACTS OF 1798

In 1798, the United States found itself embroiled in a European war that then raged between France and England. A bitter political and philosophical debate divided the Federalists, who favored the English, and the Republicans, who favored the French. The Federalists were then in power, and the administration of President John Adams initiated a sweeping series of defense measures that brought the United States into a state of undeclared war with France.

The Republicans opposed these measures, leading Federalists to accuse them of disloyalty. President Adams, for example, declared that the Republicans "would sink the glory of our country and prostrate her liberties at the feet of France." Against this backdrop, and in a mood of patriotic fervor, the Federalists enacted the Alien and Sedition Acts of 1798.

The Alien Friends Act empowered the President to deport any non-citizen he judged to be dangerous to the peace and safety of the United States. The Act applied to citizens or subjects of nations with whom we were not in a state of declared war. The Act accorded individuals detained under the Act no right to a hearing, no right to present evidence and no right to judicial review. Congressman Edward Livingston aptly observed in opposition to the Act that with "no indictment; no jury; no trial; no public procedure; no statement of the accusation; no examination of the witnesses in its support; no counsel for defense; all is darkness, silence, mystery, and suspicion." The Alien Friends Act expired on the final day of President Adams's term of office, and has never been renewed.

The Sedition Act of 1798 prohibited criticism of the government, the Congress, or the President, with the intent to bring them into contempt or disrepute. The Act was vigorously enforced, but only against supporters of the Republican Party. Prosecutions were brought against every influential Republican newspaper and the most vocal critics of the Adams administration.

The Sedition Act also expired on the last day of Adams's term of office. The new President, Thomas Jefferson, pardoned those who had been convicted under the Act, and forty years later Congress repaid all the fines. The Sedition Act was a critical factor in the demise of the Federalist Party, and the Supreme Court has often reminded us in the years since that the Sedition Act of 1798 has been judged unconstitutional in the "court of history."

B. THE CIVIL WAR: THE SUSPENSION OF *HABEAS CORPUS*

During the Civil War, the nation faced its most serious challenge. There were sharply divided loyalties, fluid military and political boundaries, and easy opportunities for espionage and sabotage. In such circumstances, and in the face of widespread and often bitter opposition to the war, the draft and the Emancipation Proclamation, President Lincoln had to balance the conflicting interests of military necessity and individual liberty.

During the course of the war, Lincoln suspended the writ of *habeas corpus* on eight separate occasions. Some of these orders were more warranted than others. The most extreme of the suspensions, which applied throughout the entire nation, declared that "all persons . . . guilty of any disloyal practice . . . shall be subject to court martial." Under this authority, military officers arrested and imprisoned as many as 38,000 civilians, with no judicial proceedings and no judicial review.

In 1866, a year after the war ended, the Supreme Court ruled in *Ex parte Milligan* that Lincoln had exceeded his constitutional authority, and held that the President could not constitutionally suspend the writ of *habeas corpus,* even in time of war, if the ordinary civil courts were open and functioning. As Chief Justice Rehnquist has observed, *Milligan* "is justly celebrated for its rejection of the government's position that the Bill of Rights has no application in wartime."

C. WORLD WAR I: THE ESPIONAGE ACT OF 1917

When the United States entered World War I, there was widespread opposition to both the war and the draft. Many citizens argued that our goal was not to "make the world safe for democracy," but to protect the investments of the wealthy, and that this cause was not worth the life of one American soldier.

President Wilson had little patience for such dissent. He warned that disloyalty "must be crushed out" of existence and declared that disloyalty "was . . . not a subject on which there was room for . . . debate." Disloyal individuals, he explained, "had sacrificed their right to civil liberties."

Shortly after the United States entered the war, Congress enacted the Espionage Act of 1917. Although the Act was not directed at dissent as such, aggressive federal prosecutors and compliant federal judges soon transformed the Act into a blanket prohibition of seditious utterance. The Wilson administration's intent was made clear in November 1917 when Attorney General Charles Gregory, referring to war dissenters, announced: "May God have mercy on them, for they need expect none from an outraged people and an avenging government."

In fact, the government worked hard to create an "outraged people." Because there had been no direct attack on the United States, and no direct threat to our national security, the Wilson administration had to generate a sense of urgency and a mood of anger in order to exhort Americans to enlist, to contribute money, and to make the many sacrifices that war demands. To this end, Wilson established the Committee for Public Information, which produced a flood of inflammatory and often misleading pamphlets, news releases, speeches, editorials, and motion pictures, all designed to instill a hatred of all things German and of all persons whose "loyalty" might be open to doubt.

The government prosecuted more than 2,000 dissenters for expressing their opposition to the war or the draft, and in an atmosphere of fear, hysteria and clamor, most judges were quick to mete out severe punishment — often 10 to 20 years in prison — to those deemed disloyal. The result was the suppression of all genuine debate about the merits, morality and progress of the war. But even this was not enough. Less than a year after adopting the Espionage Act, Congress enacted the Sedition Act of 1918, which declared it unlawful for any person to publish any disloyal, profane, scurrilous, or abusive language intended to cause contempt or scorn for the form of government, the Constitution, or the flag of the United States.

The story of the Supreme Court in this era is too familiar, and too painful, to bear repeating in detail. In a series of decisions in 1919 and 1920—most notably *Schenck, Debs,* and *Abrams*—the Court consistently upheld the convictions of individuals who had agitated against the war and the draft—individuals as obscure as Mollie Steimer, a twenty-year-old Russian-Jewish émigré who had thrown anti-war leaflets written in Yiddish from a rooftop on the lower East Side of New York, and as prominent as Eugene Debs, who had received almost a million votes in 1912 as the Socialist Party candidate for President. As Harry Kalven once observed, the Court's performance was "simply wretched."

In December 1920, after all the dust had settled, Congress quietly repealed the Sedition Act of 1918. Between 1919 and 1923, the government released from prison every individual who had been convicted under the Espionage and Sedition Acts. A decade later, President Roosevelt granted amnesty to all of these individuals, restoring their full political and civil rights. Over the next half-century, the Supreme Court overruled every one of its World War I decisions, implicitly acknowledging that the individuals who had been imprisoned for their dissent in this era had been punished for speech that should have been protected by the First Amendment.

D. THE RED SCARE: 1919–1920

The Russian Revolution generated deep anxiety in the United States. A series of violent strikes and spectacular bombings triggered the period of public paranoia that became known as the "Red Scare" of 1919–1920. Attorney General A. Mitchell Palmer announced that the bombings were an "attempt on the part of radical elements to rule the country."

Palmer established the "General Intelligence Division" within the Bureau of Investigation and appointed J. Edgar Hoover to gather and coordinate information about radical activities. The GID unleashed a horde of undercover agents to infiltrate radical organizations. From November 1919 to January 1920, the GID conducted a series of raids in thirty-three cities. More than 5,000 people were arrested on suspicion of radicalism. Attorney General Palmer described the "alien filth" captured in these raids as creatures with "sly and crafty eyes, lopsided faces, sloping brows and misshapen features" whose minds were tainted by "cupidity, cruelty, and crime." More than a thousand individuals were summarily deported.

In the spring of 1920, a group of distinguished lawyers and law professors, including Ernst Freund, Felix Frankfurter and Roscoe Pound, published a report on the activities of the Department of Justice, which carefully documented that the government had acted without legal authorization and without complying with the minimum standards of due process. This report marked the beginning of the end of this era. As the *Christian Science Monitor* observed in June 1920, "in the light of what is now known, it seems clear that what appeared to be an excess of radicalism" was met with a real "excess of suppression." In 1924, Attorney General Harlan Fiske Stone ordered an end to the Bureau of Investigation's surveillance of political radicals. "A secret police," he explained, is "a menace to free government and free institutions."

E. WORLD WAR II: INTERNMENT

On December 7, 1941, Japan attacked Pearl Harbor. Two months later, on February 19, 1942, President Roosevelt signed Executive Order 9066, which authorized the Army to "designate military areas" from which "any persons may be excluded." Although the words "Japanese" or "Japanese American" never appeared in the Order, it was understood to apply only to persons of Japanese ancestry.

Over the next eight months, 120,000 individuals of Japanese descent were forced to leave their homes in California, Washington, Oregon and Arizona. Two-thirds of these individuals were American citizens, representing almost 90% of all Japanese-Americans. No charges were brought against these individuals; there were no hearings; they did not know where they were going, how long they would be detained, what conditions they would face, or what fate would await them. Many families lost everything.

On the orders of military police, these individuals were transported to one of ten internment camps, which were located in isolated areas in wind-swept deserts or vast swamp lands. Men, women and children were placed in overcrowded rooms with no furniture other than cots. They found themselves surrounded by barbed wire and military police, and there they remained for three years.

In *Korematsu v. United States,* this Court, in a six-to-three decision, upheld the President's action. The Court offered the following explanation:

[We] are not unmindful of the hardships imposed . . . upon a large group of American citizens. But hardships are part of war, and war is an aggregation of hardships. . . .

Korematsu was not excluded from the [West Coast] because of hostility to . . . his race, [but] because . . . the military authorities . . .

decided that the [] urgency of the situation demanded that all citizens of Japanese ancestry be segregated from the [area]. . . . We cannot—by availing ourselves of the calm perspective of hindsight—say that these actions were unjustified.

On February 19, 1976, as part of the celebration of the Bicentennial of the Constitution, President Gerald Ford issued Presidential Proclamation 4417, in which he acknowledged that, in the spirit of celebrating our Constitution, we must recognize "our national mistakes as well as our national achievements." "February 19th," he noted, "is the anniversary of a sad day in American history," for it was "on that date in 1942 . . . that Executive Order 9066 was issued." President Ford observed that "we now know what we should have known then"—that the evacuation and internment of these individuals was "wrong." Ford concluded by calling "upon the American people to affirm with me this American Promise—that we have learned from the tragedy of that long-ago experience" and "resolve that this kind of action shall never again be repeated."

In 1980, Congress established the Commission on Wartime Relocation and Internment of Civilians to review the implementation of Executive Order 9066. The Commission was composed of former members of Congress, the Supreme Court and the Cabinet, as well as distinguished private citizens. In 1983, the Commission unanimously concluded that the factors that shaped the internment decision "were race prejudice, war hysteria, and a failure of political leadership," rather than military necessity.

Shortly thereafter, lower federal courts granted extraordinary writs of *coram nobis* in the *Korematsu* and *Hirabayashi* cases, finding that government officials had known at the time of the internment decision that there had been no military necessity and that government officials had intentionally deceived the Supreme Court about this state of affairs.

In vacating Fred Korematsu's forty-year-old conviction because it was the result of "manifest injustice," Federal District Judge Marilyn Hall Patel emphasized the need for both executive branch accountability and careful judicial review:

[*Korematsu*] stands as a constant caution that in times of war or declared military necessity our institutions must be vigilant in protecting constitutional guarantees. It stands as a caution that in times of distress the shield of military necessity and national security must not be used to protect governmental actions from close scrutiny and accountability. . . .

In 1988, President Reagan signed the Civil Liberties Restoration Act, which officially declared the Japanese internment a "grave injustice" that had been "carried out without adequate security reasons," and offered a formal presidential apology and reparations to each of the Japanese-American internees who had suffered discrimination, loss of liberty, loss of property, and personal humiliation because of the actions of the United States government. This Court's decision in *Korematsu* has become a constitutional pariah. The Supreme Court has never cited it with approval of its result.

F. THE COLD WAR: LOYALTY OATHS AND MCCARTHYISM

As World War II drew to a close, the nation moved almost seamlessly into the Cold War. With the glow of our wartime alliance with the Soviet Union evaporating, President Truman came under increasing attack by those who sought to exploit fears of Communist aggression. The issue of "loyalty" quickly became a shuttlecock of party politics. By 1948, President Truman was boasting on the stump that he had imposed on the federal civil service the most extreme loyalty program in the "Free World."

But there were limits to Truman's anticommunism. In 1950, he vetoed the McCarren Act, which required the registration of all Communists. Truman explained that the Act was the product of "public hysteria" and would lead to "witch hunts." Congress passed the Act over Truman's veto.

In 1954, Congress enacted the Communist Control Act, which stripped the Communist Party of "all rights, privileges, and immunities." Only one Senator, Estes Kefauver, dared to vote against it. Irving Howe lamented "this Congressional stampede to . . . trample . . . liberty in the name of destroying its enemy."

Hysteria over the "Red Menace" swept the nation and generated a wide range of federal, state and local restrictions on free expression and free association, including extensive loyalty programs for government employees; emergency detention plans for alleged "subversives"; abusive legislative investigations designed to punish by exposure; public and private blacklists of those who had been "exposed"; and criminal prosecutions of the leaders and members of the Communist Party of the United States.

This Court's response was mixed. The key decision was *Dennis v. United States,* which involved the direct prosecution under the Smith Act of the leaders of the American Communist Party. The Court held that the defendants could constitutionally be punished for their speech under the clear and present danger standard—even though the danger was neither clear nor present. It was a memorable feat of judicial legerdemain.

Over the next several years, the Court upheld far-reaching legislative investigations of "subversive" organizations and individuals and the exclusion of members of the Communist Party from the bar, the ballot and public employment. In so doing, the Court clearly put its stamp of approval on an array of actions we look back on today as models of McCarthyism. In later years, the Court effectively overruled *Dennis* and its progeny, recognizing once again that the nation had been led astray by the emotions and fears of the moment.

II.

To avoid a repetition of past mistakes, this court should closely scrutinize the government's claims of "military necessity" in these cases to ensure that civil liberties are not unnecessarily restricted.

As in past episodes, the issues raised in these cases involve a direct conflict between our most precious civil liberties and a threat to our safety and security. That we have made mistakes in the past does not mean we should make mistakes in the present. We should learn from our experience.

During World War I, John Lord O'Brian served as Special Assistant Attorney General in charge of the War Emergency Division of the Department of Justice. In this capacity, he played a central role in enforcing the Espionage Act of 1917. Four decades later, reflecting on his own experience, O'Brian cautioned against the "emotional excitement engendered . . . during a war," and warned that "the greatest danger to our institutions" may rest, not in the threat of subversion, but "in our own weaknesses in yielding" to wartime anxiety and our "readiness to . . . disregard the fundamental rights of the individual." He expressed the hope that "our judges will in the end establish principles reaffirming" our nation's commitment to civil liberties.

As Chief Justice Rehnquist has written, "[i]t is all too easy to slide from a case of genuine military necessity . . . to one where the threat is not critical and the power [sought to be exercised is] either dubious or nonexistent." It is, he added, "both desirable and likely that more careful attention will be paid by the courts to the . . . government's claims of necessity as a basis for curtailing civil liberty."

This Court has a profound responsibility to help guide our nation in the extraordinary circumstances of wartime. It has been said that in such circumstances the Court may grant too much deference to the other branches of government to avoid inadvertently hindering the war effort. *Korematsu* and *Dennis* are examples of this phenomenon.

But the lesson of those decisions is not that this Court should abdicate its responsibility. It is, rather, that the Court should bring to its responsibility an even deeper commitment to preserving the liberties for which this nation has fought. The Court's confident exercise of that responsibility is essential to enabling our nation to strike the *right* balance in times of crisis.

This Court should make clear that the United States adheres to the rule of law even in wartime, and that even in wartime the United States respects the principle that individuals may not be deprived of their liberty except for appropriate justifications that are demonstrated in fair hearings, in which they can be tested with the assistance of counsel.

This Court should make clear that, even in wartime, the United States does not abandon fundamental liberties in the absence of convincing military necessity. Our failure to hold ourselves to this standard in the past has led to many of our most painful episodes as a nation. We should not make that mistake again.

Conclusion

The petitions for writs of certiorari should be granted.

Respectfully submitted,
GEOFFREY R. STONE
DAVID A. STRAUSS
STEPHEN J. SCHULHOFER

Recommended Resources

Azuma, Eiichiro. *Between Two Empires: Race, History, and Transnationalism in Japanese America.* New York: Oxford University Press, 2005.

Bascara, Victor. *Model-Minority Imperialism.* Minneapolis: University of Minnesota Press, 2006.

Brooks, Charlotte. *Between Mao and McCarthy: Chinese American Politics in the Cold War Years.* Chicago: University of Chicago Press, 2015.

Chong, Sylvia Shin Huey. *The Oriental Obscene: Violence and Racial Fantasies in the Vietnam Era.* Durham, NC: Duke University Press, 2012.

Cumings, Bruce. *The Korean War: A History.* New York: Modern Library, 2010.

Diaz, Vicente M. *Repositioning the Missionary: Rewriting the Histories of Colonialism, Native Catholicism, and Indigeneity in Guam.* Honolulu: University of Hawaiʻi Press, 2010.

Feifer, George. *Breaking Open Japan: Commodore Perry, Lord Abe, and American Imperialism in 1853.* New York: Smithsonian Books/Collins, 2006.

Garcia, Jerry. *Looking Like the Enemy: Japanese Mexicans, the Mexican State, and US Hegemony, 1897–1945.* Tucson: University of Arizona Press, 2014.

Hein, Laura E., and Mark Selden. *Islands of Discontent: Okinawan Responses to Japanese and American Power.* Lanham, MD: Rowman & Littlefield, 2003.

Jones, Matthew. *After Hiroshima: The United States, Race and Nuclear Weapons in Asia, 1945–1965.* New York: Cambridge University Press, 2010.

Khandelwal, Madhulika S. *Becoming American, Being Indian: An Immigrant Community in New York City.* Ithaca, NY: Cornell University Press, 2002.

Kim, Jodi. *Ends of Empire: Asian American Critique and the Cold War.* Minneapolis: University of Minnesota Press, 2010.

Kina, Laura, and Wei Ming Dariotis, eds. *War Baby/Love Child: Mixed Race Asian American Art.* Seattle: University of Washington Press, 2013.

Klein, Christina. *Cold War Orientalism: Asia in the Middlebrow Imagination, 1945–1961.* Berkeley: University of California Press, 2003.

Koshiro, Yukiko. *Trans-Pacific Racisms and the U.S. Occupation of Japan.* New York: Columbia University Press, 1999.

Kramer, Paul A. *The Blood of Government: Race, Empire, the United States, & the Philippines.* Chapel Hill: University of North Carolina Press, 2006.

Moon, Katharine H. S. *Sex Among Allies: Military Prostitution in U.S.-Korea Relations.* New York: Columbia University Press, 1997.

Nguyen, Mimi Thi. *The Gift of Freedom: War, Debt, and Other Refugee Passages.* Durham, NC: Duke University Press, 2012.

Robinson, Greg. *By Order of the President: FDR and the Internment of Japanese Americans.* Cambridge, MA: Harvard University Press, 2001.

Schlund-Vials, Cathy J. *War, Genocide, and Justice: Cambodian American Memory Work.* Minneapolis: University of Minnesota Press, 2012.

Shigematsu, Setsu, and Keith L. Camacho. *Militarized Currents: Toward a Decolonized Future in Asia and the Pacific.* Minneapolis: University of Minnesota Press, 2010.

Silva, Noenoe K. *Aloha Betrayed: Native Hawaiian Resistance to American Colonialism.* Durham, NC: Duke University Press, 2004.

Takaki, Ronald. *Double Victory: A Multicultural History of America in World War II.* Boston: Little, Brown & Company, 2000.

Tanaka, Toshiyuki. *Japan's Comfort Women: Sexual Slavery and Prostitution During World War II and the US Occupation.* London: Psychology Press, 2002.

Thompson, Lanny. *Imperial Archipelago: Representation and Rule in the Insular Territories Under U.S. Dominion After 1898.* Honolulu: University of Hawai'i Press, 2010.

Wong, K. Scott. *Americans First: Chinese Americans and the Second World War.* Cambridge, MA: Harvard University Press, 2005.

Wu, Ellen D. *The Color of Success: Asian Americans and the Origins of the Model Minority.* Princeton, NJ: Princeton University Press, 2013.

Wu, Judy Tzu-Chun. *Radicals on the Road: Internationalism, Orientalism, and Feminism During the Vietnam Era.* Ithaca, NY: Cornell University Press, 2013.

Yoneyama, Lisa. *Hiroshima Traces: Time, Space, and the Dialectics of Memory.* Berkeley: University of California Press, 1999.

PART III

Race, Rights, and Representation

Chang and Eng Advertisements

Chang and Eng Bunker (1811–1874) were conjoined twin brothers born in Samutsongkram in the Kingdom of Siam (Thailand today) to a Thai Chinese father and Chinese Malay mother. In 1829, Robert Hunter, a British merchant, began exhibiting them as a sideshow curiosity; eventually, the twins terminated their contract with Hunter and went into business for themselves. They settled on a North Carolina plantation and owned slaves. In 1843, the twins married two sisters, Adelaide and Sarah Anne Yates, and became naturalized U.S. citizens. The advertisements stress the twins' "unique-

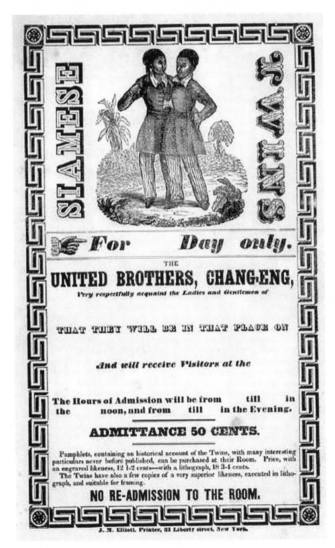

Figure 3.1
"Siamese twins. For [blank] Day Only . . ." New York: J. M. Elliott, printer, ca. 1838.

Figure 3.2 Currier and Ives, "'Chang' and 'Eng': The World Renowned United Siamese Twins," 1860. U.S. National Library of Medicine, Washington, DC.

ness" as curiosities, and they were exhibited largely because they were conjoined, but it is important to note that Chang and Eng were among the first prominent Asian immigrants to the United States (figs. 3.1 and 3.2).

Roughing It
Mark Twain

Mark Twain (Samuel Langhorne Clemens, 1835–1910) made his debut as a storyteller and chronicler of American life in his semiautobiographical travelogue Roughing It *(1872). The work details Twain's travels from the Missouri River to California from 1870 to 1871 and commences with his brother's journey into the Nevada Territory for a governmental appointment. Twain explores the rapidly changing social and political landscapes of recently conquered Mexican lands. As the following excerpt suggests, Twain frequently encountered Chinese communities, about which he held a neutral view. (Excerpted from Mark Twain [Samuel L. Clemens].* Roughing It. *Hartford, CT: American Publishing Co., 1872. Chapter LIV.)*

Of course there was a large Chinese population in Virginia [City, Nevada] — it was the case with every town and city on the Pacific coast. They are a harmless race when white men either let them alone or treat them no worse than dogs; in fact they are almost entirely harmless anyhow, for they seldom think of resenting the vilest insults or the cruelest injuries. They are quiet, peaceable, tractable, free from drunkenness, and they are as industrious as the day is long. A disorderly Chinaman is rare, and a lazy one does not exist. So long as a Chinaman has strength to use his hands he needs no support from anybody; white men often complain of want of work, but a Chinaman offers no such complaint; he always manages to find something to do. He is a great convenience to everybody — even to the worst class of white men, for he bears the most of their sins, suffering fines for their petty thefts, imprisonment for their robberies, and death for their murders. Any white man can swear a Chinaman's life away in the courts, but no Chinaman can testify against a white man. Ours is the "land of the free" — nobody denies that — nobody challenges it. (Maybe it is because we won't let other people testify.) As I write, news comes that in broad daylight in San Francisco, some boys have stoned an inoffensive Chinaman to death, and that although a large crowd witnessed the shameful deed, no one interfered.

There are seventy thousand (and possibly one hundred thousand) Chinamen on the Pacific coast. There were about a thousand in Virginia. They were penned into a "Chinese quarter"—a thing which they do not particularly object to, as they are fond of herding together. Their buildings were of wood; usually only one story high, and set thickly together along streets scarcely wide enough for a wagon to pass through. Their quarter was a little removed from the rest of town. The chief employment of Chinamen in towns is to wash clothing. They always send a bill . . . pinned to the clothes. It is mere ceremony, for it does not enlighten the customer much. Their price for washing was $2.50 per dozen—rather cheaper than white people could afford to wash for at that time. A very common sign on the Chinese houses was: "See Yup, Washer and Ironer"; "Hong Wo, Washer"; "Sam Sing & Ah Hop, Washing." The house servants, cooks, etc., in California and Nevada, were chiefly Chinamen. There were few white servants and no Chinawomen so employed. Chinamen make good house servants, being quick, obedient, patient, quick to learn and tirelessly industrious. They do not need to be taught a thing twice, as a general thing. They are imitative. If a Chinaman were to see his master break up a centre table, in a passion, and kindle a fire with it that Chinaman would be likely to resort to the furniture for fuel forever afterward.

All Chinamen can read, write and cipher with easy facility—pity but all our petted voters could. In California they rent little patches of ground and do a deal of gardening. They will raise surprising crops of vegetables on a sand pile. They waste nothing. What is rubbish to a Christian, a Chinaman carefully preserves and makes useful in one way or another. He gathers up all the old oyster and sardine cans that white people throw away, and procures marketable tin and solder from them by melting. He gathers up old bones and turns them into manure. In California he gets a living out of old mining claims that white men have abandoned as exhausted and worthless—and then the officers come down on him once a month with an exorbitant swindle to which the legislature has given the broad, general name of "foreign" mining tax, but is usually inflicted on no foreigners but Chinamen. This swindle has in some cases been repeated once or twice on the same victim in the course of the same month—but the public treasury was not additionally enriched by it, probably. . . .

They are a kindly disposed well-meaning race, and are respected and well treated by the upper classes, all over the Pacific coast. No Californian

gentleman or lady ever abuses or oppresses a Chinaman, under any circumstances, an explanation that seems to be much needed in the East.
Only the scum of the population do it—they and their children; they,
and naturally and consistently, the policemen and politicians likewise, for
these are the dust-licking pimps and slaves of the scum, there as well as
elsewhere in America.

"The Chinese Question" and Political Cartoons

*American political cartoons were ubiquitous in the second half of the nine-
teenth century and emerged as a popular platform for the production of
racial discourse in national print culture. These three cartoons demonstrate
a spectrum of political messages conveyed about Asians that highlight per-*

Figure 3.3 "The Great Fear of the Period: That Uncle Sam May Be Swallowed by
Foreigners," San Francisco: White & Bauer (between 1860 and 1869). Source:
Library of Congress. Online at http://www.loc.gov/pictures/item/98502829/.

Figure 3.4 Thomas Nast, "The Chinese Question." Caption: "Columbia. — 'Hands off gentlemen! America means fair play for all men.'" Originally published in *Harper's Weekly,* 18 Feb. 1871, p. 149.

THE YELLOW TERROR IN ALL HIS GLORY

Figure 3.5 "The Yellow Terror in All His Glory." Editorial cartoon, 1899, artist unknown, publication unknown.

ceived racial differences between Asian ethnicities as well as the position of Asians among other U.S. racial groups (figs. 3.3, 3.4, and 3.5). Images of Chinese immigrants as a racial terror and depictions of them as undeserving victims of prejudice occurred in close proximity to the depiction of other racial and ethnic groups. The swirling racial imagery of Asians during this period helped underwrite a transformation of U.S. racial codes that broadened the category of whiteness for European ethnic groups at the same time that it degraded Asians as perpetual foreigners and disciplinary subjects of imperial rule.

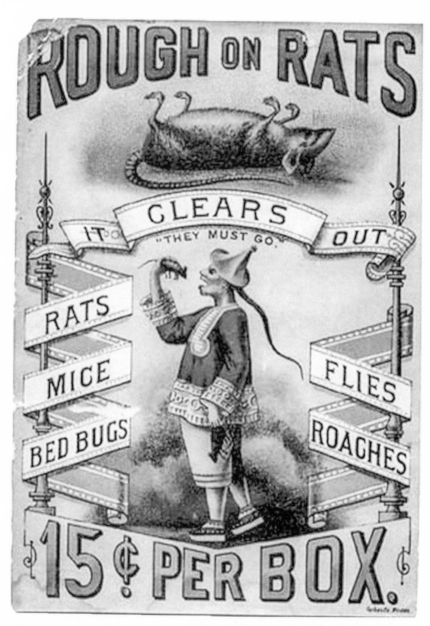

Figure 3.6 "Rough on Rats" advertising trading card, E. S. Wells, manufacturer and proprietor (ca. 1879–1890). Facsimile. Cathy J. Schlund-Vials, personal collection.

Rough on Rats

Rough on Rats was a turn-of-the-twentieth-century product intended to kill various vermin (rats, mice, bedbugs, roaches, and flies). As part of an advertising campaign, Rough on Rats issued this trading card, which features a stereotypical "Chinaman" figure (fig. 3.6). The logic of the card is clear: the Chinese subject eats a rat, thereby accessing the dominant-held notions of Chinese monstrosity, specifically in terms of culinary taste.

Rock Springs Massacre (1885)

The Rock Springs Massacre (or Rock Springs Riot) took place on September 2, 1885, in Rock Springs, Wyoming (fig. 3.7). The conflict involved Chinese miners, their white counterparts, and an increasingly violent labor dispute with the Union Pacific Coal Department. The company had been hiring more Chinese miners because they could be paid lower wages. An estimated

Figure 3.7 "Massacre of the Chinese at Rock Springs, Wyoming," drawn by T. de Thulstrup from photographs by Lt. C. A. Booth, Seventh U.S. Infantry. *Harper's Weekly,* Vol. 29, 26 Sept. 1886, p. 637. Source: Library of Congress. Online at http://www.loc.gov/pictures/item/89708533/.

twenty-eight Chinese miners were killed and fifteen injured during the riot, and Chinese homes were burned. A week later, federal troops were deployed, and Chinese miners—many of whom had escaped to nearby Evanston, Wyoming—were escorted back to Rock Springs. The massacre ushered in a wave of anti-Chinese violence in the Pacific Northwest, though it was by no means a "single" occurrence. Indeed, more than a decade before, in 1871, Los Angeles and San Francisco had been sites of similar anti-Chinese riots.

Some Reasons for Chinese Exclusion: Meat vs. Rice
American Federation of Labor

Published in 1902, the American Federation of Labor's pamphlet Some Reasons for Chinese Exclusion *tellingly carried the subtitle* Meat vs. Rice. American Manhood against Asiatic Coolieism. Which Shall Survive? *(fig. 3.8). Written to influence U.S. policymakers to extend anti-Chinese exclusion, the pamphlet emphasized—culturally, economically, and socially—the inferiority of Chinese labor while stressing the superiority of white working-class labor. As the accompanying cartoon suggests, central to claims of white superiority was the cheapness of Chinese labor (fig. 3.9).*

"La Mestización" Cartoon

By the turn of the twentieth century, Chinese immigrants had become the second-largest immigrant group in Mexico. Totaling ten thousand, most of these immigrants were male laborers or small-scale merchants. Although the Mexican government had previously embraced Chinese immigration as a key element of economic development, the majority attitude had shifted dramatically by 1910. Faced with vast inequality and increased economic competition, and in the midst of the Mexican Revolution, Chinese Mexicans were specifically targeted in violent anti-Chinese campaigns that stressed their physical, intellectual, and moral inferiority. Chinese immigration continued into the 1920s, and these campaigns became even more vociferous. The accompanying cartoon appears in a 1932 book written by José Angel

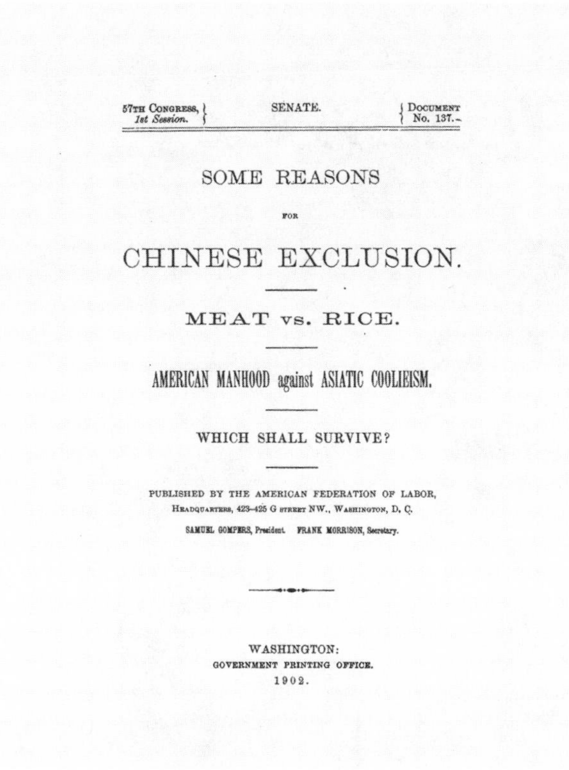

Figure 3.8
Pamphlet title page:
*Some Reasons for
Chinese Exclusion . . .*
Washington, DC:
GPO, 1902.

57TH CONGRESS, }   SENATE.   { DOCUMENT
1st Session. }   { No. 137.

SOME REASONS

FOR

CHINESE EXCLUSION.

MEAT vs. RICE.

AMERICAN MANHOOD against ASIATIC COOLIEISM.

WHICH SHALL SURVIVE?

PUBLISHED BY THE AMERICAN FEDERATION OF LABOR,
Headquarters, 423–425 G Street NW., Washington, D. C.
SAMUEL GOMPERS, President.   FRANK MORRISON, Secretary.

WASHINGTON:
GOVERNMENT PRINTING OFFICE.
1902.

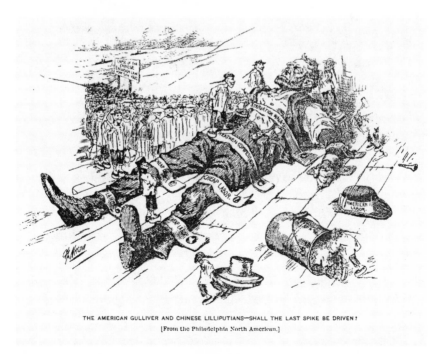

THE AMERICAN GULLIVER AND CHINESE LILLIPUTIANS—SHALL THE LAST SPIKE BE DRIVEN?
[From the Philadelphia North American.]

Figure 3.9 From American Federation of Labor, "Some Reasons for Chinese Exclusion."
Washington, DC: GPO, 1902. Caption: "The American Gulliver and Chinese
Lilliputians—Shall the Last Spike Be Driven?"

Figure 3.10 From José Angel Espinoza, *El Ejemplo de Sonoro*, Mexico City, 1933.

Espinoza, a congressman from the northern Mexican state of Sonora, where thousands of Chinese men, their Mexican wives, and their mixed-race children had been forcibly expelled (fig. 3.10). The cartoon's insistence on Chinese inferiority—manifest in the sickly depiction of the mixed-race "mestización"—links interracial reproduction to national denigration.

Four Bids for Canal Labor (1906)

New York Times

This newspaper article emphasizes the cheap nature of Chinese labor, as indicated by its subhead: "Washington Man Offers to Supply 15,000 Chinese at 9 Cents an Hour." Since President Theodore Roosevelt was committed to expanding U.S. influence into Central America, the Panama Canal figured keenly in contemporaneous U.S. foreign policy. Although the article focuses on Chinese labor as a primary workforce in the construction of the canal, the workforce was originally composed of Southern Europeans (from Spain, Italy, and Greece); it would eventually shift to include laborers from the British and French West Indies. (New York Times, 21 Sept. 1906: 6.)

WASHINGTON, September 20.—Proposals were submitted to the Isthmian Canal Commission to-day for the furnishing of Chinese labor to be employed in the construction of the Panama Canal. The requirements were, in brief, that the contractors should agree to supply the commission with at least 2,500 Chinese, the commission having the privilege of calling up on the successful contractor for additional labor, not exceeding 15,000. It further specified that the laborers should be on the Isthmus ready for work within three and a half months of the opening of the proposals, and that the contractors should deposit with their proposals a bond of $50,000 as a guarantee to faithfully carry out the terms of the contract.

At the conclusion of the reading of the only four proposals submitted it was announced that no award would be made until they had been examined by the commission and its general counsel. In accordance with the specifications the proposals were made for the furnishing of different classes of labor at a price fixed by the hour in American gold.

The following is a summary of the four proposals:

The America-China Contracting Company, represented by James R. Morse of Englewood, N.J.—Common laborers, 10 cents per hour; foremen and interpreters, 20 cents per hour; physicians, 40 cents per hour; cooks and barbers, 15 cents per hour.

International Contracting Company, Washington, D.C., represented by Carroll Purman, President.—Laborers and cooks, 13 cents per hour; physicians, 39 cents per hour; assistant physicians, 26 cents per hour; interpreters, 32½ cents per hour; foremen 10½ cents per hour.

Wu Ne Lee Hing & Co., Baltimore, Md.—Laborers, clerks, and barbers, 12½ cents per hour; foremen and interpreters, 15 cents per hour; physicians, 25 cents per hour.

Joel Julian Reuben, Washington, D.C.—For the first 2,500 Chinese—Laborers, 11 cents per hour; foremen, 40 cents per hour; physicians, 60 cents per hour; interpreters, 60 cents per hour; cooks and barbers, 30 cents per hour.

Mr. Reuben makes a fractional decrease in his proposal for each additional thousand common laborers after the first thousand. This is assumed by the department to mean that if the commission enters into a contract with him and wants the full quota of 15,000 Chinese he will furnish them at the rate of 9 cents per hour for common laborers.

The Unparalleled Invasion (1910)
Jack London

Jack London's short story "The Unparalleled Invasion" was published in 1910 as part of a collection titled The Strength of the Strong. *A science fiction narrative, this story is very much a "yellow peril" story in its emphasis on uncontained Japanese and Chinese global power. This racial anxiety is in part fixed to the Japanese victory in the Russo-Japanese War (1904-1905). It is also linked to London's consistent support of white working-class labor via anti-Chinese exclusion. The "solution" to the Chinese problem is extermination through biological warfare. (Jack London. "The Unparalleled Invasion."* McClure's Magazine, *July 1910: 308-16.)*

It was in the year 1976 that the trouble between the world and China reached its culmination. It was because of this that the celebration of the Second Centennial of American Liberty was deferred. Many other plans of the nations of the earth were twisted and tangled and postponed for the same reason. The world awoke rather abruptly to its danger; but for over seventy years, unperceived, affairs had been shaping toward this very end.

The year 1904 logically marks the beginning of the development that, seventy years later, was to bring consternation to the whole world. The Japanese-Russian War took place in 1904, and the historians of the time gravely noted it down that that event marked the entrance of Japan into the comity of nations. What it really did mark was the awakening of China.

This awakening, long expected, had finally been given up. The Western nations had tried to arouse China, and they had failed. Out of their native optimism and race-egotism they had therefore concluded that the task was impossible, that China would never awaken.

What they had failed to take into account was this: THAT BETWEEN THEM AND CHINA WAS NO COMMON PSYCHOLOGICAL SPEECH. Their thought processes were radically dissimilar. There was no intimate vocabulary. The Western mind penetrated the Chinese mind but a short distance when it found itself in a fathomless maze. The Chinese mind penetrated the Western mind an equally short distance when it fetched up against a blank, incomprehensible wall. It was all a matter of language. There was no way to communicate Western ideas to the Chinese mind. China remained asleep. The material achievement and progress of the West was a closed book to her; nor could the West open the book. Back and deep down on the tie-ribs of consciousness, in the mind, say, of the English-speaking race, was a capacity to thrill to short, Saxon words; back and deep down on the tie-ribs of consciousness of the Chinese mind was a capacity to thrill to its own hieroglyphics; but the Chinese mind could not thrill to short, Saxon words; nor could the English-speaking mind thrill to hieroglyphics. The fabrics of their minds were woven from totally different stuffs. They were mental aliens. And so it was that Western material achievement and progress made no dent on the rounded sleep of China.

Came Japan and her victory over Russia in 1904. Now the Japanese race was the freak and paradox among Eastern peoples. In some strange way Japan was receptive to all the West had to offer. Japan swiftly assimilated the Western ideas, and digested them, and so capably applied them that she suddenly burst forth, full-panoplied, a world-power. There is no explaining this peculiar openness of Japan to the alien culture of the West. As well might be explained any biological sport in the animal kingdom.

Having decisively thrashed the great Russian Empire, Japan promptly set about dreaming a colossal dream of empire for herself. Korea she had made into a granary and a colony; treaty privileges and vulpine diplomacy gave her the monopoly of Manchuria. But Japan was not satisfied. She turned her eyes upon China. There lay a vast territory, and in that territory were the hugest deposits in the world of iron and coal—the backbone of industrial civilization. Given natural resources, the other great factor in industry is labour. In that territory was a population of 400,000,000 souls—one quarter of the then total population of the earth. Furthermore, the Chinese were excellent workers, while their fatalistic philosophy (or religion) and their stolid nervous organization constituted them splendid soldiers—if they were properly managed. Needless to say, Japan was prepared to furnish that management.

But best of all, from the standpoint of Japan, the Chinese was a kindred race. The baffling enigma of the Chinese character to the West was no baffling enigma to the Japanese. The Japanese understood as we could never school ourselves or hope to understand. Their mental processes were the same. The Japanese thought with the same thought-symbols as did the Chinese, and they thought in the same peculiar grooves. Into the Chinese mind the Japanese went on where we were balked by the obstacle of incomprehension. They took the turning which we could not perceive, twisted around the obstacle, and were out of sight in the ramifications of the Chinese mind where we could not follow. They were brothers. Long ago one had borrowed the other's written language, and, untold generations before that, they had diverged from the common Mongol stock. There had been changes, differentiations brought about by diverse conditions and infusions of other blood; but down at the bottom of their beings, twisted into the fibres of them, was a heritage in common, a sameness in kind that time had not obliterated.

And so Japan took upon herself the management of China. In the years immediately following the war with Russia, her agents swarmed over the Chinese Empire. A thousand miles beyond the last mission station toiled her engineers and spies, clad as coolies, under the guise of itinerant merchants or proselytizing Buddhist priests, noting down the horse-power of every waterfall, the likely sites for factories, the heights of mountains and passes, the strategic advantages and weaknesses, the wealth of the farming valleys, the number of bullocks in a district or the number of labourers that could be collected by forced levies. Never was there such a census, and it could have been taken by no other people than the dogged, patient, patriotic Japanese.

But in a short time secrecy was thrown to the winds. Japan's officers reorganized the Chinese army; her drill sergeants made the mediaeval warriors over into twentieth century soldiers, accustomed to all the modern machinery of war and with a higher average of marksmanship than the soldiers of any Western nation. The engineers of Japan deepened and widened the intricate system of canals, built factories and foundries, netted the empire with telegraphs and telephones, and inaugurated the era of railroad-building. It was these same protagonists of machine-civilization that discovered the great oil deposits of Chunsan, the iron mountains of

Whang-Sing, the copper ranges of Chinchi, and they sank the gas wells of Wow-Wee, that most marvelous reservoir of natural gas in all the world.

In China's councils of empire were the Japanese emissaries. In the ears of the statesmen whispered the Japanese statesmen. The political reconstruction of the Empire was due to them. They evicted the scholar class, which was violently reactionary, and put into office progressive officials. And in every town and city of the Empire newspapers were started. Of course, Japanese editors ran the policy of these papers, which policy they got direct from Tokio. It was these papers that educated and made progressive the great mass of the population.

China was at last awake. Where the West had failed, Japan succeeded. She had transmuted Western culture and achievement into terms that were intelligible to the Chinese understanding. Japan herself, when she so suddenly awakened, had astounded the world. But at the time she was only forty millions strong. China's awakening, with her four hundred millions and the scientific advance of the world, was frightfully astounding. She was the colossus of the nations, and swiftly her voice was heard in no uncertain tones in the affairs and councils of the nations. Japan egged her on, and the proud Western peoples listened with respectful ears.

China's swift and remarkable rise was due, perhaps more than to anything else, to the superlative quality of her labour. The Chinese was the perfect type of industry. He had always been that. For sheer ability to work no worker in the world could compare with him. Work was the breath of his nostrils. It was to him what wandering and fighting in far lands and spiritual adventure had been to other peoples. Liberty, to him, epitomized itself in access to the means of toil. To till the soil and labour interminably was all he asked of life and the powers that be. And the awakening of China had given its vast population not merely free and unlimited access to the means of toil, but access to the highest and most scientific machine-means of toil.

China rejuvenescent! It was but a step to China rampant. She discovered a new pride in herself and a will of her own. She began to chafe under the guidance of Japan, but she did not chafe long. On Japan's advice, in the beginning, she had expelled from the Empire all Western missionaries, engineers, drill sergeants, merchants, and teachers. She now began to expel the similar representatives of Japan. The latter's advisory statesmen were showered with honours and decorations, and sent home. The West had awakened Japan, and, as Japan had then requited the West, Japan was not requited by China. Japan was thanked for her kindly aid and flung out bag and baggage by her gigantic protégé. The Western nations chuckled. Japan's rainbow dream had gone glimmering. She grew angry. China laughed at her. The blood and the swords of the Samurai would out, and Japan rashly went to war. This occurred in 1922, and in seven bloody months Manchuria, Korea, and Formosa were taken away from her and she was hurled back, bankrupt, to stifle in her tiny, crowded islands. Exit Japan from the world drama. Thereafter she devoted herself to art, and her task became to please the world greatly with her creations of wonder and beauty.

Contrary to expectation, China did not prove warlike. She had no Napoleonic dream, and was content to devote herself to the arts of peace. After a time of disquiet, the idea was accepted that China was to be feared, not in war, but in commerce. It will be seen that the real danger was not apprehended. China went on consummating her machine-civilization. Instead of a large standing army, she developed an immensely larger and splendidly efficient militia. Her navy was so small that it was the laughing stock of the world; nor did she attempt to strengthen her navy. The treaty ports of the world were never entered by her visiting battleships.

The real danger lay in the fecundity of her loins, and it was in 1970 that the first cry of alarm was raised. For some time all territories adjacent to China had been grumbling at Chinese immigration; but now it suddenly came home to the world that China's population was 500,000,000. She had increased by a hundred millions since her awakening. Burchaldter called attention to the fact that there were more Chinese in existence than white-skinned people. He performed a simple sum in arithmetic. He added together the populations of the United States, Canada, New Zealand, Australia, South Africa, England, France, Germany, Italy, Austria, European Russia, and all Scandinavia. The result was 495,000,000. And the population of China overtopped this tremendous total by 5,000,000. Burchaldter's figures went round the world, and the world shivered.

For many centuries China's population had been constant. Her territory had been saturated with population; that is to say, her territory, with the primitive method of production, had supported the maximum limit of population. But when she awoke and inaugurated the machine-civilization, her productive power had been enormously increased. Thus, on the same territory, she was able to support a far larger population. At once the birth rate began to rise and the death rate to fall. Before, when population pressed against the means of subsistence, the excess population had been swept away by famine. But now, thanks to the machine-civilization, China's means of subsistence had been enormously extended, and there were no famines; her population followed on the heels of the increase in the means of subsistence.

During this time of transition and development of power, China had entertained no dreams of conquest. The Chinese was not an imperial race. It was industrious, thrifty, and peace-loving. War was looked upon as an unpleasant but necessary task that at times must be performed. And so, while the Western races had squabbled and fought, and world-adventured against one another, China had calmly gone on working at her machines and growing. Now she was spilling over the boundaries of her Empire—that was all, just spilling over into the adjacent territories with all the certainty and terrifying slow momentum of a glacier.

Following upon the alarm raised by Burchaldter's figures, in 1970 France made a long-threatened stand. French Indo-China had been over-run, filled up, by Chinese immigrants. France called a halt. The Chinese wave flowed on. France assembled a force of a hundred thousand on the boundary between her unfortunate colony and China, and China sent down an army of militia-soldiers a million strong. Behind came the wives and sons and daughters and relatives, with their personal household luggage, in a second army. The French force was brushed aside like a fly. The Chinese militia-soldiers, along with their families, over five millions all told, coolly took possession of French Indo-China and settled down to stay for a few thousand years.

Outraged France was in arms. She hurled fleet after fleet against the coast of China, and nearly bankrupted herself by the effort. China had no navy. She withdrew like a turtle into her shell. For a year the French fleets blockaded the coast and bombarded exposed towns and villages. China did not mind. She did not depend upon the rest of the world for anything. She calmly kept out of range of the French guns and went on working. France wept and wailed, wrung her impotent hands and appealed to the dumfounded nations. Then she landed a punitive expedition to march to Peking. It was two hundred and fifty thousand strong, and it was the flower of France. It landed without opposition and marched into the interior. And that was the last ever seen of it. The line of communication was snapped on the second day. Not a survivor came back to tell what had happened. It had been swallowed up in China's cavernous maw, that was all.

In the five years that followed, China's expansion, in all land directions, went on apace. Siam was made part of the Empire, and, in spite of all that England could do, Burma and the Malay Peninsula were overrun;

while all along the long south boundary of Siberia, Russia was pressed severely by China's advancing hordes. The process was simple. First came the Chinese immigration (or, rather, it was already there, having come there slowly and insidiously during the previous years). Next came the clash of arms and the brushing away of all opposition by a monster army of militia-soldiers, followed by their families and household baggage. And finally came their settling down as colonists in the conquered territory. Never was there so strange and effective a method of world conquest.

Napal and Bhutan were overrun, and the whole northern boundary of India pressed against by this fearful tide of life. To the west, Bokhara, and, even to the south and west, Afghanistan, were swallowed up. Persia, Turkestan, and all Central Asia felt the pressure of the flood. It was at this time that Burchaldter revised his figures. He had been mistaken. China's population must be seven hundred millions, eight hundred millions, nobody knew how many millions, but at any rate it would soon be a billion. There were two Chinese for every white-skinned human in the world, Burchaldter announced, and the world trembled. China's increase must have begun immediately, in 1904. It was remembered that since that date there had not been a single famine. At 5,000,000 a year increase, her total increase in the intervening seventy years must be 350,000,000. But who was to know? It might be more. Who was to know anything of this strange new menace of the twentieth century—China, old China, rejuvenescent, fruitful, and militant!

The Convention of 1975 was called at Philadelphia. All the Western nations, and some few of the Eastern, were represented. Nothing was accomplished. There was talk of all countries putting bounties on children to increase the birth rate, but it was laughed to scorn by the arithmeticians, who pointed out that China was too far in the lead in that direction. No feasible way of coping with China was suggested. China was appealed to and threatened by the United Powers, and that was all the Convention of Philadelphia came to; and the Convention and the Powers were laughed at by China. Li Tang Fwung, the power behind the Dragon Throne, deigned to reply.

"What does China care for the comity of nations?" said Li Tang Fwung. "We are the most ancient, honourable, and royal of races. We have our own destiny to accomplish. It is unpleasant that our destiny does not tally with the destiny of the rest of the world, but what would you? You have talked windily about the royal races and the heritage of the earth, and we can only reply that that remains to be seen. You cannot invade us. Never mind about your navies. Don't shout. We know our navy is small. You see we use it for police purposes. We do not care for the sea. Our strength is in our population, which will soon be a billion. Thanks to you, we are equipped with all modern war-machinery. Send your navies. We will not notice them. Send your punitive expeditions, but first remember France. To land half a million soldiers on our shores would strain the resources of any of you. And our thousand millions would swallow them down in a mouthful. Send a million; send five millions, and we will swallow them down just as readily. Pouf! A mere nothing, a meager morsel. Destroy, as you have threatened, you United States, the ten million coolies we have forced upon your shores—why, the amount scarcely equals half of our excess birth rate for a year."

So spoke Li Tang Fwung. The world was nonplussed, helpless, terrified. Truly had he spoken. There was no combating China's amazing birth rate. If her population was a billion, and was increasing twenty millions a year, in twenty-five years it would be a billion and a half—equal to the total population of the world in 1904. And nothing could be done. There was no way to dam up the over-spilling monstrous flood of life. War was futile. China laughed at a blockade of her coasts. She welcomed invasion. In her capacious maw was room for all the hosts of earth that could be hurled at her. And in the meantime her flood of yellow life poured out and on over Asia. China laughed and read in their magazines the learned lucubrations of the distracted Western scholars.

But there was one scholar China failed to reckon on—Jacobus Laningdale. Not that he was a scholar, except in the widest sense. Primarily, Jacobus Laningdale was a scientist, and, up to that time, a very obscure scientist, a professor employed in the laboratories of the Health Office of New York City. Jacobus Laningdale's head was very like any other head, but in that head was evolved an idea. Also, in that head was the wisdom to keep that idea secret. He did not write an article for the magazines. Instead, he asked for a vacation. On September 19, 1975, he arrived in Washington. It was evening, but he proceeded straight to the White House, for he had already arranged an audience with the President. He was closeted with President Moyer for three hours. What passed between them was not learned by the rest of the world until long after; in fact, at that time the world was not interested in Jacobus Laningdale. Next day the President called in his Cabinet. Jacobus Laningdale was present. The proceedings were kept secret. But that very afternoon Rufus Cowdery, Secretary of State, left Washington, and early the following morning sailed for England. The secret that he carried began to spread, but it spread only among the heads of Governments. Possibly half-a-dozen men in a nation were entrusted with the idea that had formed in Jacobus Laningdale's head. Following the spread of the secret, sprang up great activity in all the dock-yards, arsenals, and navy-yards. The people of France and Austria became suspicious, but so sincere were their Governments' calls for confidence that they acquiesced in the unknown project that was afoot.

This was the time of the Great Truce. All countries pledged themselves solemnly not to go to war with any other country. The first definite action was the gradual mobilization of the armies of Russia, Germany, Austria, Italy, Greece, and Turkey. Then began the eastward movement. All rail-roads into Asia were glutted with troop trains. China was the objective, that was all that was known. A little later began the great sea movement. Expeditions of warships were launched from all countries. Fleet followed fleet, and all proceeded to the coast of China. The nations cleaned out their navy-yards. They sent their revenue cutters and dispatch boats and lighthouse tenders, and they sent their last antiquated cruisers and battle-ships. Not content with this, they impressed the merchant marine. The statistics show that 58,640 merchant steamers, equipped with searchlights and rapid-fire guns, were dispatched by the various nations to China.

And China smiled and waited. On her land side, along her boundaries, were millions of the warriors of Europe. She mobilized five times as many millions of her militia and awaited the invasion. On her sea coasts she did the same. But China was puzzled. After all this enormous preparation, there was no invasion. She could not understand. Along the great Siberian frontier all was quiet. Along her coasts the towns and villages were not even shelled. Never, in the history of the world, had there been so mighty a gathering of war fleets. The fleets of all the world were there, and day and night millions of tons of battleships ploughed the brine of her coasts, and nothing happened. Nothing was attempted. Did they think to make her emerge from her shell? China smiled. Did they think to tire her out, or starve her out? China smiled again.

But on May 1, 1976, had the reader been in the imperial city of Peking, with its then population of eleven millions, he would have witnessed a curious sight. He would have seen the streets filled with the chattering yel-low populace, every queued head tilted back, every slant eye turned sky-ward. And high up in the blue he would have beheld a tiny dot of black, which, because of its orderly evolutions, he would have identified as an airship. From this airship, as it curved its flight back and forth over the city, fell missiles — strange, harmless missiles, tubes of fragile glass that shattered into thousands of fragments on the streets and house-tops. But there was nothing deadly about these tubes of glass. Nothing happened. There were no explosions. It is true, three Chinese were killed by the tubes dropping on their heads from so enormous a height; but what were three Chinese against an excess birth rate of twenty millions? One tube struck perpendicularly in a fish-pond in a garden and was not broken. It was dragged ashore by the master of the house. He did not dare to open it, but, accompanied by his friends, and surrounded by an ever-increasing crowd, he carried the mysterious tube to the magistrate of the district. The latter was a brave man. With all eyes upon him, he shattered the tube with a blow from his brass-bowled pipe. Nothing happened. Of those who were very near, one or two thought they saw some mosquitoes fly out. That was all. The crowd set up a great laugh and dispersed.

As Peking was bombarded by glass tubes, so was all China. The tiny airships, dispatched from the warships, contained but two men each, and over all cities, towns, and villages they wheeled and curved, one man directing the ship, the other man throwing over the glass tubes.

Had the reader again been in Peking, six weeks later, he would have looked in vain for the eleven million inhabitants. Some few of them he would have found, a few hundred thousand, perhaps, their carcasses festering in the houses and in the deserted streets, and piled high on the abandoned death wagons. But for the rest he would have had to seek along the highways and byways of the Empire. And not all would he have found fleeing from plague-stricken Peking, for behind them, by hundreds of thousands of unburied corpses by the wayside, he could have marked their flight. And as it was with Peking, so it was with all the cities, towns, and villages of the Empire. The plague smote them all. Nor was it one plague, nor two plagues; it was a score of plagues. Every virulent form of infectious death stalked through the land. Too late the Chinese government apprehended the meaning of the colossal preparations, the marshaling of the world-hosts, the flights of the tin airships, and the rain of the tubes of glass. The proclamations of the government were vain. They could not stop the eleven million plague-stricken wretches, fleeing from the one city of Peking to spread disease through all the land. The physicians and health officers died at their posts; and death, the all-conqueror, rode over the decrees of the Emperor and Li Tang Fwung. It rode over them as well, for Li Tang Fwung died in the second week, and the Emperor, hidden away in the Summer Palace, died in the fourth week.

Had there been one plague, China might have coped with it. But from a score of plagues no creature was immune. The man who escaped small-pox went down before scarlet fever. The man who was immune to yellow fever was carried away by cholera; and if he were immune to that, too, the Black Death, which was the bubonic plague, swept him away. For it was these bacteria, and germs, and microbes, and bacilli, cultured in the laboratories of the West, that had come down upon China in the rain of glass.

All organization vanished. The government crumbled away. Decrees and proclamations were useless when the men who made them and signed them one moment were dead the next. Nor could the maddened millions, spurred on to flight by death, pause to heed anything. They fled from the cities to infect the country, and wherever they fled they carried the plagues with them. The hot summer was on—Jacobus Laningdale had selected the time shrewdly—and the plague festered everywhere. Much is conjectured of what occurred, and much has been learned from the stories of the few survivors. The wretched creatures stormed across the Empire in many-millioned flight. The vast armies China had collected on her frontiers melted away. The farms were ravaged for food, and no more crops were planted, while the crops already in were left unattended and never came to harvest. The most remarkable thing, perhaps, was the flights. Many millions engaged in them, charging to the bounds of the Empire to be met and turned back by the gigantic armies of the West. The slaughter of the mad hosts on the boundaries was stupendous. Time and again the guarding line was drawn back twenty or thirty miles to es-cape the contagion of the multitudinous dead.

Once the plague broke through and seized upon the German and Aus-trian soldiers who were guarding the borders of Turkestan. Preparations had been made for such a happening, and though sixty thousand soldiers of Europe were carried off, the international corps of physicians isolated the contagion and dammed it back. It was during this struggle that it was suggested that a new plague-germ had originated, that in some way or other a sort of hybridization between plague-germs had taken place, pro-ducing a new and frightfully virulent germ. First suspected by Vomberg, who became infected with it and died, it was later isolated and studied by Stevens, Hazenfelt, Norman, and Landers.

Such was the unparalleled invasion of China. For that billion of people there was no hope. Pent in their vast and festering charnel house, all or-ganization and cohesion lost, they could do naught but die. They could not escape. As they were flung back from their land frontiers, so were they flung back from the sea. Seventy-five thousand vessels patrolled the coasts. By day their smoking funnels dimmed the sea-rim, and by night their flashing searchlights ploughed the dark and harrowed it for the tiniest escaping junk. The attempts of the immense fleets of junks were pitiful. Not one ever got by the guarding sea-hounds. Modern war-machinery held back the disorganized mass of China, while the plagues did the work.

But old War was made a thing of laughter. Naught remained to him but patrol duty. China had laughed at war, and war she was getting, but it was ultra-modern war, twentieth century war, the war of the scientist and the laboratory, the war of Jacobus Laningdale. Hundred-ton guns were toys compared with the micro-organic projectiles hurled from the laboratories, the messengers of death, the destroying angels that stalked through the empire of a billion souls.

During all the summer and fall of 1976 China was an inferno. There was no eluding the microscopic projectiles that sought out the remotest hiding-places. The hundreds of millions of dead remained unburied and the germs multiplied themselves, and, toward the last, millions died daily of starvation. Besides, starvation weakened the victims and destroyed their natural defences against the plagues. Cannibalism, murder, and madness reigned. And so perished China.

Not until the following February, in the coldest weather, were the first expeditions made. These expeditions were small, composed of scientists and bodies of troops; but they entered China from every side. In spite of the most elaborate precautions against infection, numbers of soldiers and a few of the physicians were stricken. But the exploration went bravely on. They found China devastated, a howling wilderness through which wandered bands of wild dogs and desperate bandits who had survived. All survivors were put to death wherever found. And then began the great task, the sanitation of China. Five years and hundreds of millions of treasure were consumed, and then the world moved in—not in zones, as was the idea of Baron Albrecht, but heterogeneously, according to the democratic American program. It was a vast and happy intermingling of nationalities that settled down in China in 1982 and the years that followed—a tremendous and successful experiment in cross-fertilization. We know to-day the splendid mechanical, intellectual, and art output that followed.

It was in 1987, the Great Truce having been dissolved, that the ancient quarrel between France and Germany over Alsace-Lorraine recrudesced. The war-cloud grew dark and threatening in April, and on April 17, the Convention of Copenhagen was called. The representatives of the nations of the world, being present, all nations solemnly pledged themselves never to use against one another the laboratory methods of warfare they had employed in the invasion of China.

—Excerpt from WALT MERVIN's "Certain Essays in History"

In the Land of the Free (1909)
Sui Sin Far

Sui Sin Far (1865-1914; born Edith Maude Eaton) was a Chinese Canadian short story writer, journalist, and essayist. Far's father was British and her mother was Chinese; her work consistently focused on the experiences of Chinese immigrants in the United States and Canada. "In the Land of the Free" was published in The Independent, *a progressive New York weekly known for advocating abolition and women's suffrage. The story's plot pivots on the detention of a Chinese child and his parents' efforts to negotiate U.S. immigration policy through bureaucratic red tape. (Sui Sin Far [Edith Maude Eaton]. "In the Land of the Free."* The Independent, *2 Sept. 1909: 504-8.)*

I.

"See, Little One—the hills in the morning sun. There is thy home for years to come. It is very beautiful and thou wilt be very happy there."

The Little One looked up into his mother's face in perfect faith. He was engaged in the pleasant occupation of sucking a sweetmeat; but that did not prevent him from gurgling responsively. "Yes, my olive bud; there is where thy father is making a fortune for thee. Thy father! Oh, wilt thou not be glad to behold his dear face. 'Twas for thee I left him."

The Little One ducked his chin sympathetically against his mother's knee. She lifted him on to her lap. He was two years old, a round, dimple-cheeked boy with bright brown eyes and a sturdy little frame.

"Ah! Ah! Ah! Ooh! Ooh! Ooh!" puffed he, mocking a tugboat steaming by.

San Francisco's water front was lined with ships and steamers, while other craft, large and small, including a couple of white transports from the Philippines, lay at anchor here and there off shore. It was some time before the "Eastern Queen" could get docked, and even after that was accomplished, a lone Chinaman who had been waiting on the wharf for an hour was detained that much longer by men with the initials U. S. C. on their caps, before he could board the steamer and welcome his wife and child.

"This is thy son," announced the happy Lae Choo.

Hom Hing lifted the child, felt his little body and limbs, gazed into his face with proud and joyous eyes, then turned inquiringly to a customs officer at his elbow.

"That's a fine boy you have there," said the man. "Where was he born?"

"In China," answered Hom Hing, swinging the Little One on his right shoulder, preparatory to leading his wife off the steamer.

"Ever been to America before?"

"No, not he," answered the father with a happy laugh.

The customs officer beckoned to another.

"This little fellow," said he, "is visiting America for the first time."

The other customs officer stroked his chin reflectively.

"Good day," said Hom Hing.

"Wait!" commanded one of the officers, "You cannot go just yet."

"What more now?" asked Hom Hing. "I'm afraid," said the first customs officer, "that we cannot allow the boy to go ashore. There is nothing in the papers that you have shown us—your wife's papers and your own—having any bearing upon the child."

"There was no child when the papers were made out," returned Hom Hing. He spoke calmly; but there was apprehension in his eyes and in his tightening grip on his son.

"What is it? What is it?" quavered Lae Choo, who understood a little English.

The second customs officer regarded her pityingly.

"I don't like this part of the business," he muttered.

The first officer turned to Hom Hing and in an official tone of voice, said:

"Seeing that the boy has no certificate entitling him to admission to this country, you will have to leave him with us."

"Leave my boy," exclaimed Hom Hing.

"Yes; he will be well taken care of and just as soon as we can hear from Washington he will be handed over to you."

"But," protested Hom Hing, "he is my son."

"We have no proof," answered the man with a shrug of his shoulders, "and even if so, we cannot let him pass without orders from the Government."

"He is my son," reiterated Hom Hing, slowly and solemnly. "I am a Chinese merchant and have been in business in San Francisco for many years. When my wife told to me one morning that she dreamed of a green tree with spreading branches and one beautiful red flower growing thereon, I answered her that I wished my son to be born in our country, and for her to prepare to go to China. My wife complied with my wish. After my son was born, my mother fell sick and my wife nursed and cared for her; then my father, too, fell sick, and my wife also nursed and cared for him. For twenty moons my wife care for and nurse the old people, and when they die, they bless her and my son, and I send for her to return to me. I had no fear of trouble. I was a Chinese merchant and my son was my son."

"Very good, Hom Hing," replied the first officer. "Nevertheless, we take your son."

"No, you not take him; he my son, too."

It was Lae Choo. Snatching the child from its father's arms, she held and covered it with her own.

The officers conferred together for a few moments; then one drew Hom Hing aside and spoke in his ear.

Resignedly Hom Hing bowed his head, then approached his wife. "'Tis the law," said he, speaking in Chinese, "and 'twill be but for a little while — until tomorrow's sun arises."

"You, too," reproached Lae Choo, in a voice eloquent with pain. But accustomed to obedience, she yielded the boy to her husband, who in turn delivered him to the first officer. The Little One protested lustily against the transfer; but his mother covered her face with her sleeve and his father silently led her away. Thus was the law of the land to be complied with.

II.

Day was breaking. Lae Choo, who had been awake all night, dressed herself, then awoke her husband.

"'Tis the morn," she cried, "Go, bring our son."

The man rubbed his eyes and arose upon his elbow so that he could see out of the window. A pale star was visible in the sky. The petals of a lily in a bowl on the window sill were unfurled.

"'Tis not yet time," said he, laying his head down again.

"Not yet time. Ah, all the time that I lived before yesterday is not so much as the time that has been since my little one was taken from me."

The mother threw herself down beside the bed and covered her face.

Hom Hing turned on the light and touching his wife's bowed head with a sympathetic hand inquired if she had slept.

"Slept!" she echoed, weepingly. "Ah, how could I close my eyes with my arms empty of the little body that has filled them every night for more than twenty moons. You do not know—man—what it is to miss the feel of the little fingers and the little toes and the soft round limbs of your little one. Even in the darkness, his darling eyes used to shine up to mine and often have I fallen into slumber with his pretty babble at my ear. And now, I see him not—I touch him not; I hear him not. My baby, my little fat one!"

"Now! Now! Now!" consoled Hom Hing, patting his wife's shoulder reassuringly; "there is no need to grieve so; he will soon gladden you again. There cannot be any law that would keep a child from its mother!"

Lae Choo dried her tears.

"You are right, my husband," she meekly murmured. She arose and stepped about the apartment setting things right. The box of presents she had brought for her California friends had been opened the evening before; and silks, embroideries, carved ivories, ornamental lacquer ware, brasses, camphor wood boxes, fans and chinaware were scattered around in confused heaps. In the midst of unpacking, the thought of her child in the hands of strangers had overpowered her and she had left everything to crawl into bed and weep.

Having arranged her gifts in order she stepped out on to the deep balcony.

The stars had faded from view and there were bright streaks in the Western sky. Lae Choo looked down the street and around. Beneath the flat occupied by her and her husband were quarters for a number of bachelor Chinamen, and she could hear them from where she stood, taking their early morning breakfast. Below their dining room was her husband's grocery store. Across the way was a large restaurant. Last night it had been resplendent with gay colored lanterns and the sound of music. The rejoicings over "the completion of the moon" by Quong Sum's first born had been long and loud, and had caused her to tie a handkerchief over her ears. She, a bereaved mother, had it not in her heart to rejoice with other parents. This morning, the place was more in accord with her mood. It was still and quiet. The revelers had dispersed or were asleep.

A roly-poly woman in black sateen, with long pendant earrings in her ears, looked up from the street below and waved her a smiling greeting. It was her old neighbor, Kuie Hoe, the wife of the gold embosser, Mark

Sing. With her was a little boy in yellow jacket and lavender pantaloons. Lae Choo remembered him as a baby. She used to like to play with him in those days when she had no child of her own. What a long time ago that seemed! She caught her breath in a sigh, and laughed instead.

"Why are you so merry?" called her husband from within.

"Because my Little One is coming home," answered Lae Choo. "I am a happy mother—a happy mother."

She pattered into the room with a smile on her face.

The noon hour had arrived. The rice was steaming in the bowls and a fragrant dish of chicken and bamboo shoots was awaiting Hom Hing. Not for one moment had Lae Choo paused to rest during the morning hours; her activity had been ceaseless. Every now and again, however, she had raised her eyes to the gilded clock on the curiously carved mantelpiece. Once, she had exclaimed:

"Why so long, Oh, why so long?" Then apostrophizing herself: "Lae Choo, be happy. The Little One is coming! The Little One is coming!" Several times she burst into tears and several times she laughed aloud.

Hom Hing entered the room; his arms hung down by his side.

"The Little One!" shrieked Lae Choo.

"They bid me call tomorrow."

With a moan the mother sank to the floor.

The noon hour passed. The dinner remained on the table.

III.

The winter rains were over; the spring had come to California, flushing the hills with green and causing an ever changing pageant of flowers to pass over them. But there was no spring in Lae Choo's heart, for the Little One remained away from her arms. He was being kept in a mission. White women were caring for him, and tho for one full moon he had pined for his mother and refused to be comforted, he was now apparently happy and contented. Five moons or five months had gone by, since the day he had passed with Lae Choo thru the Golden Gate; but the great Government at Washington still delayed sending the answer which would return him to his parents.

Hom Hing was disconsolately rolling up and down the balls in his abacus box when a keen-faced young man stepped into his store.

"What news?" asked the Chinese merchant.

"This!" The young man brought forth a typewritten letter. Hom Hing read the words:

"Re Chinese child, alleged to be the son of Hom Hing, Chinese merchant, doing business at 425 Clay street, San Francisco.

"Same will have attention as soon as possible."

Hom Hing returned the letter and without a word continued his manipulation of the counting machine.

"Have you anything to say?" asked the young man.

"Nothing. They have sent the same letter fifteen times before. Have you not yourself showed it to me?"

"True!" The young man eyed the Chinese merchant furtively. He had a proposition to make and he was pondering whether or not the time was opportune.

"How is your wife?" he inquired solicitously and diplomatically.

Hom Hing shook his head mournfully. "She seems less every day," he replied. "Her food she takes only when I bid her and her tears fall continually. She finds no pleasure in dress or flowers and cares not to see her friends. Her eyes stare all night. I think, before another moon, she will pass into the land of spirits."

"No!" exclaimed the young man, genuinely startled.

"If the boy not come home I lose my wife sure," continued Hom Hing with bitter sadness.

"It's not right," cried the young man, indignantly. Then he made his proposition.

The Chinese father's eyes brightened exceedingly.

"Will I like you to go to Washington and make them give you the paper to restore my son?" cried he. "How can you ask when you know my heart's desire?"

"Then," said the young fellow, "I will start next week. I am anxious to see this thing thru if only for the sake of your wife's peace of mind."

"I will call her. To hear what you think to do will make her glad," said Hom Hing.

He called a message to Lae Choo upstairs thru a tube in the wall.

In a few moments she appeared, listless, wan and hollow-eyed; but when her husband told her the young lawyer's suggestion, she became as one electrified; her form straightened, her eyes glistened; the color flushed to her cheeks. "Oh," she cried, turning to James Clancy, "You are a hundred man good."

The young man felt somewhat embarrassed; his eyes shifted a little under the intense gaze of the Chinese mother.

"Well, we must get your boy for you," he responded. "Of course," turning to Hom Hing, "it will cost a little money. You can't get fellows to hurry the Government for you without gold in your pocket."

Hom Hing stared blankly for a moment. Then: "How much do you want, Mr. Clancy?" he asked quietly.

"Well I need at least five hundred to start with."

Hom Hing cleared his throat.

"I think I told you the time I last paid you for writing letters for me and seeing the custom boss here that nearly all I had was gone!"

"Oh well then, we won't talk about it, old fellow. It won't harm the boy to stay where he is, and your wife may get over it alright."

"What that you say?" quavered Lae Choo.

James Clancy looked out of the window.

"He says," explained Hom Hing in English, "that to get our boy we have to have much money."

"Money! Oh yes." Lae Choo nodded her head.

"I have not got the money to give him."

For a moment Lae Choo gazed wonderingly from one face to the other, then comprehension dawning upon her; with swift anger, pointing to the lawyer, she cried: "You are not one hundred man good; you just common white man."

"Yes, ma'am," returned James Clancy, bowing and smiling ironically.

Hom Hing pushed his wife behind him and addressed the lawyer again: "I might try," said he, "to raise something; but five hundred—it is not possible."

"What about four?"

"I tell you I have next to nothing left and my friends are not rich."

"Very well!"

The lawyer moved leisurely toward the door, pausing on its threshold to light a cigarette.

"Stop, white man; white man stop!"

Lae Choo, panting and terrified, had started forward and now stood beside him, clutching his sleeve excitedly.

"You say you can go to get paper to bring my Little One to me if Hom Hing give you five hundred dollars?"

The lawyer nodded carelessly; his eyes were intent upon the cigarette which would not take the fire from the match.

"Then you go get paper. If Hom Hing not can give you five hundred dollars—I give you perhaps what more that much."

She slipped a heavy gold bracelet from her wrist and held it out to the man. Mechanically he took it.

"I go get more."

She scurried away, disappearing behind the door thru which she had come.

"Oh, look here, I can't accept this," said James Clancy, walking back to Hom Hing and laying down the bracelet before him.

"It's all right," said Hom Hing, seriously, "pure China gold. My wife's parents give it to her when we married."

"But I can't take it anyway," protested the young man.

"It is all same as money. And you with money to go to Washington," replied Hom Hing in a matter of fact manner.

"See, my jade earrings—my gold buttons—my comb of pearl and my rings—one, two three, four, five rings; very good—very good—all same much money. I give them all to you. You take and bring me paper for my Little One."

Lae Choo piled up her jewels before the lawyer.

Hom Hing laid a restraining hand upon her shoulder. "Not all, my wife," he said in Chinese. He selected a ring—his gift to Lae Choo when she dreamed of the tree with the red flower. The rest of the jewels he pushed toward the white man.

"Take them and sell them," said he. "They will pay your fare to Washington and bring you back with the paper."

For one moment James Clancy hesitated. He was not a sentimental man; but something within him arose against accepting such payment for his services.

"They are good, good," pleadingly asserted Lae Choo, seeing his hesitation.

Whereupon he seized the jewels, thrusting them into his coat pocket and walked rapidly away from the store.

IV.

Lae Choo followed after the missionary woman thru the mission nursery school. Her heart was beating so high with happiness that she could scarcely breathe. The paper had come at last—the precious paper which gave Hom Hing and his wife the right to the possession of their own child.

It was ten months now since he had been taken from them—ten months since the sun had ceased to shine for Lae Choo.

The room was filled with children—most of them wee tots, but none so wee as her own. The mission woman talked as she walked. She told Lae Choo that little Kim, as he had been named by the school, was the pet of the place, and that his little tricks and ways amused and delighted every one. He had been rather difficult to manage at first and had cried much for his mother; "but children so soon forget, and after a month he seemed quite at home, and played around as bright and happy as a bird."

"Yes," responded Lae Choo, "Oh, yes, yes!"

But she did not hear what was said to her. She was walking in a maze of anticipatory joy.

"Wait here, please," said the mission woman, placing Lae Choo in a chair, "the very youngest ones are having their breakfast."

She withdrew for a moment—it seemed like an hour to the mother— then she reappeared leading by the hand a little boy dressed in blue cotton overalls and white soled shoes. The little boy's face was round and dimpled and his eyes were very bright.

"Little One, ah, my Little One!" cried Lae Choo.

She fell on her knees and stretched her hungry arms toward her son.

But the Little One shrunk from her and tried to hide himself in the folds of the white woman's skirt.

"Go 'way, go 'way!" he bade his mother.

Japs Keep Moving—This Is a White Man's Neighborhood (ca. 1920)

Although many people characterize the rise of anti-Japanese sentiment in the twentieth century as fixed to the bombing of Pearl Harbor on December 7, 1941, this 1920s photograph (taken in West Hollywood, California) makes clear a decades-long nativism and racism that preceded World War II (fig. 3.11).

Figure 3.11 "Japs Keep Moving—This Is a White Man's Neighborhood" (ca. 1920).
Courtesy of the National Japanese American Historical Society, San Francisco.

Watsonville Riots (1930)

Los Angeles Times

Late in the evening on January 18, 1930, five hundred white men and youths gathered outside a Filipino dance hall in Watsonville, California. Increasingly resentful of the use of Filipino farm labor and angered by the employment of white women at the dance hall, those gathered threatened to storm the club and destroy it. Police attempted to disperse the crowd with gas bombs; however, tensions continued to escalate. Over five days (January 19–23), rioters targeted Filipino residents, dragging them from their homes and beating them. One Filipino, Fermin Tovera, was fatally shot on the last day of the riots. News quickly spread, and many Filipinos fled the country; Filipino migration to the United States greatly decreased in the immediate aftermath of the violence. ("Riot Patrol Mobilizes." Los Angeles Times, 24 Jan. 1930: 1+. Reprinted courtesy of the Los Angeles Times.)

241

Watsonville Squad Organized by Sheriff as Fears of Reprisals for Filipino's Death Grow

Watsonville, Jan. 23. (Exclusive) — Fifteen picked men were mobilized here tonight by Sheriff Abbott and the American Legion, and Spanish-American War veterans offered their services to Chief of Police Hastings as preparations were made to prevent expected violence in the nature of reprisals for the death of a Filipino in race rioting which began five nights ago and flared into open warfare Wednesday night.

The body of Fermin Tovera, 22 years of age, a lettuce picker, was found in a Filipino ranch bunkhouse three miles south of the city after the quarters of the field workers had been made the butt of a mob attack during the night. Tovera had been shot to death, police said.

SEVEN ARRESTED

Some time later seven Watsonville youths, some of them high school students, were arrested as they drove into the city in two automobiles. They are R. A. Smith, George Barnes, Ramon Davis, George Slas, Charles Morrison, Theodore Spanger, and Fred Majors.

They denied knowledge, police say, of the means by which Tovera came to his death, but admitted, according to Dist.-Atty. Warth, going to the bunkhouse in search of a Filipino who allegedly insulted a young woman friend of Smith on a Watsonville street last Sunday night. Smith said he and his friends intended to turn the Filipino over to police but they did not find him.

Filipinos began flocking into the city from all directions tonight. Most of them said they came for protection afforded by peace officers as they feared further violence.

CLUB LEADER SPEAKS

President Cruz of the Filipino Club, after issuing a call for a mass meeting, gave out a statement saying his countrymen are not seeking violence. He defended the employment of white girls in the Filipino dancing club on the outskirts of the city, asserting the Filipinos as a rule are more courteous to the dancing girls than white men.

The employment of the white girls at the club is said to have been the real reason for the outbreak of race feeling. The club is owned by William

Locke-Paddon, San Francisco real estate dealer, whose family troubles have been dragged through the courts for several years.

MORE EXPECTED

The arrival of 1,000 blanket rolls from Yuma, Ariz., was taken as indication more Filipino workers are en route here to be employed in the fields, and the news did not serve to lessen an evident tension throughout the surrounding countryside.

The matron of the club said the girls work on a percentage basis, are not vicious in any sense, and no intoxicating liquors are sold in the place. She said many of them are extra girls from the motion-picture lots of Hollywood, temporarily out of work. They sometimes earn as much as $15 and $20 a day at the club, she stated. The matron added she has a daughter of her own there.

Watsonville police said most of the girls came from Guadalupe, where a Filipino club was driven out of business recently at the conclusion of trouble similar to that experienced here.

Be American
Carlos Bulosan

Filipino writer/activist Carlos Sampayan Bulosan (1913–1956) came to the United States in 1930 at the age of seventeen; he originally arrived in Seattle and worked low-wage jobs. He was active in the Pacific Coast labor movement as an organizer and Popular Front writer. "Be American" incorporates these autobiographical elements. Of equal significance is the story's revelation of contemporaneous naturalization law, which, until 1943, prohibited Filipino migrants from obtaining U.S. citizenship. (Carlos Bulosan. "Be American." In On Becoming Filipino: Selected Writings of Carlos Bulosan, *ed. E. San Juan Jr. Philadelphia: Temple University Press, 1995, 66–72. Courtesy of the University of Washington Libraries, Special Collections, Carlos Bulosan Papers MS Collection No. 0581-012.)*

It was not Consorcio's fault. My cousin was an illiterate peasant from the vast plains of Luzon. When he came off the boat in San Francisco, he could neither read nor write English or Ilocano, our dialect. I met him when he arrived, and right away he had bright ideas in his head.

"Cousin, I want to be American," he told me.

"Good," I said. "That is the right thing to do. But you have plenty of time. You are planning to live permanently in the United States, are you not?"

"Sure, cousin," he said. "But I want to be American right away. On the boat, I say, 'Consorcio stoody Engleesh right away.' Good ideeyas, eh, cousin?"

"It is," I said. "But the first thing for you to do is look for a job."

"Sure, cousin. You have job for me?"

I did. I took him to a countryman of ours who owned a small restaurant on Kearny Street. He had not done any dishwashing in the Philippines, so he broke a few dishes before he realized that the dishes were not coconut shells that he could flagrantly throw around the place, the way he used to do in his village where coconut shells were plates and carved trunks of trees were platters and his fingers were spoons. He had never seen bread and butter before, so he lost some weight before he realized that he had to eat these basic things like the rest of us, and be an American, which was his own idea in the first place. He had never slept in a bed with a mattress before, so he had to suffer from severe cold before he realized that he had to sleep inside the bed, under the blankets, but not on top of the spread, which was what he had done during his first two weeks in America. And of course he had never worn shoes before, so he had to suffer a few blisters on both feet before he realized that he had to walk lightfooted, easy, and even graceful, but not the way he used to do it in his village, which was like wrestling with a carabao [water buffalo] or goat.

All these natural things he had to learn during his first two weeks. But he talked about his Americanization with great confidence.

"You see, cousin," he told me, "I have earned mony quick. I poot the hoot dashes in the sink, wash-wash, day come, day out, week gone— mony! Simple?"

"Fine," I said.

"You know what I done with mony?"

"No."

"I spent all."

"On what?"

"Books. Come see my room."

I went with him to his small room at the back of the restaurant where he was working, near the washrooms. And sure enough, he had lined the four walls of his room with big books. I looked at the titles. He had a cheap edition of the classics, books on science, law and mathematics. He even had some brochures on political and governmental matters. All were books that a student or even a professor would take time to read.

I turned to my cousin. He was smiling with pride.

"Well, I hope these big books will make you an American faster," I told him.

"Sure, cousin. How long I wait?"

"Five years."

"Five years?" There was genuine surprise in his dark peasant face. "Too long. I do not wait. I make faster—one year."

"It is the law," I assured him.

"No good law. One year enough for Consorcio. He make good American citizen."

"There is nothing you can do about it."

"I change law."

"Go ahead."

"You see, cousin."

But he was puzzled. So I left him. I left San Francisco. When I saw him a year later, he was no longer washing dishes. But he still had the pardonable naivete of a peasant from the plains of Luzon.

"Where are you working now?" I asked him.

"Bakery," he said. "I make da bread. I make da donot. I made da pys."

"Where?"

"Come, cousin, I show you."

It was a small shop, a three-man affair. Consorcio was the handyboy in the place scrubbing the floor, washing the pots and pans; and he was also the messenger. The owner was the baker, while his wife was the saleswoman. My cousin lived at the back of the building, near the washrooms. He had a cot in a corner of the dark room. But the books were gone.

"What happened to your books?" I asked him.

He looked sad. Then he said, "I sold, cousin."

"Why?"

"I cannot read. I cannot understand. Words too big and too long."

"You should begin with the simple grammar books."

"Those cannot read also. What to do now, cousin?"

"You still want to be an American citizen?"

"Sure."

"Go to night school."

"Is a place like that?"

"Yes."

"No use, cousin, no money."

"The school is free," I told him. "It is for foreign-born people. For adults, so they could study American history."

"Free? I go now."

"The school opens only at night."

"I work night."

"Well, work in the daytime. Look for another job. You still want to be an American, don't you?"

"Sure, but I like boss-man. What to do?"

"Tell him the truth."

"You help me?"

I did. We went to the boss-man. I explained the matter as truthfully as I could and he understood Consorcio's problems. But he asked me to find someone to take the place of my cousin's place, which I did too, so we shook hands around and departed in the best of humor. I helped Consorcio register at the night school, and looked for another job for him as a janitor in an apartment building. Then I left him, wishing him the best of luck.

I worked in Alaska the next two years. When I returned to the mainland, I made it my duty to pass through San Francisco. But my cousin had left his janitor job and the night school. I could not find his new address, and it seemed that no one knew him well enough in the Filipino community.

I did not think much of his disappearance because we are a wandering people due to the nature of our lowly occupations, which take us from place to place, following the seasons. When I received a box of grapes from a friend, I knew he was working in the grape fields in either Fresno or Delano, depending on the freight mark. When I received a box of asparagus, I knew he was working in Stockton. But when it was a crate of lettuce, he was working in Santa Maria or Salinas, depending on the freight mark again. And in the summertime when I received a large barrel of salmon, I knew he was working the salmon canneries in Alaska. There were no letters, no post cards—nothing. But these surprising boxes, crates, and barrels that arrived periodically were the best letters in the world. What they contained were lovingly distributed among my city friends. Similarly, when I was in one of my own wanderings, which were done in cities and large towns, I sent my friend or friends unsealed envelopes bursting with the colored pictures of actresses and other beautiful women. I addressed these gifts to poolrooms and restaurants in towns where my friends had lived or worked for a season, because they were bound to go to any of these havens of the homeless wanderer. However, when another curious wanderer opened the envelopes and pilfered the pictures, it was not a crime. The enjoyment which was originally intended for my friends was his and his friends. That is the law of the nomad: finders keepers.

But Consorcio had not yet learned the unwritten law of the nomad. I did not expect him to send me boxes, crates, and barrels from faraway Alaska. So I did not know where I could locate him.

I wandered in and out of Los Angeles the next two years. At the beginning of the third year, when I was talking to the sleeping birds in Pershing Square, I felt a light hand on my shoulders. I was not usually curious about hands, but it was well after midnight and the cops were wandering in and out of the place. So I turned around—and found Consorcio.

I found a new Consorcio. He had aged and the peasant naivete was gone from his face. In his eyes was now a hidden fear. His hands danced and flew when he was talking, and even when he was not talking, as though he were slapping the wind with both hands or clapping with one hand. Have you ever heard the noise of one hand clapping?

This was Consorcio after five years in America. He was either slapping the wind with both hands or clapping with one hand. So I guided him out of the dark park to a lighted place, where we had coffee until the city awoke to give us another day of hope. Of course, I sat in silence for a long time because it was the fear of deep silence. And Consorcio sat for a long time too, because by now he had learned to hide in the deep silence that was flung like a mourning cloak across the face of the land. When we talked our sentences were short and punctuated by long silences. So we conversed somewhat like this:

"Been wandering everywhere."

"No job."

"Nothing anywhere."

"Where have you been all these years?"

Silence.

"No finished school?"

Silence.

"Not American citizen yet?"

"You should have told me."

"Told you want?"

"Filipinos can't become American citizens."

"Well, I could have told you. But I wanted you to learn."

"At least I speak better English now."

"This is a country of great opportunity."

Silence.

"No work?"

"No work."

"How long?"

"I have forgotten."

"Better times will come."

"You have a wonderful dream, cousin," he told me and left. He left Los Angeles for a long time. Then two years later, I received a crate of oranges from him. The freight mark was San Jose. Now I knew he was working and had learned the unwritten law of the wanderers on this troubled earth. So as I ate the oranges, I recalled his last statement: you have a wonderful dream, cousin . . .

I had a wonderful dream. But I dreamed it for both of us, for many of us who wandered in silence.

Then the boxes and crates became more frequent. Then a barrel of salmon came from Alaska. And finally, the letters came. My cousin Consorcio, the one-time illiterate peasant from the vast plains of Luzon, had indeed become an American without knowing it. His letters were full of wondering and pondering about many things in America. How he realized his naivete when he landed in San Francisco. But he realized also that he could not ask too much in a strange land. And it was this realization that liberated him from his peasant prison, his heritage, and eventually led him to a kind of work to which he dedicated his time and life until the end.

I was in Oregon when I received a newspaper from Consorcio, postmarked Pismo Beach. It was the first issue of his publication for agricultural workers in California. It was in English. From then on, I received all issues of his publication. For five years it existed defending the workers and upholding the rights and liberties of all Americans, native or foreign born, so that, as he began to understand the nature of American society, he became more belligerent in his editorials and had to go to jail a few times for his ideas about freedom and peace.

Yes, indeed Consorcio: you have become an American, a real American. And this land that we have known too well is not yet denuded by the rapacity of men. Rolling like a beautiful woman with an overflowing abundance of fecundity and murmurous with her eternal mystery, there she lies before us like a great mother. To her we always return from our prodigal wanderings and searchings for an anchorage in the sea of life; from her we always drew our sustenance and noble thoughts, to add to her glorious history.

But the war came. And war ended Consorcio's newspaper work and his crusade for a better America. And it ended his life also. When he was brought back from overseas, he knew he would not last long. But he talked the way he had written his editorials, measured sentences that rang like music, great poetry, and soft, soft. He would not shed a tear; but his heart must have been crying, seeing eternal darkness coming toward him, deep, deep in the night of perpetual sleep. Yes he would not shed a tear; but he must have been crying, seeing that there was so much to do with so little time left. There was in his voice a kindness for me—unhappy, perhaps, that he could not impart what he had learned from his wanderings on this earth; unhappy, also, because he knew that it would take all the people to unmake the unhappiness which had caught up with us. And now, fifteen years after his arrival in San Francisco, he was dying.

And he died. But at least he received his most cherished dream: American citizenship. He did realize later that he had become an American before he received his papers, when he began to think and write lovingly about *our* America. He gave up many things, and finally his own life, to realize his dream.

But Consorcio is not truly dead. He lives again in my undying love for the American earth. And soon, when I see the last winter coming to the last leaf, I will be warm with the thought that another wanderer shall inherit the wonderful dream which my cousin and I had dreamed and tried to realize in America.

Success Story of One Minority Group in U.S.

U.S. News and World Report

Published on December 26, 1966, this article—along with sociologist William Petersen's "Success Story, Japanese-American Style" (published in the New York Times *in January 1966)—is credited with the mainstream articulation of the so-called model minority myth. It should be noted that*

*neither article used the term "model minority"; this idea is more character-
ized than overtly named. Concentrated on the alleged socioeconomic success
of Asian Americans due to hard work, patience, perseverance, and strong
cultural values, the model minority myth on one level accesses past stereotypes of Jewish Americans during the 1920s. On another level, the stereotype's insistence that this group of color has achieved success ignores the
asymmetrical histories of African Americans, Native Americans, and Latinos and Latinas and denies the existence of ongoing systemic racism. (From*
U.S. News and World Report, *26 Dec. 1966: 73–76. Reprinted courtesy of*
U.S. News and World Report.)

At a time when Americans are awash in worry over the plight of racial
minorities—one such minority, the nation's 300,000 Chinese-Americans,
is winning wealth and respect by dint of its own hard work. In any Chinatown from San Francisco to New York, you discover youngsters at grips
with their studies. Crime and delinquency are found to be rather minor in
scope. Still being taught in Chinatown is the old idea that people should
depend on their own efforts—not a welfare check—in order to reach
America's "promised land." Visit "Chinatown U.S.A." and you find an important racial minority pulling itself up from hardship and discrimination
to become a model of self-respect and achievement in today's America. At
a time when it is being proposed that hundreds of billions be spent to uplift Negroes and other minorities, the nation's 300,000 Chinese-Americas
are moving ahead on their own—with no help from anyone else.

Low Rate of Crime

In crime-ridden cities, Chinese districts turn up as islands of peace and
stability. Of 4.7 million arrests reported to the Federal Bureau of Investigation in 1965, only 1,293 involved persons of Chinese ancestry. A Protestant pastor in New York City's Chinatown said: "This is the safest place
in the city." Few Chinese-Americans are getting welfare handouts—or
even want them. Within a tight network of family and clan loyalties, relatives continue to help each other. Mrs. Jean Ma, publisher of a Chinese-
language newspaper in Los Angeles, explained: "We're a big family. If
someone has trouble, usually it can be solved within the family. There is
no need to bother someone else. And nobody will respect any member of
the family who does not work and who just plays around."

Today, Chinese-American parents are worrying somewhat about their young people. Yet, in every city, delinquency in Chinatown is minor compared with what goes on around it.

Strict Discipline

Even in the age of television and fast automobiles, Chinese-American children are expected to attend school faithfully, work hard at their studies—and stay out of trouble. Spanking is seldom used, but supervision and verbal discipline are strict.

A study of San Francisco's Chinatown noted that "if school performance is poor and the parents are told, there is an immediate improvement." And, in New York City, schoolteachers reportedly are competing for posts in schools with large numbers of Chinese-American children.

Recently, Dr. Richard T. Sollenberger, professor of psychology at Mount Holyoke College, made a study of New York City's Chinatown and concluded: "There's a strong incentive for young people to behave. As one informant said, 'When you walk around the streets of Chinatown, you have a hundred cousins watching you.'"

What you find, in back of this remarkable group of Americans, is a story of adversity and prejudice that would shock those now complaining about the hardships endured by today's Negroes. It was during California's gold rush that large numbers of Chinese began coming to America. On the developing frontier, they worked in mines, on railroads and in other hard labor. Moving to the cities, where the best occupations were closed to them, large numbers became laundrymen and cooks because of the shortage of women in the West.

Past Handicaps

High value was placed on Chinese willingness to work long hours for low pay. Yet Congress, in 1882, passed an Exclusion Act denying naturalization to Chinese immigrants and forbidding further influx of laborers. A similar act in 1924, aimed primarily at the Japanese, prohibited laborers from bringing in wives.

In California, the first legislature slapped foreign miners with a tax aimed at getting Chinese out of the gold-mining business. That State's highest court ruled Chinese could not testify against whites in court. Chinese-Americans could not own land in California, and no corporation or public agency could employ them. These curbs, in general, applied also to Japanese-Americans, another Oriental minority that has survived discrimination to win a solid place in the nation.

The curbs, themselves, have been discarded in the last quarter century. And, in recent years, immigration quotas have been enlarged with 8,800 Chinese allowed to enter the country this year. As a result, the number of persons of Chinese ancestry living in the United States is believed to have almost doubled since 1950. Today, as in the past, most Chinese are to be found in Hawaii, California, and New York. Because of the ancient emphasis on family and village, most of those on the U.S. mainland trace their ancestry to communities southwest of Canton.

How Chinese Get Ahead

Not all Chinese-Americans are rich. Many, especially recent arrivals from Hong Kong, are poor and cannot speak English. But the large majority are moving ahead by applying the traditional virtues of hard work, thrift, and morality.

Success stories have been recorded in business, science, architecture, politics, and other professions. Dr. Sollenberger said of New York's China-town: "The Chinese people here will work at anything. I know of some who were scholars in China and are now working as waiters in restaurants. That's a stopgap for them, of course, but the point is that they're willing to do something—they don't sit around moaning."

The biggest and most publicized of all Chinatowns is San Francisco. Since 1960, the inflow of immigrants has raised the Chinese share of San Francisco's population from 4.9 per cent to 5.7 per cent. Altogether 42,600 residents of Chinese ancestry were reported in San Francisco last year.

Shift to Suburbs

As Chinese-Americans gain in affluence, many move to the suburbs. But about 30,000 persons live in 25 blocks of San Francisco's Chinatown. Sixty-three per cent of these are foreign-born, including many who are being indoctrinated by relatives in the American way of life. Irivin Lum, an official of the San Francisco Federal Savings and Loan Community House, said: "We follow the custom of being good to our relatives. There is not a very serious problem with our immigrants. We're a people of ability, adaptable and easy to satisfy in material wants. I know of a man coming here from China who was looked after by his sister's family, worked in

Chinatown for two years, then opened a small restaurant of his own." Problems among newcomers stir worries, however. A minister said, "Many are in debt when they arrive. They have a language problem. They are used to a rural culture, and they have a false kind of expectation."

A youth gang of foreign-born Chinese, known as "the Bugs" or "Tong San Tsai," clashes occasionally with a gang of Chinese-American youngsters. And one group of Chinese-American teenagers was broken up after stealing as much as $5,800 a week in burglaries this year.

Yet San Francisco has seen no revival of the "tong wars" or opium dens that led to the organizing of a "Chinese squad" of policemen in 1875. The last trouble between Chinese clans or "tongs" was before World War II. The special squad was abolished in 1956.

"Streets Are Safer"

A University of California team making a three-year study of Chinatown in San Francisco reported its impression "that Chinatown streets are safer than most other parts of the city" despite the fact that it is one of the most densely populated neighborhoods in the United States. In 1965, not one San Francisco Chinese—young or old—was charged with murder, manslaughter, rape, or an offense against wife or children. Children accounted for only two adult cases out of 252 of assault with a deadly weapon. Only one of San Francisco's Chinese youths, who comprise 17 per cent of the city's high-school enrollment, was among 118 juveniles arrested last year for assault with a deadly weapon. Meantime, 25 per cent of the city's semifinalists in the California State scholarship competition were Chinese.

Most Chinese-Americans continue to send their youngsters to Chinese schools for one or two hours a day so they can learn Chinese history, culture and—in some cases—language. A businessman said: "I feel my kids are Americans, which is a tremendous asset. But they're also Chinese, which is another great asset. I want them to have and keep the best of both cultures." Much of the same picture is found in mainland America's other big Chinatowns—Los Angeles and New York.

Riots of 1871

Los Angeles has a memory of riots in 1871 when white mobs raged through the Chinese section. Twenty-three Chinese were hanged, beaten, shot or stabbed to death.

Today, 25,000 persons of Chinese ancestry live in Los Angeles County—20,000 in the city itself. About 5,000 alien Chinese from Hong Kong and Formosa are believed to be in Southern California.

In Los Angeles, as elsewhere, Chinese-Americans are worrying about their children. Superior Judge Delbert E. Wong said: "Traditionally, the family patriarch ruled the household, and the other members of the family obeyed and followed without questioning his authority. "As the Chinese become more Westernized, women leave the home to work and the younger generation finds greater mobility in seeking employment, we see greater problems within the family unit—and a corresponding increase in crime and divorce."

A Chinese-American clergyman complained that "the second and third-generation Chinese feel more at home with Caucasians. They don't know how to act around the older Chinese anymore because they don't understand them."

The Family Unit

On the other hand, Victor Wong, president of the Chinese Consolidated Benevolent Association in Los Angeles said: "Basically, the Chinese are good citizens. The parents always watch out for the children, train them, send them to school and make them stay home after school to study. When they go visiting, it is as a family group. A young Chinese doesn't have much chance to go out on his own and get into trouble."

A high-ranking police official in Los Angeles found little evidence of growing trouble among Chinese. He reported: "Our problems with the Chinese are at a minimum. This probably is due to strict parental supervision. There is still a tradition of respect for parents."

New York City, in 1960, had a population of 32,831 persons of Chinese ancestry. Estimates today run considerably higher, with immigrants coming in at the rate of 200 or 300 a month.

Many Chinese have moved to various parts of the city and to the suburbs. But newcomers tend to settle in Chinatown, and families of 8 and 10 have been found living in two-room apartments. "The housing shortage here is worse than in Harlem," one Chinese-American said. Altogether, about 20,000 persons are believed living in the eight-block area of New York's Chinatown at present. The head of the Chinatown Planning Council said recently that, while most Chinese are still reluctant to accept public welfare, somewhat more are applying for it than in the past. "We are trying to let Chinese know that accepting public welfare is not necessarily the worst thing in the world," he said.

However, a Chinese-American banker in New York took this view: "There are at least 60 associations here whose main purpose is to help our own people. We believe welfare should be used only as a last resort." A sizable number of Chinese-Americans who could move out if they wanted to are staying in New York's Chinatown — not because of fears of discrimination on the outside, but because they prefer their own people and culture. And Chinatown, despite its proximity to the Bowery, remains a haven of law and order. Dr. Sollenberger said: "If I had a daughter, I'd rather have her live in Chinatown than any place else in New York City." A police lieutenant said: "You don't find any Chinese locked up for robbery, rape or vagrancy."

There has been some rise in Chinese-American delinquency in recent years. In part, this is attributed to the fact that the ratio of children in Chinatown's total population is going up as more women arrive and more families are started.

Even so, the proportion of Chinese-American youngsters getting into difficulty remains low. School buildings used by large numbers of Chinese are described as the cleanest in New York. Public recreational facilities amount to only one small part, but few complaints are heard.

Efforts at Progress

Over all, what observers are finding in America's Chinatowns are a thrifty, law-abiding and industrious people — ambitious to make progress on their own. In Los Angeles, a social worker said: "If you had several hundred thousand Chinese-Americans subjected to the same economic and societal pressures that confront Negroes in major cities, you would have a good deal of unrest among them. At the same time, it must be recognized that the Chinese and other Orientals in California were faced with even more prejudice than faces the Negro today. We haven't stuck Negroes in concentration camps, for instance, as we did the Japanese in World War II. The Orientals came back, and today they have established themselves as strong contributors to the health of the whole community."

The Basis of Black Power

Stokely Carmichael

In 1966, Stokely Carmichael (in his work with the Student Nonviolent Co-ordinating Committee, or SNCC) authored a position paper titled "The Basis of Black Power." Carmichael, who would later be known as Kwame Ture (1941–1998), focuses on the need to shift the purview of the civil rights movement away from integration and toward self-determination. Influenced by the "Third World" struggles for independence, Carmichael's assertion of black power pivots on the idea that one must organize according to racial lines in order to achieve liberation. Carmichael's call for self-determination reflects an increased disillusionment with the integrationist civil rights movement. The tenets of the Black Power movement profoundly influenced the Yellow Power movement, which was likewise invested in organizing along racial lines and racial liberation. (Stokely Carmichael. "The Basis of Black Power." Student Nonviolent Coordinating Committee Position Paper, 1966. Online at "Civil Rights Movement Veterans." http://www.crmvet.org/docs/blackpwr.htm.)

The myth that the Negro is somehow incapable of liberating himself, is lazy, etc., came out of the American experience. In the books that children read, whites are always "good" (good symbols are white), blacks are "evil" or seen as savages in movies, their language is referred to as a "dialect," and black people in this country are supposedly descended from savages.

Any white person who comes into the movement has the concepts in his mind about black people, if only subconsciously. He cannot escape them because the whole society has geared his subconscious in that direction.

Miss America coming from Mississippi has a chance to represent all of America, but a black person from either Mississippi or New York will never represent America. Thus the white people coming into the movement cannot relate to the black experience, cannot relate to the word "black," cannot relate to the "nitty gritty," cannot relate to the experience that brought such a word into existence, cannot relate to chitterlings, hog's head cheese, pig feet, ham hocks, and cannot relate to slavery, because these things are not a part of their experience. They also cannot relate to the black religious experience, nor to the black church, unless, of course, this church has taken on white manifestations.

White Power

Negroes in this country have never been allowed to organize themselves because of white interference. As a result of this, the stereotype has been reinforced that blacks cannot organize themselves. The white psychology that blacks have to be watched, also reinforces this stereotype. Blacks, in fact, feel intimidated by the presence of whites, because of their knowledge of the power that whites have over their lives. One white person can come into a meeting of black people and change the complexion of that meeting, whereas one black person would not change the complexion of that meeting unless he was an obvious Uncle Tom. People would immediately start talking about "brotherhood," "love," etc.; race would not be discussed.

If people must express themselves freely, there has to be a climate in which they can do this. If blacks feel intimidated by whites, then they are not liable to vent the rage that they feel about whites in the presence of whites — especially not the black people whom we are trying to organize, i.e., the broad masses of black people. A climate has to be created whereby blacks can express themselves. The reasons that whites must be excluded is not that one is anti-white, but because the effects that one is trying to achieve cannot succeed because whites have an intimidating effect. Oftentimes, the intimidating effect is in direct proportion to the amount of degradation that black people have suffered at the hands of white people.

Roles of Whites and Blacks

It must be offered that white people who desire change in this country should go where that problem (racism) is most manifest. The problem is not in the black community. The white people should go into white communities where the whites have created power for the express purpose of denying blacks human dignity and self-determination. Whites who come into the black community with ideas of change seem to want to absolve the power structure of its responsibility for what it is doing and saying that change can only come through black unity, which is the worst kind of paternalism. This is not to say that whites have not had an important role in the movement. In the case of Mississippi, their role was very key in that they helped give blacks the right to organize, but that role is now over, and it should be.

People now have the right to picket, the right to give out leaflets, the right to vote, the right to demonstrate, the right to print.

These things which revolve around the right to organize have been accomplished mainly because of the entrance of white people into Mississippi, in the summer of 1964. Since these goals have now been accomplished, whites' role in the movement has now ended. What does it mean if black people, once having the right to organize, are not allowed to organize themselves? It means that blacks' ideas about inferiority are being reinforced. Shouldn't people be able to organize themselves? Blacks should be given this right. Further, white participation means in the eyes of the black community that whites are the "brains" behind the movement, and that blacks cannot function without whites. This only serves to perpetuate existing attitudes within the existing society, i.e., blacks are "dumb," "unable to take care of business," etc. Whites are "smart," the "brains" behind the whole thing.

How do blacks relate to other blacks as such? How do we react to Willie Mays as against Mickey Mantle? What is our response to Mays hitting a home run against Mantle performing the same deed? One has to come to the conclusion that it is because of black participation in baseball. Negroes still identify with the Dodgers because of Jackie Robinson's efforts with the Dodgers. Negroes would instinctively champion all-black teams if they opposed all-white or predominantly white teams. The same principle operates for the movement as it does for baseball: a mystique must be created whereby Negroes can identify with the movement.

Thus an all-black project is needed in order for the people to free themselves. This has to exist from the beginning. This relates to what can be called "coalition politics." There is no doubt in our minds that some whites are just as disgusted with this system as we are. But it is meaningless to talk about coalition if there is no one to align ourselves with, because of the lack of organization in the white communities. There can be no talk of "hooking up" unless black people organize blacks and white people organize whites. If these conditions are met, then perhaps at some later date—and if we are going in the same direction—talks about exchange of personnel, coalition, and other meaningful alliances can be discussed.

In the beginning of the movement, we had fallen into a trap whereby we thought that our problems revolved around the right to eat at certain lunch counters or the right to vote, or to organize our communities. We have seen, however, that the problem is much deeper. The problem of this country, as we had seen it, concerned all blacks and all whites and therefore if decisions were left to the young people, then solutions would be arrived at. But this negates the history of black people and whites. We have dealt stringently with the problem of "Uncle Tom," but we have not yet gotten around to Simon Legree. We must ask ourselves, who is the real villain—Uncle Tom or Simon Legree? Everybody knows Uncle Tom, but who knows Simon Legree? So what we have now in SNCC is a closed society, a clique. Black people cannot relate to SNCC because of its unrealistic, nonracial atmosphere; denying their experience of America as a racist society. In contrast, the Southern Christian Leadership Conference of Martin Luther King, Jr., has a staff that at least maintains a black facade. The front office is virtually all black, but nobody accuses SCLC of being racist.

If we are to proceed toward true liberation, we must cut ourselves off from white people. We must form our own institutions, credit unions, co-ops, political parties, write our own histories.

To proceed further, let us make some comparisons between the Black Movement of the early 1900s and the movement of the 1960s—i.e., compare the National Association for the Advancement of Colored People with SNCC. Whites subverted the Niagara movement (the forerunner of the NAACP) which, at the outset, was an all-black movement. The name of the new organization was also very revealing, in that it presupposed blacks have to advance to the level of whites. We are now aware that the NAACP has grown reactionary, is controlled by the black power structure itself, and stands as one of the main roadblocks to black freedom. SNCC, by allowing the whites to remain in the organization, can have its efforts subverted in much the same manner, i.e., through having them play important roles such as community organizers, etc. Indigenous leadership cannot be built with whites in the positions they now hold.

These facts do not mean that whites cannot help. They can participate on a voluntary basis. We can contract work out to them, but in no way can they participate on a policy-making level.

Black Self-Determination

The charge may be made that we are "racists," but whites who are sensitive to our problems will realize that we must determine our own destiny.

In an attempt to find a solution to our dilemma, we propose that our organization (SNCC) should be black-staffed, black-controlled, and black-financed. We do not want to fall into a similar dilemma that other civil rights organizations have fallen into. If we continue to rely upon white financial support we will find ourselves entwined in the tentacles of the white power complex that controls this country. It is also important that a black organization (devoid of cultism) be projected to our people so that it can be demonstrated that such organizations are viable.

More and more we see black people in this country being used as a tool of the white liberal establishment. Liberal whites have not begun to address themselves to the real problem of black people in this country—witness their bewilderment, fear, and anxiety when nationalism is mentioned concerning black people. An analysis of the white liberal's reaction to the word "nationalism" alone reveals a very meaningful attitude of whites of an ideological persuasion toward blacks in this country. It means previous solutions to black problems in this country have been made in the interests of those whites dealing with these problems and not in the best interests of black people in the country. Whites can only subvert our true search and struggles for self-determination, self-identification, and liberation in this country. Reevaluation of the white and black roles must *now* take place so that whites no longer designate roles that black people play but rather black people define white people's roles.

Too long have we allowed white people to interpret the importance and meaning of the cultural aspects of our society. We have allowed them to tell us what was good about our Afro-American music, art, and literature. How many black critics do we have on the "jazz" scene? How can a white person who is not part of the black psyche (except in the oppressor's role) interpret the meaning of the blues to us who are manifestations of the song themselves?

It must be pointed out that on whatever level of contact blacks and whites come together, that meeting or confrontation is not on the level of the blacks but always on the level of the whites. This only means that our everyday contact with whites is a reinforcement of the myth of white supremacy. Whites are the ones who must try to raise themselves to our humanistic level. We are not, after all, the ones who are responsible for a genocidal war in Vietnam; we are not the ones who are responsible for neocolonialism in Africa and Latin America; we are not the ones who held a people in animalistic bondage over 400 years. We reject the American dream as defined by white people and must work to construct an American reality defined by Afro-Americans.

White Radicals

One of the criticisms of white militants and radicals is that when we view the masses of white people we view the overall reality of America, we view the racism, the bigotry, and the distortion of personality, we view man's inhumanity to man; we view in reality 180 million racists. The sensitive white intellectual and radical who is fighting to bring about change is conscious of this fact, but does not have the courage to admit this. When he admits this reality, then he must also admit his involvement because he is a part of the collective white America. It is only to the extent that he recognizes this that he will be able to change this reality.

Another common concern is, how does the white radical view the black community, and how does he view the poor white community, in terms of organizing? So far, we have found that most white radicals have sought to escape the horrible reality of America by going into the black community and attempting to organize black people while neglecting the organization of their own people's racist communities. How can one clean up someone else's yard when one's own yard is untidy? Again we feel that SNCC and the civil rights movement in general is in many aspects similar to the anticolonial situations in the African and Asian countries. We have the whites in the movement corresponding to the white civil servants and missionaries in the colonial countries who have worked with the colonial people for a long period of time and have developed a paternalistic attitude toward them. The reality of the colonial people taking over their own lives and controlling their own destiny must be faced. Having to move aside and letting the natural process of growth and development take place must be faced.

These views should not be equated with outside influence or outside agitation but should be viewed as the natural process of growth and development within a movement; so that the move by the black militants and SNCC in this direction should be viewed as a turn toward self-determination.

It is very ironic and curious that aware whites in the country can champion anticolonialism in other countries in Africa, Asia, and Latin America, but when black people move toward similar goals of self-determination in this country they are viewed as racists and anti-white by these same progressive whites. In proceeding further, it can be said that this attitude derives from the overall point of view of the white psyche as it concerns the black people. This attitude stems from the era of the slave revolts when every white man was a potential deputy or sheriff or guardian of the state. Because when black people get together among themselves to work out their problems, it becomes a threat to white people, because such meetings were potential slave revolts.

It can be maintained that this attitude or way of thinking has perpetuated itself to this current period and that it is part of the psyche of white people in this country whatever their political persuasion might be. It is part of the white fear-guilt complex resulting from the slave revolts. There have been examples of whites who stated that they can deal with black fellows on an individual basis but become threatened or menaced by the presence of groups of blacks. It can be maintained that this attitude is held by the majority of progressive whites in this country.

Black Identity

A thorough re-examination must be made by black people concerning the contributions that we have made in shaping this country. If this re-examination and re-evaluation is not made, and black people are not given their proper due and respect, then the antagonisms and contradictions are going to become more and more glaring, more and more intense, until a national explosion may result.

When people attempt to move from these conclusions it would be faulty reasoning to say they are ordered by racism, because, in this country and in the West, racism has functioned as a type of white nationalism when dealing with black people. We all know the habit that this has created throughout the world and particularly among nonwhite people in this country.

Therefore any re-evaluation that we must make will, for the most part, deal with identification. Who are black people, what are black people, what is their relationship to America and the world?

It must be repeated that the whole myth of "Negro citizenship," perpetuated by the white elite, has confused the thinking of radical and progressive blacks and whites in this country. The broad masses of black people react to American society in the same manner as colonial peoples react to the West in Africa and Latin America, and had the same relationship—that of the colonized toward the colonizer.

The Emergence of Yellow Power in America
Amy Uyematsu

Published in 1969, Japanese American poet/activist Amy Uyematsu's "The Emergence of Yellow Power in America" opens with Stokely Carmichael's characterization of black power and self-determination. This manifesto, which encapsulates the politics of the Third World Liberation Front and lays bare the tenets of Yellow Power, appeared in the activist newspaper Gidra. *Integral to Uyematsu's manifesto is a critique of model minoritization and internalized racism. (Excerpt from Amy Uyematsu. "The Emergence of Yellow Power in America."* Gidra, *Oct. 1969: 8–10. Reprinted with permission from the author.)*

Asian Americans can no longer afford to watch the black-and-white struggle from the sidelines. They have their own cause to fight, since they are also victims—with less visible scars—of the white institutionalized racism. A yellow movement has been set into motion by the black power movement. Addressing itself to the unique problems of Asian Americans, this "yellow power" movement is relevant to the black power movement in that both are part of the Third World struggle to liberate all colored people.

Part 1: Mistaken Identity

The Yellow Power movement has been motivated largely by the problem of self-identity in Asian Americans. The psychological focus of this movement is vital, for Asian Americans suffer the critical mental crises of having "integrated" into American society—

> No person can be healthy, complete, and mature if he must deny a part of himself; this is what "integration" has required so far.
> —Stokely Carmichael and Charles V. Hamilton

The Asian Americans' current position in America is not viewed as a social problem. Having achieved middle-class incomes while presenting no real threat in numbers to the white majority, the main body of Asian Americans (namely, the Japanese and the Chinese) have received the token acceptance of white America.

Precisely because Asian Americans have become economically secure, do they face serious identity problems. Fully committed to a system that subordinates them on the basis of non-whiteness, Asian Americans still try to gain complete acceptance by denying their yellowness. They have become white in every respect but color.

ASIAN AMERICANS ASSUME WHITE IDENTITIES

However, the subtle but prevailing racial prejudice that "yellows" experience restricts them to the margins of the white world. Asian Americans have assumed white identities, that is, the values and attitudes of the majority of Americans. Now they are beginning to realize that this nation is a "White democracy" and that yellow people have a mistaken identity.

Within the past two years, the "Yellow Power" movement has developed as a direct outgrowth of the "Black Power" movement. The "Black Power" movement caused many Asian Americans to question themselves. "Yellow Power" is just now at the stage of an articulated mood rather than a program—disillusionment and alienation from white America and independence, race pride, and self-respect. Yellow consciousness is the immediate goal of concerned Asian Americans.

In the process of Americanization, Asians have tried to transform themselves into white men—both mentally and physically. Mentally, they have adjusted to the white man's culture by giving up their own languages, customs, histories, and cultural values. They have adopted the "American way of life" only to discover that this is not enough.

Next, they have rejected their physical heritages, resulting in extreme self-hatred. Yellow people share with the blacks the desire to look white. Just as blacks wish to be light-complected with thin lips and unkinky hair, "yellows" want to be tall with long legs and large eyes. The self-hatred is also evident in the yellow male's obsession with unobtainable white women, and in the yellow female's attempt to gain male approval by aping white beauty standards. Yellow females have their own "conking" techniques—they use "peroxide, foam rubber, and scotch tape to give them light hair, large breasts, and double lidded eyes."

SELF-ACCEPTANCE FIRST STEP

The "Black is Beautiful" cry among black Americans has instilled a new awareness in Asian Americans to be proud of their physical and cultural heritages. Yellow Power advocates self-acceptance as the first step toward strengthening the personalities of Asian Americans.

Since the Yellow Power movement is thus far made up of students and young adults, it is working for Asian-American ethnic studies centers on college campuses such as Cal and U.C.L.A. The re-establishment of ethnic identity through education is being pursued in classes like U.C.L.A.'s "Orientals in America." As one student in the course relates:

264

I want to take this course for a 20–20 realization, and not a passive glance in the ill-reflecting mirror; the image I see is W.A.S.P., but the yellow skin is not lily white . . . I want to find out what my voluntarily or subconsciously suppressed Oriental self is like; also what the thousands of other suppressed Oriental selves are like in a much larger mind and body—America . . . I want to establish my ethnic identity not merely for the sake of such roots, but for the inherent value that such a background merits.

The problem of self-identity in Asian Americans also requires the removal of stereotypes. The yellow people in America seem to be silent citizens. They are stereotyped as being passive, accommodating, and unemotional. Unfortunately, this description is fairly accurate, for Asian Americans have accepted these stereotypes and are becoming true to them.

The "silent" Asian Americans have rationalized their behavior in terms of cultural values which they have maintained from the old country. For example, the Japanese use the term "enryo" to denote hesitation in action or expression. A young Buddhist minister, Reverend Mas Kodani of the Los Angeles Senshin Buddhist Temple, has illustrated the difference between Japanese "enryo" and Japanese-American "enryo": in Japan, if a teacher or lecturer asks, "Are there any questions?" several members of the class or audience respond; but in the United States, the same question is followed by a deathly silence.

Reverend Kodani has also commented on the freedom of expression between family members that is absent in Asian Americans. As an American-born student in Japan, he was surprised at the display of open affection in Japanese families. This cultural characteristic is not shown in Japanese-American families, who react with embarrassment and guilt toward open feelings of love and hate.

SILENT, PASSIVE IMAGE

This uneasiness in admitting and expressing natural human feelings has been a factor in the negligible number of Asian Americans in the theater, drama, and literary arts. Not discounting the race prejudice and competition in these fields, yellow Americans cannot express themselves honestly, or in the works of Chinese-American actor James Hong, they cannot feel "from the gut level."

The silent, passive image of Asian Americans is understood not only in terms of their cultural backgrounds, but by the fact that they are scared. The earliest Asians in America were Chinese immigrants who began settling in large numbers on the West Coast from 1850 through 1880. They were subjected to extreme white racism, ranging from economic subordination, to the denial of rights of naturalization, to physical violence. During the height of anti-Chinese mob action of the 1880s, whites were "stoning the Chinese in the streets, cutting off their queues, wrecking their shops and laundries." The worst outbreak took place in Rock Springs, Wyoming, in 1885, when twenty-eight Chinese residents were murdered. Perhaps, surviving Asians learned to live in silence, for even if "the victims of such attacks tried to go to court to win protection, they could not hope to get a hearing. The phrase, 'not a Chinaman's chance' had a grim and bitter reality."

ASIAN AMERICANS ARE STILL SCARED

Racist treatment of "yellows" still existed during World War II, with the unjustifiable internment of 110,000 Japanese into detention camps. When Japanese Americans were ordered to leave their homes and possessions behind within short notice, they co-operated with resignation and did not even voice opposition. According to Frank Chumann, one-time president of the Japanese American Citizens League, they "used the principle of *shikataganai*—realistic resignation—and evacuated without protest."

Today the Asian Americans are still scared. Their passive behavior serves to keep national attention on the black people. By being as inconspicuous as possible, they keep pressure off of themselves at the expense of the blacks. Asian Americans have formed an uneasy alliance with white Americans to keep the blacks down. They close their eyes to the latent white racism toward them which has never changed.

Frightened "yellows" allow the white public to use the "silent Oriental" stereotype against the black protest. The presence of twenty million blacks in America poses an actual physical threat to the white system. Fearful whites tell militant blacks that the acceptable criterion for behavior is exemplified in the quiet, passive Asian American.

The Yellow Power movement envisages a new role for Asian Americans:

It is a rejection of the passive oriental stereotype and symbolizes the birth of a new Asian—one who will recognize and deal with injustices. The shout of Yellow Power, symbolic of our new direction, is reverberating in the quiet corridors of the Asian community.

FALSE PRIDE IN OWN ECONOMIC PROGRESS

As expressed in the Black Power writings, Yellow Power also says that "When we begin to define our own image, the stereotypes—that is, lies—that our oppressor has developed will begin in the white community and end there."

Another obstacle to the creation of yellow consciousness is the well-incorporated white racist attitudes which are present in Asian Americans. They take much false pride in their own economic progress and feel that blacks could succeed similarly if they only followed the Protestant ethic of hard work and education. Many Asians support S. I. Hayakawa, the so-called spokesman of yellow people, when he advises the black man to imitate the Nisei [second-generation Asian Americans]: "Go to school and get high grades, save one dollar out of every ten you earn to capitalize your business." But the fact is that the white power structure allowed Asian Americans to succeed through their own efforts while the same institutions persist in denying these opportunities to black Americans.

Certain basic changes in American society made it possible for many Asian Americans to improve their economic condition after the war. In the first place, black people became the target group of West Coast discrimination. During and after World War II, a huge influx of blacks migrated to the West, taking racist agitation away from the yellows and onto the blacks. From 1940 to 1950, there was a gain of 85.2 percent in the black population of the West and North; from 1950 to 1960, a gain of 71.6 percent; and from 1960 to 1966, a gain of 80.4 percent.

ASIAN AMERICANS PERPETUATE WHITE RACISM

The other basic change in society was the shifting economic picture. In a largely agricultural and rural West, Asian Americans were able to find employment. First- and second-generation Japanese and Filipinos were hired as farm laborers and gardeners, while Chinese were employed in laundries and restaurants. In marked contrast is the highly technological and urban society which today faces unemployed black people. "The Negro migrant, unlike the immigrant, found little opportunity in the city; he had arrived too late, and the unskilled labor he had to offer was no longer needed." Moreover, blacks today are kept out of a shrinking labor market, which is also closing opportunities for white job-seekers.

Asian Americans are perpetuating white racism in the United States as they allow white America to hold up the "successful" Oriental image before other minority groups as the model to emulate. White America justifies the blacks' position by showing that other non-whites—yellow people—have been able to "adapt" to the system. The truth underlying both the yellows' history and that of the blacks has been distorted. In addition, the claim that black citizens must "prove their rights to equality" is fundamentally racist.

Unfortunately, the Yellow Power movement is fighting a well-developed racism in Asian Americans who project their own frustrated attempts to gain white acceptance onto the black people. They nurse their own feelings of inferiority and insecurity by holding themselves as superior to blacks. Since they feel they are in a relatively secure economic and social position, most Asian Americans overlook the subtle but damaging racism that confronts them. They do not want to upset their present ego systems by honest self-appraisal. They would rather fool themselves than admit that they have prostituted themselves to white society.

Part 2: The Relevance of Power for Asians in America

The emerging movement among Asian Americans can be described as "Yellow Power" because it is seeking freedom from racial oppression through the power of a consolidated yellow people. As derived from the black power ideology, yellow power implies that Asian Americans must control the decision-making processes affecting their lives.

One basic premise of both Black Power and Yellow Power is that ethnic political power must be used to improve the economic and social conditions of blacks and yellows. In considering the relevance of power for Asian Americans, two common assumptions will be challenged: first, that the Asian Americans are completely powerless in the United States; and second, the assumption that Asian Americans have already obtained "economic" equality.

While the Black Power movement can conceivably bargain from a position of strength, Yellow Power has no such potential to draw from. A united black people would comprise over ten percent of the total American electorate; this is a significant enough proportion of the voting population to make it possible for blacks to be a controlling force in the power structure. In contrast, the political power of yellows would have little effect on state and national contests. The combined populations of Chinese, Japanese, and Filipinos in the United States in 1960 was only 887,834—not even one-half percent of the total population.

POTENTIAL POLITICAL POWER ON WEST COAST

However, Asian Americans are not completely weaponless, in the local political arena. For instance, in California, the combined strength of Chinese, Japanese, and Filipinos in 1960 was two percent of the state population. Their possible political significance lies in the fact that there are heavy concentrations of these groups in San Francisco and Los Angeles. In the San Francisco–Oakland metropolitan area, 55% of the Chinese, 16% of the Japanese, and 33% of the Filipinos live. . . . On an even more local level, Japanese and Chinese in the Crenshaw area of Los Angeles form about one-third of the total residents; and Japanese in the city of Gardena own forty percent of that city's property.

In city and county government, a solid yellow voting bloc could make a difference. As has been demonstrated by the Irish, Italians, Jews, and Poles, the remarkable fact of ethnic political power is its ability to "control a higher proportion of political control and influence than their actual percentage in the population warrants."

"MORE OF THE MONEY PIE"

Even under the assumption that yellow political power could be significant, how will it improve the present economic situation of Asian Americans? Most yellow people have attained middle-class incomes and feel that they have no legitimate complaint against the existing capitalist structure.

The middle-class attainment of Asian Americans has also made certain blacks unsympathetic to the yellow power movement. In the words of one B.S.U. member, it looks like Asian Americans "just want more of the money pie." It is difficult for some blacks to relate to the yellow man's problems next to his own total victimization.

Although it is true that some Asian minorities lead all other colored groups in America in terms of economic progress, it is a fallacy that Asian Americans enjoy full economic opportunity. If the Protestant ethic is truly a formula for economic success, then why don't Japanese and Chinese who work harder and have more education than whites earn just as much?

Statistics on unemployment, educational attainment, and median annual income reveal an inconsistency in this "success" formula when it applies to non-whites.

STATISTICAL DISCREPANCIES

In 1960, unemployment rates for Japanese and Chinese males were lower than those for white males in California:

2.6 percent for Japanese
4.9 percent for Chinese
5.5 percent for whites

In the same year, percentage rates for Japanese and Chinese males who had completed high school or college were higher than those for white males:

High School
34.3 percent for Japanese
24.4 percent for Chinese

College (4 years or more)
13.3 percent for Chinese
11.9 percent for Japanese
10.7 percent for whites

Despite these figures, the median annual income of Japanese and Chinese was considerably lower than the median annual income of whites. Chinese men in California earned $3,803; Japanese men earned $4,388; and white men earned $5,109.

The explanation for this discrepancy lies in the continuing racial discrimination toward yellows in upper-wage level and high-status positions. White America praises the success of Japanese and Chinese for being highest among all other colored groups. Japanese and Chinese should feel fortunate that they are accepted more than any other non-white ethnic groups, but they should not step out of place and compare themselves with whites. In essence, the American capitalistic dream was never meant to include non-whites.

The myth of Asian American success is most obvious in the economic and social position of Filipino Americans. In 1960, the 65,459 Filipino residents of California earned a median annual income of $2,925, as compared to $3,553 for blacks and $5,109 for whites. Over half of the total Filipino male working force was employed in farm labor and service work; over half of all Filipino males received less than 8.7 years of school education. Indeed, Filipinos are a forgotten minority in America. Like blacks, they have many legitimate complaints against American society.

MYTH OF ASIAN AMERICAN SUCCESS

A further example of the false economic and social picture of Asian Americans exists in the ghetto communities of Little Tokyo in Los Angeles and Chinatown in San Francisco. In the former, elderly Japanese live in rundown hotels in social and cultural isolation. And in the latter, Chinese families suffer the poor living conditions of a community that has the second highest tuberculosis rate in the nation.

Thus, the use of yellow political power is valid, for Asian Americans do have definite economic and social problems which must be improved. By organizing around these needs, Asian Americans can make the Yellow Power movement a viable political force in their lives. . . .

San Francisco State College Strike (1968–1969)

In 1968, soon after the assassination of Martin Luther King Jr. and in the midst of an escalated war in Southeast Asia, student members of the Black Student Union and the Third World Liberation Front began pushing for the formation of ethnic studies programs (particularly African American studies, Asian American studies, Chicano studies, and Native studies) at San Francisco State College. Central to their demands was the need to make education relevant by offering courses and having faculty that reflected their experiences as people of color in the United States (fig. 3.12). The strike, which ended March 20, 1969, represents the longest student strike in U.S. history and culminated in the institutionalization of ethnic studies at not only San Francisco State College, but also other American universities.

THIRD WORLD LIBERATION FRONT NOTICE:

This College's Faculty, Administrators, Trustees, and Chancellor
NEVER WERE AND ARE NOT NOW prepared to relate to the needs and the desires of the Third World People. They have attempted to disrupt

THIRD WORLD LIBERATION FRONT

NOTICE:

28

This College's Faculty, Administrators, Trustees, and Chancellor

NEVER WERE AND ARE NOT NOW prepared to relate to the needs

and the desires of the Third World People. They have attempted

to disrupt and confuse the work and directions of the Third

World People of this school, and are in the process of

MAKING IT IMPOSSIBLE FOR THIRD WORLD PEOPLE TO REMAIN in this

school.

THE THIRD WORLD LIBERATION FRONT HAS VOTED UNANIMOUSLY TO

SUPPORT THE POSITION OF THE BLACK STUDENTS UNION and to parti-

cipate, and to encourage our people to work and participate in

the strike, in whatever level of involvement they are prepared

to fulfill.

In order to protect Third World People from the pigs con-

tinuing to run our schools and dictating our education, the

THIRD WORLD LIBERATION FRONT DEMANDS THE FOLLOWING:

From the Administration and Trustees of this college:

- That a School of Ethnic Studies for the ethnic groups

involved in the Third World be set up with the students in each

particular ethnic organization having the authority and control

of the hiring and retention of any faculty member, director and

administrator, as well as the curriculum in a specific area study.

- That 50 faculty positions be appropriated to the School

of Ethnic Studies, 20 of which would be for the Black Studies

program.

- That, in the Spring semester, the College fulfill its

committment to the non-white students in admitting those that

apply.

(continued)

Figure 3.12 "Third World Liberation Front Notice" (recto and verso). Third World Liberation Front folder, item #28. Courtesy University Archives, "SF State Strike Collection," J. Paul Leonard Library, San Francisco State University.

and confuse the work and directions of the Third World People of this school, and are in the process of MAKING IT IMPOSSIBLE FOR THIRD WORLD PEOPLE TO REMAIN in this school.

THE THIRD WORLD LIBERATION FRONT HAS VOTED UNANI-MOUSLY TO SUPPORT THE POSITION OF THE BLACK STUDENTS

Page 2

THIRD WORLD LIBERATION FRONT   NOTICE OF DEMANDS continued

- That, in the Fall of 1969, all applications of non-white students be accepted.

- That George Murray, and any other faculty person chosen by non-white people as their teacher, be retained in their position.

Figure 3.12 *Continued.*

UNION and to participate, and to encourage our people to work and participate in the strike, in whatever level of involvement they are prepared to fulfill.

In order to protect Third World People from the pigs continuing to run our schools and dictating our education, the THIRD WORLD LIBERATION FRONT DEMANDS THE FOLLOWING:

From the Administration and Trustees of this college:

— That a School of Ethnic Studies for the ethnic groups involved in the Third World be set up with the students in each particular ethnic organization having the authority and control of the hiring and retention of any faculty member, director and administrator, as well as the curriculum in a specific area study.

— That 50 faculty positions be appropriated to the School of Ethnic Studies, 20 of which would be for the Black Studies program.

— That, in the Spring semester, the College fulfill its commitment to the non-white students in admitting those that apply.

— That, in the Fall of 1969, all applications of non-white students be accepted.

— That George Murray, and any other faculty person chosen by non-white people as their teacher, be retained in their position.

ALL POWER TO THE PEOPLE

Interview with Yuri Kochiyama (2006)

The human rights activist Yuri Kochiyama (1921–2014) and her family were, like other Japanese Americans, specifically targeted by the U.S. federal government after the Japanese bombing of Pearl Harbor on December 7, 1941. Her father was detained soon after the attacks and denied medical care while under interrogation; he died soon after his release in 1942. Kochiyama and the surviving members of her family were originally relocated to Santa Anita Assembly Center; they would eventually end up in an internment camp in Jerome, Arkansas. In 1960, Kochiyama and her husband moved to Harlem, where they joined Malcolm X's Organization of Afro-American Unity. She was with Malcolm X when he was assassinated on February 21, 1965. What follows is an excerpt of an interview with Kochiyama specifically focusing on her father's experience. She served as a foundational figure for Asian American activists and was a key figure in the Japanese American redress movement. ("Yuri Kochiyama Remembers Malcolm X's Assassination & Living at WWII Japanese-American Detention Camp." Interview by Amy Goodman. Democracynow.org. Democracy Now!, 27 Jan. 2006. On-

Interview with Yuri Kochiyama

line at http://www.democracynow.org/2006/2/21/civil_rights_activist_yuri _kochiyama_remembers. Courtesy of Democracy Now!)

...YURI KOCHIYAMA: I lived in San Pedro, California, which is, you know, on the west side of California, and it's where many, many Japanese lived. Well, the Japanese were mostly all living on the West Coast: Washington, Oregon, California and parts of Arizona. And that's the number one war zone. But immediately, the newspaper headlines were "Get the Japs Out!" and people like—who is the guy, that general on the West Coast, the top one, the top general? I can't think of his name. He said, "The only good Jap is a dead Jap." And, anyway, not just the newspaper headlines, but there were signs all over. "Get the Japs out! Get the Japs out!" And—

AMY GOODMAN: You were a teacher? You were teaching that day that Pearl Harbor was bombed?

YK: No. No. I had just finished junior college. No, I wasn't teaching. But I was teaching Sunday school. And I had been teaching about a year-and-a-half. It was a place where I felt very comfortable. But that day, when I went in, I could just feel something was different. And, of course, because that's all people were thinking about is—

AG: Were you the only Japanese American at the Sunday school?

YK: Oh, yeah. It was really what's called a white church. So I took all the kids home, as I usually do. They pack in the car, sit on top of each other, and I take about ten of the kids home. And then, when I came home . . . I knew my father had come back from the hospital, so I came back early, too. And just a few minutes later, three tall white men, I could see through the window. They were right there at the door.

And so I went there to see who they were. And they all, you know, put their—like a wallet out, which had the F.B.I. card. And they said, "Is there a Seichi Nakahara living here?" I said, "Yes, that's my father." They said, "Where is he right now? We need to see him." I said, "Oh, he's sleeping in bed." I said, "He just came home." I don't know if it was that morning or the day before, he came home from ulcer surgery. And they said, "Well, where is he?" And I pointed to one of the bedrooms.

And they went in and got—it was done so quickly, it didn't even take a half of a minute, I don't think. And I didn't dare ask a question. They were going out the door immediately. And then, I just called my mother, who was right down the street to say, "Come home quick. The F.B.I. just came and took Pop." And—

AG: He was the first person, Japanese American, arrested after the bombing of Pearl Harbor?

YK: That's what we heard, but I don't know if it was the first. They could have been doing it all over, but I think he was one of the first . . . they did find the Japanese still very quickly. So I'm sure they had a list. . . . Well, he was in the fishing business. That's why it hit all fishermen, because they knew then that the fishermen knew the waters, and if the Japanese ships got close enough, would the Japanese fishermen in America help the Japanese? But, actually, I tell you, the Japanese Americans and even the Isseis, first generation, who could not become Americans, they were so American. And yet, the hysteria about the suspicion of Japanese people was very, very strong. And, anyway, by the end of the day, I think all the Japanese people were calling their friends to say, "Did anyone come to your home and take your father or mother?"

AG: How long was your father held for?

YK: Well, he was picked up on December 7. And, of course, he wasn't getting any better, because they didn't do anything for him while he was—first, he was in prison. And my mother kept begging, "Please let him go to a hospital, and then when he gets some treatment, then he could go back to the prison." But we didn't realize that when they did take him to the hospital, he was the only Japanese that was taken there, and all the other prisoners, every single one of the prisoners, were Americans, all white, no black or brown or anyone else. And I—

AG: In the hospital.

YK: Yes, in the only hospital in our town, San Pedro Hospital. And then they put a sheet around his bed, and it said, "prisoner of war." And . . . us kids didn't get to go see my father yet, but my mother got permission, and she said when she saw the sheet with the "prisoner of war," and she saw the reaction of all the American prisoners who were just brought in from Wake Island, she didn't think he was going to last. And so, she asked the head of that hospital, could he be given a room by himself and get some medication or something, and then when he was feeling better, could they take him back to the prison, because that hospital, she said, was probably worse than prison, because here were all these Americans who had been injured . . . in Wake Island or other islands, and at least in the prison, he would be in a—probably in a cell by himself.

AG: When, ultimately, did he get released? How long was he held?

YK: . . . He was home not even twelve hours. He came home, it was around dinner time, 5:30. And they had a nurse come with him. And we put him in his own bedroom. And the nurse was the only one that stayed in that room. And by the next morning, she woke us up and said, "He's gone."

AG: Were you rounded up, as well?

YK: Not then. No. They were only rounding up first generation Japanese.

AG: So your father died—

YK: We were American citizens.

AG: Your father died after being released?

YK: Yeah.

AG: Immediately after.

YK: He was only home not even twelve hours, and he was gone. So, we didn't get to talk to him. We don't think he could have talked the way he looked, jumbled or mumbled. We couldn't tell if he could see. We would put our hands in front of him. We didn't know if he could hear. And it was so fast, he was gone.

AG: We only have a minute. But were you detained, your family, after?

YK: Everybody was. Every person of Japanese ancestry, 120,000. . . .

The Civil Liberties Act of 1988

Set against the backdrop of the midcentury civil rights movement, Japanese Americans (particularly third-generation Japanese Americans, or Sansei) began pushing for what would eventually be known as the redress movement, which sought apologies and reparations from the federal government for the forced relocation/incarceration of Aleut Indians in Alaska and Japanese and Japanese Americans during World War II. In 1978, the Japanese American Citizens League (JACL) led the campaign for redress, requesting the following reparations: $25,000 for each person detained, a congressional apology for abuse of civil liberties, and the establishment of an educational foundation for Japanese American youth. In 1988, President Ronald Reagan signed the Civil Liberties Act of 1988, which provided a $20,000 reparation for those interned. (The Civil Liberties Act of 1988 [Restitution for World War II Internment of Japanese-Americans and Aleuts]. Pub. L. 100-383; 102 Stat. 903. 10 Aug. 1988.)

The purposes of this Act are to—

(1) acknowledge the fundamental injustice of the evacuation, relocation, and internment of United States citizens and permanent resident aliens of Japanese ancestry during World War II;

(2) apologize on behalf of the people of the United States for the evacuation, relocation, and internment of such citizens and permanent resident aliens;

(3) provide for a public education fund to finance efforts to inform the public about the internment of such individuals so as to prevent the recurrence of any similar event;

(4) make restitution to those individuals of Japanese ancestry who were interned;

(5) make restitution to Aleut residents of the Pribilof Islands and the Aleutian Islands west of Unimak Island, in settlement of United States obligations in equity and at law, for—

    (A) injustices suffered and unreasonable hardships endured while those Aleut residents were under United States control during World War II;

    (B) personal property taken or destroyed by United States forces during World War II;

      (C) community property, including community church property, taken or destroyed by United States forces during World War II; and

      (D) traditional village lands on Attu Island not rehabilitated after World War II for Aleut occupation or other productive use;

  (6) discourage the occurrence of similar injustices and violations of civil liberties in the future; and

  (7) make more credible and sincere any declaration of concern by the United States over violations of human rights committed by other nations.

(a) With Regard to Individuals of Japanese Ancestry

The Congress recognizes that, as described by the Commission on Wartime Relocation and Internment of Civilians, a grave injustice was done to both citizens and permanent resident aliens of Japanese ancestry by the evacuation, relocation, and internment of civilians during World War II. As the Commission documents, these actions were carried out without adequate security reasons and without any acts of espionage or sabotage documented by the Commission, and were motivated largely by racial prejudice, wartime hysteria, and a failure of political leadership. The excluded individuals of Japanese ancestry suffered enormous damages, both material and intangible, and there were incalculable losses in education and job training, all of which resulted in significant human suffering for which appropriate compensation has not been made. For these fundamental violations of the basic civil liberties and constitutional rights of these individuals of Japanese ancestry, the Congress apologizes on behalf of the Nation.

(b) With Respect to the Aleuts

The Congress recognizes that, as described by the Commission on Wartime Relocation and Internment of Civilians, the Aleut civilian residents of the Pribilof Islands and the Aleutian Islands west of Unimak Island were relocated during World War II to temporary camps in isolated regions of southeast Alaska where they remained, under United States control and in the care of the United States, until long after any potential danger to their home villages had passed. The United States failed to provide reasonable care for the Aleuts, and this resulted in widespread illness, disease, and death among the residents of the camps; and the United States further failed to protect Aleut personal and community property while such property was in its possession or under its control. The United States has not compensated the Aleuts adequately for the conversion or destruction of personal property, and the conversion or destruction of community property caused by the United States military occupation of Aleut villages during World War II. There is no remedy for injustices suffered by the Aleuts during World War II except an Act of Congress providing appropriate compensation for those losses which are attributable to the conduct of United States forces and other officials and employees of the United States. . . .

(a) Review of Convictions

The Attorney General is requested to review any case in which an individual living on the date of the enactment of this Act [Aug. 10, 1988] was, while a United States citizen or permanent resident alien of Japanese ancestry, convicted of a violation of—

(1) Executive Order Numbered 9066, dated February 19, 1942;

(2) the Act entitled "An Act to provide a penalty for violation of restrictions or orders with respect to persons entering, remaining in, leaving, or committing any act in military areas or zones," approved March 21, 1942 (56 Stat. 173); or

(3) any other Executive order, Presidential proclamation, law of the United States, directive of the Armed Forces of the United States, or other action taken by or on behalf of the United States or its agents, representatives, officers, or employees, respecting the evacuation, relocation, or internment of individuals solely on the basis of Japanese ancestry;

on account of the refusal by such individual, during the evacuation, relocation, and internment period, to accept treatment which discriminated against the individual on the basis of the individual's Japanese ancestry.

(b) Recommendations for Pardons

Based upon any review under subsection (a), the Attorney General is requested to recommend to the President for pardon consideration those convictions which the Attorney General considers appropriate.

(c) Action by the President

In consideration of the statement of the Congress set forth in section 2(a), the President is requested to offer pardons to any individuals recommended by the Attorney General under subsection (b). . . .

(a) Location and Payment of Eligible Individuals
(1) IN GENERAL

Subject to paragraph (7), the Attorney General shall, subject to the availability of funds appropriated to the Fund for such purpose, pay out of the Fund to each eligible individual the sum of $20,000, unless such individual refuses, in the manner described in paragraph (5), to accept the payment.

(2) LOCATION OF ELIGIBLE INDIVIDUALS

The Attorney General shall identify and locate, without requiring any application for payment and using records already in the possession of the United States Government, each eligible individual. The Attorney General should use funds and resources available to the Attorney General, including those described in subsection (c), to attempt to complete such identification and location within 12 months after the date of the enactment of this Act [Aug. 10, 1988]. Any eligible individual may notify the Attorney General that such individual is an eligible individual, and may provide documentation therefor. The Attorney General shall designate an officer or employee to whom such notification and documentation may be sent, shall maintain a list of all individuals who submit such notification and documentation, and shall, subject to the availability of funds appropriated for such purpose, encourage, through a public awareness campaign, each eligible individual to submit his or her current address to such officer or employee. To the extent that resources referred to in the second sentence of this paragraph are not sufficient to complete the identification and location of all eligible individuals, there are authorized to be appropriated such sums as may be necessary for such purpose. In any case, the identification and location of all eligible individuals shall be completed within 12 months after the appropriation of funds under the preceding sentence. Failure to be identified and located by the end of the 12-month period specified in the preceding sentence shall not preclude an eligible individual from receiving payment under this section.

(3) BENEFIT OF THE DOUBT

When, after consideration of all evidence and relevant material for determining whether an individual is an eligible individual, there is an approximate balance of positive and negative evidence regarding the merits of an issue material to the determination of eligibility, the benefit of the doubt in resolving each such issue shall be given to such individual.

(4) NOTICE FROM THE ATTORNEY GENERAL

The Attorney General shall, when funds are appropriated to the Fund for payments to an eligible individual under this section, notify that eligible individual in writing of his or her eligibility for payment under this section. Such notice shall inform the eligible individual that—

- (A) acceptance of payment under this section shall be in full satisfaction of all claims against the United States arising out of acts described in section 108(2)(B), and
- (B) each eligible individual who does not refuse, in the manner described in paragraph (5), to accept payment under this section within 18 months after receiving such written notice shall be deemed to have accepted payment for purposes of paragraph (6).

(5) EFFECT OF REFUSAL TO ACCEPT PAYMENT

If an eligible individual refuses, in a written document filed with the Attorney General, to accept any payment under this section, the amount of such payment shall remain in the Fund and no payment may be made under this section to such individual at any time after such refusal.

(6) PAYMENT IN FULL SETTLEMENT OF CLAIMS AGAINST THE UNITED STATES

The acceptance of payment by an eligible individual under this section shall be in full satisfaction of all claims against the United States arising out of acts described in section 108(2)(B). This paragraph shall apply to any eligible individual who does not refuse, in the manner described in paragraph (5), to accept payment under this section within 18 months after receiving the notification from the Attorney General referred to in paragraph (4).

(7) EXCLUSION OF CERTAIN INDIVIDUALS

No payment may be made under this section to any individual who, after September 1, 1987, accepts payment pursuant to an award of a final judgment or a settlement on a claim against the United States for acts described in section 108(2)(B), or to any surviving spouse, child, or parent of such individual to whom paragraph (8) applies.

Japanese Latin Americans to Receive Compensation for Internment During World War II
Department of Justice

As the following news release from the Department of Justice underscores, the internment of people of Japanese descent during World War II was by no means limited to the United States; Japanese Canadians and Japanese Latin Americans were also incarcerated. An estimated twenty-two hundred Japanese Latin Americans were interned in New Mexico and Texas; the majority came from Peru, but others hailed from Bolivia, Colombia, Costa Rica, Cuba, Ecuador, El Salvador, Mexico, Nicaragua, Panama, and Venezuela. (United States Department of Justice. "Japanese Latin Americans to Receive Compensation for Internment During World War II." Washington, DC: GPO, 12 June 1998.)

WASHINGTON, D.C.—Nearly 600 Japanese Latin Americans who were interned during World War II will each be able to receive $5,000 and an apology under an agreement reached today with the Justice Department.

Today's agreement resolves a 1996 civil suit filed by five Japanese Latin Americans who were deported from their homes in Latin America during World War II and held in internment camps in the United States. The five, who had been denied redress under the Civil Liberties Act of 1988, claimed that they deserved to be compensated along with Japanese American internees during the war.

"This was a tragic chapter in the history of our nation," said Attorney General Janet Reno. "It's time to right this wrong and close the book."

The Civil Liberties Act, which was signed into law on August 10, 1988, acknowledges, apologizes, and makes restitution for the fundamental injustice of the evacuation, relocation and internment of Japanese Americans during World War II.

Under the law, claimants can receive compensation if they were alive at the time of the signing of the law, were a U.S. citizen or permanent resident alien during internment, and are a person of Japanese ancestry or the spouse or parent of a person of Japanese ancestry.

The Justice Department's Office of Redress Administration (ORA) is charged with administering the 10-year program which ends on August 10, 1998.

During the war, Latin American nations deported more than 2,000 of their citizens or residents of Japanese ancestry to the United States to be held in internment camps. Over the past eight years, ORA denied the claims of many of these internees because they were not U.S. citizens or permanent resident aliens during their internment, as the law requires. After ORA's rulings, the five individuals filed suit on behalf of all Japanese Latin Americans who were interned under similar circumstances.

Under today's settlement, these internees will each receive $5,000, to the extent funds are available, as well as an apology.

To date, ORA has received approximately 600 claims from Japanese Latin Americans who have been denied redress under the Act. The plaintiffs estimated that more than 2,000 Japanese Latin Americans were interned during the war, but that only 1,300 may still be living.

The program has paid out nearly $1.65 billion in reparations to 81,664 eligible claimants. More than $11 million now remains in the redress fund.

"Time is running out," said Acting Assistant Attorney General for Civil Rights Bill Lann Lee. "I urge anyone who may be eligible to come forward soon."

In February, Reno announced that six months remained in the redress program and urged any potential claimant to come forward.

Since her announcement nearly 400 claimants have been compensated.

"We will work hard to reach any Japanese Latin American who may be eligible under this settlement," said DeDe Greene, ORA Administrator. "As long as there's time, we will keep searching for claimants."

Persons who may be eligible for payments under this settlement but who have not yet come forward will need to postmark their claims by August 10, 1998. Claims must be received by September 4."

U.A.W. Says, "If You Sell in America, Build in America" (1981)

In the early 1980s, the U.S. auto industry suffered enormous setbacks due to the 1979 OPEC (Organization of the Petroleum Exporting Countries) oil crisis and experienced increased competition from automakers overseas, particularly those in Japan. Detroit, known as the Motor City, was especially hit: in the early 1980s, unemployment had risen to epic proportions, contributing to a dramatic increase in anti-Japanese and anti–Asian American sentiment. Such "Japan-bashing," linked to a trade war between the United States and Japan, is evident in the accompanying photograph, which shows an anti–foreign-made product rally that took place on March 3, 1981 (fig. 3.13).

Figure 3.13 Pictured are members of the United Automobile Workers Local 588 (of the Ford Motor Company) bashing a 1975 Toyota Corolla with sledgehammers and bars. AP Photo/Str. Reprinted with permission from the Associated Press.

The Wheel of Justice

THE KILLING OF VINCENT CHIN AND
THE DEATH OF THE MOTOR CITY

Frank H. Wu

On June 23, 1982, Vincent Chin (a Chinese American) died of injuries he had incurred four days before when he was assaulted by two out-of-work Detroit autoworkers: Ronald Ebens and his stepson, Michael Nitz. Chin was celebrating his upcoming wedding at a local adult entertainment establishment; Ebens and Nitz allegedly mistook Chin for Japanese and blamed him for the fact that they were unemployed. Chin eventually left the establishment; Ebens and Nitz followed him to a fast food restaurant and beat him with a baseball bat in the parking lot. The two men were originally charged with second-degree murder, but this charge was subsequently reduced to manslaughter. Both were fined but given no jail time. Chin's mother, Lily Chin, appealed for justice on the national stage, and the crime is credited with reinvigorating the Asian American movement. Frank H. Wu's essay, written for this anthology, recalls the case and its aftermath.

Wu served on the faculty of Howard University Law School for a decade and as dean of Wayne State University Law School in Detroit before being named in 2009 as the chancellor and dean of the University of California Hastings, College of the Law. He is the author of Yellow: Race in America Beyond Black and White *(2001). (Research associate Chelsea Zuzindlak helped with sources. An earlier version of this essay appeared under the title "Embracing Mistaken Identity: How the Vincent Chin Case Unified Asian Americans," in* Asian American Policy Review, *2010, Harvard Kennedy School of Government.)*

What Is Known

This much is certain.

On June 19, 1982, in Detroit, Michigan, an individual named Vincent Chin—twenty-seven years old, of Chinese ancestry, an American citizen, from a working-class background, engaged to be married the following week—went out with a few friends for a bachelor's party to celebrate his upcoming wedding. At a strip club, Chin and his pals encountered two other gentlemen, Ronald Ebens and Michael Nitz, father and stepson, similarly out enjoying the evening.

There was an altercation that would have continued in the parking lot but for Mr. Ebens retrieving a baseball bat from his automobile. Upon seeing the weapon, Chin did what any reasonable person would do if an armed, angry, intoxicated man were charging toward him; he ran to avoid the assailant.

After a spell, another confrontation between these parties came about. The sun had set over Woodward Avenue, the major thoroughfare of the Motor City, when these strangers met again.

And this is what went down: Mr. Ebens swinging the baseball bat, Mr. Nitz having pushed down Chin, the bridegroom ended up with his head literally cracked open. Blood, spinal fluid, and cerebral matter pooling on the pavement under his body, he collapsed into a coma.

He uttered the last words, "It's not fair."

Chin lingered for four days before he expired, four being an inauspicious number in Chinese culture because it is a homonym for "death." He had never regained consciousness.

The emergency medical technician who had been the first responder on the scene had predicted as much. Nobody recovers from wounds such as that.

The guests who would have attended his wedding went to his funeral instead.

Later. In state court, Mr. Ebens and Mr. Nitz faced criminal charges. Represented by experienced legal counsel, sobered up, dressed in business suits, they agreed to a plea bargain.

They would have been foolish otherwise. Witnesses were abundant. An off-duty police officer had had to pull his sidearm to enforce his order that Mr. Ebens drop the baseball bat. They did not deny their actions.

At the hearing, the prosecutors failed to show up. Detroit was the murder capital of the era. The docket was too crowded to bother with the cases that had been settled.

The judge, the Honorable Charles Kaufman, imposed on each of the men the sentence of probation and a $3000 fine, plus court costs. This decision would come to summarize his career. He subsequently explained that Asian Americans might well be grateful to him for providing the catalyst for their unity.

What Is Not Known

Everything else is in doubt.

Eventually there would transpire two federal prosecutions, two civil lawsuits, a national protest movement—more attention than had ever been paid by the body politic to any single incident involving an Asian American.

According to those who were there, Messrs. Ebens and Nitz had used racial slurs to refer to Chin inside the strip club; they had suggested pursuing one of Chin's Asian American friends if they weren't able to catch Chin, once they were outside; then they had offered a bystander twenty dollars to help them find "the Chinaman," as they drove around.

Among the barrage of fighting words inside the strip club, they ultimately had said, "It's because of you little motherfuckers, we're out of work."

That coded comment was made at a time when the nation was experiencing double-digit unemployment and matching high inflation. It was all the worse in a place that had prospered because of "the Big Four"—Ford, General Motors, Chrysler, and AMC—the domestic automobile manufacturers, until imported cars became popular. Japan was feared as the Land of the Rising Sun taking economic vengeance for its World War II defeat. American iron, the mighty V-8 engine, suddenly and inexplicably could not hold its own in the market against the ugly, puny, cheap but efficient products with names that sounded so comically foreign: Honda and Subaru.

To reiterate: "It's because of you little motherfuckers, we're out of work."

To Messrs. Ebens and Nitz, the implication was, Chin stood for Tokyo and Toyota.

The effort to discredit the woman who overheard the interjection is sleazy to the edge of contemptible. She is said to have come to the courthouse for the trial *sans* panties.

The abiding local narrative, undisturbed by the truth, was that Detroit faced the beginning of the end in 1967, on the occasion of the riots. The flickering images of armored personnel carriers patrolling the curfew, the burning businesses, and the looting, transfixed viewers of black and white televisions. What happened there prefigured what would ensue elsewhere in the long, hot summer of 1968 when MLK and RFK were assassinated in turn.

The data show that the downfall began much earlier. As soon as the highways crossed Eight Mile Road, which separated the city from the suburbs, middle-class families were able to move to expansive lots on what had been cornfields. The oil embargo of 1973, and the ensuing energy crisis, accelerated the demise. Gasoline had never been free, but it had flowed freely. An American land yacht might attain miles per gallon in the single digits if anyone cared to calculate "mpg," compared to the "Jap crap" that would travel three times farther on a full tank and was advertised as capable of doing so.

The locale that introduced Chin to Messrs. Ebens and Nitz was Highland Park, an especially seedy neighborhood, a separate municipality contained inside Detroit proper. The Fancy Pants Lounge was topless and bottomless, suspected by law enforcement as a front for prostitution. The abandoned structures nearby would not have been anticipated in contemporary America, and the scale of devastation was not manifested even where there had been natural disaster. Hence the residents of East Detroit, where Mr. Ebens was domiciled, elected to change their town's name to "Eastgate," the better to disown the adjoining city.

Autoworkers were the epitome of the blue-collar middle class until then. Henry Ford had not invented the assembly line, nor the automobile, but he perfected the mass manufacturing of what had been a rich man's toy, as the twentieth century opened. His offer of $5 per day to any man who would endure the exertion of his factories transformed the economy. A person without a high school diploma could earn enough to purchase the very automobile he had had a hand in constructing, buy a fine home within a subdivision of Macomb County or Downriver, even a modest hunting cabin up north—all before retiring at under fifty years of age, on a pension no less.

The loss of such opportunities leads to communal despair. The 24/7 cycle of shifts could be interrupted by layoffs, but those pauses were not supposed to be permanent. Loyal Americans were obliged to "Buy American." When families turned their backs on the Ford Pinto, with its exploding gas tank of cost-benefit analysis disgrace, and the Chevy Vega, reputed to commence rusting before it was even sold, they had lost faith.

Asian Americans wore the face of the enemy.

What Cannot Be Known

Whether it was a bar brawl, a hate crime, or perhaps both, the context, the causes, the consequences of the Vincent Chin case have been the center of controversy without ceasing. Throughout, Messrs. Ebens and Nitz insisted under oath that they were no bigots. Without wavering, they reported that Chin had decided to accost them for no discernible purpose, coming over to "sucker punch" Mr. Ebens, whereupon the older man "just snapped."

By their understanding, the community had drummed up the accusation of "racism" and thereby wronged them. Mr. Ebens was terminated from his job as a plant foreman. He filed suit, alleging he had been discriminated against and denied due process. His complaint was dismissed. Just the same, his attitude was that of the aggrieved.

It had been a fight. Everyone was sorry about the outcome.

The Double Jeopardy Clause of the Constitution did not prevent the federal government from coming in. Its terms preclude two prosecutions by the same government for the same crime. The federal government is reluctant to intervene, and it must make it over a high bar: to prove a homicide was a hate crime necessitates proof of not only the *actus rea* (the act) but also the *mens rea* (the motive).

The first federal jury convicted Mr. Ebens and acquitted Mr. Nitz. The appeals court, rejecting the averment that "Orientals" were not protected by civil rights statutes, nonetheless reversed the judgment.

The trial judge, the Honorable Anna Diggs Taylor, admonished for the publicity that had made it unfair for the defendants, switched the venue to Cincinnati, Ohio. The Queen City, with Southern sensibilities and scant contact with automobile manufacturing, brought forth a jury pool in which hardly anyone was even acquainted with an Asian American.

The second jury acquitted Mr. Ebens, too.

The Asian American movement began with the Vincent Chin case.

To be sure, Asian Americans existed before then. They were politically active. It was not until the Chin case, however, that they formed "the Asian American movement" as such.

Asian immigrants had begun coming to the United States in meaningful numbers in the 1830s. They and their native-born descendants participated in public life to an extent beyond what stereotypical images would allow. They organized themselves into civic associations, agitated for their rights, started businesses, supported politicians. For the male workers who formed the bulk of the new arrivals, racial restrictions made it difficult to bring their wives or find mates across the color line. Despite such formal barriers, they founded families and formed communities.

For 150 years when Asian Americans described themselves, they did not use the title "Asian American." Scholar Yuji Ichioka invented the term in epochal 1968.

No, these "strangers from a different shore," as characterized by the leading history, preferred to identify themselves by what would come to be reduced to ethnicity, or even more precisely culture, clan, language, province, family. They were as distinct from each other as they were separate from whites and blacks, the divisions as obvious to them as they were obscure to outsiders: Chinese from Japanese, and vice versa; among the Chinese, the Mandarin-speaking middle-class professionals who arrived as students on scholarships from the Cantonese-speaking lower-class laborers who had opened restaurants and operated laundries in the inner city.

Some members of these groups in America remained active in what has been termed "homeland politics." The Korean independence movement of 1919 relied on leaders who had nurtured blood ties to America and a trans-Pacific network of support. At other times they disassociated themselves from one another. During World War II, Chinese Americans explained who they were, in an effort to distinguish themselves as the good Asians compared with the Japanese (and tacitly the Japanese Americans) who were the bad Asians. Overseas conflicts were grounds to distance one subgroup from other subgroups, whether it was Communism versus Nationalism as to the China-Taiwan Straits or the partitioning of the Indian subcontinent between Hindus and Muslims.

Nor were Asian Americans unique. European immigrants constituted discrete races in the scientific typology of humankind—the "Irish race" and so on—prior to their assimilation into and enjoyment of the benefits of the classification of white. Even the cynical would be incredulous about the naked chauvinism. There was a time, though, when experts spoke without embarrassment about hierarchies that were biological and immutable, that arrayed people as phrenology would have, by physiognomic particularities of the skull and the brow.

Asian Americans were invisible as Asian Americans. They were a minority among minorities.

There were Asians, foreign Asians, who were prominent as adversaries.

Movies reflected the recurring theme of Asian treachery. The Japanese Imperial Navy sailed across the Pacific Ocean to launch the sneak attack on Pearl Harbor, as seen in *Tora! Tora! Tora!* The North Koreans backed by the Red Chinese "brainwashed" American servicemen such as Frank Sinatra, as seen in *The Manchurian Candidate*. The Viet Cong destroyed the psyche of even those who survived guerilla combat, as seen in *The Deer Hunter* and *Apocalypse Now*.

The Chin case changed all that. Its violence highlighted the importance of both aspects of "Asian American" as a self-proclaimed name: it was crucial to be enveloped by the status of a "real American," for protection if no other rationale, as well as to build bridges to other Asians, even if one's grandparents may have been at war with their grandparents.

Asian Americans had to assert themselves. It was not enough to succeed in school and at work. As might be expected of any group extolled for its overachievement in a society that favors the underdog, the very image of Asian Americans doing well as a collective could be the undoing of an individual.

Before the Chin case, it must be acknowledged, there had been efforts to bring together Asian Americans. The Yellow Power movement flourished briefly in the 1960s, originating in California. Filipino Americans, Chinese Americans, and Japanese Americans, primarily young people, copied the example of Black Power radicalism. A few Nisei (second-generation Japanese Americans) even became militants, actually joining the Black Panthers and brandishing firearms. They did not want to forget the internment camps, nor to be deceived that the mass incarceration had been a vacation in the outdoors.

Activists could boast of underground magazines, folk music, and authentic social gatherings, but for all that their activities were circumscribed by duration, geography, and generation. Theirs was among the transitory phenomena of the Summer of Love, centered on San Francisco, and it generated slight enthusiasm among the elders. These predecessors deserve respect; they were vital. They created the conditions that were needed.

What made the Chin case so significant is that the legal proceedings took so many years, allowing the protest effort to expand from its Midwestern roots to the East Coast and West Coast, enlisting young and old, American and immigrant. Liza Chan, Roland Hwang, Jimmy Shimoura, and Helen Zia devoted themselves to the endeavor.

The Chin case was so compelling it overcame other considerations. It was irrelevant if one was a "banana," yellow on the outside, white on the inside, in the pejorative phrase; if one had ever marched before; or if one had spurned civil rights as a black issue. Immigrant engineers who were conservative in their lifestyles, comfortable in the suburbs, and ambitious for their children, who spoke with accents and apart from that counseled shying away from controversy, were invested in the Chin case, even if they had never heard of the Yellow Power movement or would have found it anathema.

The Vincent Chin case was imperative to average Asian Americans because it was exemplary, as much as they might resist its definitive quality. The killing of Chin displayed all of the characteristics of hostility toward Asian Americans, assuredly if the facts put forth by the protest and the prosecution were given credence, and even to an extent on the hypothesis of the defense. There have been casualties beyond Chin, who bear a family resemblance, selected by belligerents who recalled the Vietnam War and so on.

Most importantly, the killing of Chin was mistaken identity twice over. Chin was singled out not as who he understood himself to be, but rather as a representative of Asia—possessing yellow skin, coarse black hair, slanted eyes. The assault appeared to have been incited by the association of an American citizen with another sovereignty, solely on the basis of race. Chin had been adopted at a young age by a Chinese-American World War II veteran father and a Chinese immigrant mother unable to bear children, and none of them had any relationship with Japan whatsoever. The targeting also seemed to confirm the cliché "you all look alike" that rendered the Far East the source of a faceless horde. Chin was of Chinese descent, but he was assumed to be of Japanese lineage.

The campaign for justice also attracted the sympathy of many others. The Detroit City Council, the city's chapter of the NAACP (National Association for the Advancement of Colored People), Christian, Jewish, and labor groups, for example, endorsed the cause.

Whites and blacks who had not hitherto been aware of Asian Americans recognized the universal nature of the appeals made by Chin's grieving mother. Crying, scarcely able to control her lamentations, she admitted candidly she wished she could kill her son's killers as she sought an explanation of how they could escape punishment.

The Chin case, especially within the context of the severe recession of the early 1980s and its effect on Detroit as the Motor City identified with automobile manufacturing, showed the enthralling effects of scapegoating. The rage directed toward "little yellow men," in the phrase of Congressman John Dingell, who represented part of the region over a record tenure, held them responsible for the genuine concerns about plant closures and downward mobility.

Asians were blamed for a complex of problems. Corporate leadership had refused to consider fuel-efficient cars. Consumer habits took for granted the abundance of imported oil. The absence of universal health care imposed the insurance costs on employers. The populace was uninterested in diversifying the economic base of an industrial metropolis. Cultural expectations about wages could not be sustained in the face of global competition.

Asians—by extension, Asian Americans—were resented, because, it was believed, even as everyone else suffered, *those people* persisted in doing well. The bulk of Asian Americans who called Detroit their home were exactly like their co-workers, dependent on the automobile industry for their livelihoods. If they were to disappear overnight, much of the research and development capability of their employers would be lost.

The legal proceedings in the Chin case revealed how difficult it was for Asian Americans to be taken seriously, even in what was among the more clear cases, that they were subject to genuine racial discrimination. Asian Americans did not strike others as the victims of bigotry. They had been ruled inherently not credible by the courts in the nineteenth century and deemed untrustworthy under the Exclusion Acts; their testimony had to be corroborated by white witnesses.

The state court proceedings demonstrated that the government would not respect Asian Americans. The federal court proceedings showed that even the admission by the perpetrators that they had killed Chin was insufficient to substantiate that any offense had been committed. The result left many Asian Americans with the sense that if even someone who had been brutally bludgeoned to death with a baseball bat, to the accompaniment of plain slurs, could be deemed to not have had his civil rights violated, then it was impossible in practice for an Asian American to prevail under the law. Observers did not need to be Asian to be shocked.

Race begets logical error. To acquiesce to the proposition that Messrs. Ebens and Nitz were not hardcore bigots, aiming to put to death anyone Asian that night, is not to pronounce that they were innocent. They killed. There may be reasonable doubt about whether race played a role, but that is not to say that it is beyond reasonable doubt that race played no role.

People have said, "Wait, an American would not be accepted as an equal in Asia." One could be skeptical about that contention empirically, given how Americans have been received as superiors rather than inferiors.

Be that as it may, the appropriate analogy between how an American of European descent is treated in Asia is how an American of Asian descent is treated in Europe. The alternative involves an implicit commitment to an America delimited by a racial character, that a (white) American would not be treated well in an Asian nation, so an (Asian) American should not count on any better in a (white?) nation. Asian Americans touring Europe probably are taken to be Americans in any event, at least as soon as they open their mouths or move about occupying the space that Americans demand around themselves.

Other Americans were not regarded in an equivalent manner. Lee Iacocca was a high-profile businessman-pundit. The straight-talking, tough, cigar-smoking, confidant chairman of Chrysler was prideful about ethnicity: he was Italian in descent. His memoirs mentioned his youthful embarrassment of explaining what pizza was, when it was an ethnic dish not yet ubiquitous through speedy delivery. Notwithstanding his affiliation of his corporation with his heritage (the coupe designed by Maserati, he announced, would be the prettiest Italian to come to America since his mother), it would be laughable if a journalist were to take him to task over Mussolini and Fascism or the Mafia and corruption. He was not at fault, and he could revel in Italian nationality without compromising his American citizenship.

Finally, the Chin case exposed the futility of assimilation. Asian Americans did not find refuge by downplaying their roots. The Japanese American Citizens League (JACL), established long before the Day of Infamy that brought America into World War II, expressed in its creed a confidence in the fair play of baseball. Chinese Americans in the American armed forces then were patriots who had an additional inducement to serve the United States, liberating China from Japan. Japanese American families looked forward to their Independence Day picnic, as Chinese American families yearned for their gatherings on Belle Isle.

The defense lawyers did not comprehend the irony when they noted that Chin was not so different from Messrs. Ebens and Nitz. After all, they were blue-collar men fond of taking a drink at strip clubs, they were full of testosterone, and they did not lack tempers. The advocates were proud to have scored a point. They were not incorrect.

The Chinese colloquialism "eating bitterness" is apt. Chin was very much like Messrs. Ebens and Nitz. Except for race. And in the end that was all that counted.

What Is Known by Some

The cultural response to the Vincent Chin case gives solace. It has passed into myth among Asian Americans and Detroiters. The smiling Chin, innocent in his high school photograph, became an iconic image through its replication on homemade flyers and in the mainstream media alike.

"Remember Vincent Chin" is a rallying cry and an allusion to him is a synecdoche for prejudice toward Asian Americans in all its forms. American Citizens for Justice (ACJ), the advocacy group set up to advance the Chin cause, is memorialized in a series of pictures by Corky Lee, the "official" photographer of Asian America. They pledged: signs and leaflets had to be in English only; nothing in Chinese. Lee has captured them with their banner unfurled: "It's Not Fair!" Nobody had seen Asian Americans converge on downtown, unless they were peddling eggrolls at the Far East Festival.

There are two documentary movies about Chin. *Who Killed Vincent Chin?* was nominated for an Academy Award and has turned into the most widely used text in Asian American Studies courses, likely watched by every student enrolled in such a class. *Vincent Who?* was produced by the scion of a Detroit Chinatown restaurant family intent on transmitting the story to the next generation.

An episode of the "Twilight Zone" television series, entitled "Wong's Lost and Found Emporium," based on a science fiction vignette by William F. Wu, was inspired by the case. A play, *Carry the Tiger to the Mountain,* has been staged. A children's book, *A Day for Vincent Chin and Me,* has been published.

Paintings commemorate Chin, one a pop art rendering by Roger Shimomura, another a cityscape by Evri Kwong. Two murals in Detroit exist, though one has been defaced by vandalism.

Chin lurks as a cameo, popping up in a rap at the opening of the 2007 comedy movie *Ping Pong Playa.*

A historical marker in Ferndale was erected in 2010 as a monument to Chin—he had worked nearby.

Conferences and a pilgrimage to the gravesite are held on the anniversaries of the crime. Through the Internet, T-shirts are available, with simple white lettering against a black background, "V. Chin, 1955–1982."

What Is Known to Me

I know I risk confusing my own coming of age with history. I grew up in Detroit, and I was there in 1982. My father was an engineer at Ford Motor Company ("Ford's," as it was known) for virtually his whole career. He designed brakes.

I remember the place and the time that are integral to this account, and I doubt I could forget either. Although I did not know Vincent Chin, I can identify with him. At a visceral level, I feel as if he could be my cousin—or, for that matter, even me, with the circumstances altered imperceptibly.

The Vincent Chin case changed my life. As a child, like almost all children, I hoped merely to be normal. I would have wanted to discuss neither race nor civil rights, and I would have studiously steered clear of the host of issues that any invocation of race requires us to own up to. I wanted to ride my bicycle around the block with my friends, all of whom, perforce, were white, and, when I was an adolescent, hang out at video game arcades with them.

The details that make up the Vincent Chin case made me realize that the childhood cruelties I experienced, the teasing and the taunting on the playground with the same epithets Chin heard, could and should not be remedied by or erased with the teacher's intonation to retort that "sticks and stones can break my bones but words can never hurt me."

Kids suffer all sorts of bodily harm—falling off swing sets, breaking bones, enduring high fevers—and in general they heal just fine, even if an adult could not do the likewise. Against all outward appearances, youngsters experience psychological trauma that may have been relegated to the trivial and momentary, beneath notice much less remarked upon, but that turns out in fact to be much more severe and lasting.

The risk of physical attack arises from verbal abuse. A beating emanates from slurs often enough. The transgression differs in degree but not in kind. Race is complex.

Yet nobody desires to declare himself or herself a victim either. To be pitied is to be powerless. It remains by no means easy for Asian immigrants and their American-born progeny, most of whom tried to identify with the dominant majority and few of whom aspired to stand up and speak out, to organize themselves into a cause. The protest in this situation had never been seen before by Asian Americans, any more than it had by others. We hesitated then and do still, from causes internal as well as external, the traditions of cultures that did not embrace democracy and the newcomer's striving to meet basic material needs, coupled with the heckler's jeer that we go back to where we came from.

The Vincent Chin case has never come to closure. That has always been why the dead haunt the living. A ghost enjoys no repose. At least we can honor in our memory what is true and right.

Korean American Businessman Recalls L.A. Riots

Theresa Walker

On March 3, 1991, Rodney King, an African American, was stopped by police following a high-speed car chase through a Los Angeles suburb. It seemed routine, but then five police officers surrounded King and began striking him repeatedly. George Holliday, a private citizen, videotaped the assault, which lasted at least ten minutes. Four of the officers involved in the attack were charged with assault with a deadly weapon and use of excessive force; on April 29, 1992, they were each acquitted of these charges. Soon after, people gathered to protest the verdict; events quickly turned to widespread looting, assault, and arson. Korean shop owners and Korean Americans were particularly targeted. What follows is a retrospective account of the uprisings on the twentieth anniversary of what Korean immigrants call Sa-I-Gu. *(Theresa Walker. "Korean American Businessman Recalls L.A. Riots."* Orange County Register, *29 Apr. 2012. Online at http:// www.ocregister.com/articles/cha-351233-says-angeles.html. Reprinted with permission from the* Orange County Register.*)*

LOS ANGELES—Inside the cavernous building with the grungy pink exterior, Ellis Yunseong Cha squints out through metal bars at the traffic zooming on Florence Avenue.

The cars are a blur, but Cha's memory of this place is clear.

Twenty years ago, he ran a furniture store in this building, in this South Los Angeles neighborhood, just 1.5 miles away from the flash point for one of the worst urban riots in U.S. history.

Not much has changed, he says. The city has put up some signs to designate the area a "Furniture and Decorative Arts District," but otherwise the neighborhood still bears the signs of economic struggle and the omni-present threat of crime.

Cha, 59, was luckier than many merchants. His furniture store, and the mattress factory he owned nearby, weren't touched during the days of violence that some prefer to call "civil unrest." In particular, he remem-bers a woman he called "Sister," a Korean immigrant like himself. Her hamburger stand, a couple of blocks from this building—a place he fre-quented regularly—was torched.

So, too, was his sense of place, and the sense of security he'd felt as an immigrant working to improve his economic lot in his adopted country.

"The Rodney King case, the riots, got me all mixed up," he says. "Where am I? What am I supposed to be?"

Cha, who lived in Anaheim at the time, soon sold his factory and leased out his store. Before 1992 ended, he bought ABC Liquor & Mini Mart in Orange across the street from the Crystal Cathedral.

He is still there.

Cha is reluctant to improve his Florence Avenue property. His ten-ant sublets the forlorn space for Victory Outreach church services and weddings. Sunday afternoons, he stages Lucha Libre wrestling matches, a reflection of the neighborhood's demographic shift from predominantly black to Hispanic.

Weeds push through cracks in sidewalks lined by a hodgepodge of small shops—beauty salons, used auto lots, dry cleaners, fried chicken and hamburger joints. In nearby neighborhoods, the homes are protected with bars on the windows and security doors.

"When I think about doing something, the riot is still here," Cha says, pointing to his head. "It's like building a castle in the sand—it can be blown away. Driving down the street, it doesn't look safe."

Cha instead found a way to reinvent himself and to start building the kind of community relationships that didn't exist in the world he fled.

That's what brought him back to South Los Angeles a few days before the 20th anniversary of what Korean immigrants refer to as "Sa-i-Gu," or 4-29.

A Fiery Fallout

Cha was in downtown Los Angeles on April 29, 1992, having a couple of beers with his lawyer to celebrate a victory in a lawsuit. At 3:15 p.m., the TV riveted his lawyer's attention.

A court clerk was reading the verdicts in the criminal trial of the one Hispanic and three white Los Angeles police officers charged with assault and use of excessive force in subduing black motorist Rodney G. King, an ex-con on parole who led California Highway Patrol officers on a high-speed chase in 1991.

"He was looking at the TV. 'Not guilty. Not guilty. Not guilty . . .' He said, 'Wow, there's going to be a riot.'"

Cha was puzzled. He had immigrated to the United States from Korea in 1973 at the age of 21, served in the Army and earned a master's degree from UC Berkeley. Still, he didn't understand the racial tensions surrounding the King case.

"I said, 'What are you talking about?'"

Cha left to check on his businesses and say hello to his friend at the hamburger shop. He saw nothing disquieting.

He was home with his wife and two children by the time overwhelmed Los Angeles Police Department officers responded to the first reports of looting and beer cans being thrown at Florence and Normandie.

Worried about filling customer orders, Cha went the next day to his mattress factory on Avalon Boulevard. His employees, about 15 Hispanic men who lived in the area, came to work. But trouble was brewing when Cha looked outside and saw a small crowd gathering, shouting and waving their fists.

"I thought, 'Oh, my God.' . . . I closed it up and got the hell out of there."

He stayed away for days, unsure what to do. "I always thought I could handle any situation. I was thinking of my safety first. Everything was burning."

Once it was safe to return, he found his friend's hamburger stand at Florence and Avalon completely destroyed. The kindhearted woman who ran it, a single mom struggling to raise four kids, was nice to her customers and always willing to listen to his troubles, Cha says.

"That really made me sad. Why burn it down? For what?"

He never saw or heard from her again. The corner lot sat empty for years. Now it is home to a Yoshinoya beef bowl restaurant, a Subway sandwich shop and a Boost Mobile store.

"It's better to be rebuilt," Cha says. The vacant lot, he added, reminded him of the riots "again and again and again."

"Can We All Get Along?"

Cha moved from Anaheim to Fullerton in 1995. Over the years, he's decided not to dwell on what's not coming back. He started thinking more along the lines of what a clearly shaken Rodney King asked the world at a news conference on the third day of the riot, the line about everybody getting along and "not making it horrible for the older people and the kids."

"Just working hard and pursuing a career is not everything," Cha says. "You have to participate, politically and in local activities."

Galvanized by the debate over the Coyote Hills development in Fullerton, Cha in 2004 became a member of the city's Redevelopment Design Review Committee. Before that, during the 10th anniversary of the L.A. riots, he'd served as president of the Korean American Grocers Association.

Cha says he heard plenty about confrontations between Korean liquor-store owners and their local communities, and attended some intercultural events with leaders of other organizations. Many, he says, didn't go beyond "boom, boom, take a picture and split."

Better, he decided, to foster ties through young people.

In 2005, Cha started the nonprofit Youth Empowerment Scholarship program in Fullerton to provide resources for playing soccer, a sport he has enjoyed since childhood. Cha worked with residents and local businesses to start a soccer league that he says now involves about 500 underprivileged children in the city's mostly Hispanic Richman Park neighborhood.

Last week, Cha returned to South Los Angeles to meet with several Korean-American retailers seeking his advice.

Over lunch at Kang Nam Restaurant in Koreatown, Cha tells them that if they start a new organization in the neighborhoods where their businesses are located, they need to nurture relationships with residents, police and local politicians.

One of the merchants, Sang Yoon Lee, runs Fiesta Rancho liquor store and mini market, not far from Cha's old furniture store. Lee and his wife had developed a good relationship before the riots with customers at a fast food stand they once owned. Their business was not harmed, but the violence scared away the Lees until about five years ago.

Since returning, they attend an annual gathering where local residents, business owners and police share food and talk.

"I still worry about (a riot) happening again," Lee says. "But the Police

Department, the neighbors, they already saw what happened after that. The most important thing is to communicate."

Cha heads home after the luncheon feeling more positive about the future of South Los Angeles.

"I want to help them," he says. "Little things like that kind of community relationship makes a big difference."

Battle Hymn of the Tiger Mother (Interview with Amy Chua)

In 2011, author, lawyer, and legal scholar Amy Chua published Battle Hymn of the Tiger Mother, *a provocative memoir that drew great media attention and generated considerable debate over parenting techniques and different cultural perspectives (particularly those involving Asians and Asian Americans). Michel Martin, host of National Public Radio's "Tell Me More," interviewed Chua in January 2011. On its website NPR introduced the interview: "Strict, uncompromising values and discipline are what makes children raised by Chinese parents successful. That's the message in a new parenting book by Yale Law Professor Amy Chua.* Battle Hymn of the Tiger Mother, *is based on Chua's personal experiences and has raised questions about whether the book reinforces stereotypes of the unsparing Asian parent." In addition to* Battle Hymn of the Tiger Mother, *Chua is the author of three other books:* World on Fire: How Exporting Free Market Democracy Breeds Ethnic Hatred and Global Instability *(2003),* Day of Empire: How Hyperpowers Rise to Global Dominance—and Why They Fail *(2007), and with Jed Rubenfeld* The Triple Package: How Three Unlikely Traits Explain the Rise and Fall of Cultural Groups in America *(2014). (© 2011. NPR News report "Battle Hymn of the Tiger Mother" was originally broadcast on NPR's* Tell Me More *on January 13, 2011, and is used with the permission of NPR. Any unauthorized duplication is strictly prohibited.)*

MICHEL MARTIN: And now a conversation about pressure, a very different kind of pressure: the pressure to perform. Earlier this week, we spoke to the secretary of Education Arne Duncan about efforts to reach agreement on a new version of the Bush administration's signature education initiative, No Child Left Behind. We talked about the perception that the U.S. is falling behind on many key international indicators of academic performance. And a lot of critics blame No Child Left Behind for squeezing the creativity out of education, for too much emphasis on rote learning, for making school all about tests, for amping up the pressure.

Today we have a very different conversation, a provocative one, that pressure is good, that demanding perfection is good, that nothing is fun until you're good at it, even if you have to take what other people say are extreme steps to get there.

Yale law professor Amy Chua calls it the Chinese parenting model. She's written a book about her adventures in parenting that's getting a lot of attention and some rave, very conflicted reviews. And she's with us now. Amy Chua, thanks so much for joining us.

AMY CHUA: Thanks so much for having me.

MARTIN: Now, let me just say up front, I think this book is very brave. I think you are very brave because you are opening the door to something that I think a lot of people talk about privately. But let me also say, I'm not going to ask you any tough questions that you have not already asked yourself.

CHUA: OK.

MARTIN: So with that being said, these are some of the things that you say you did: Threatened—*threatened*—to put your three-year-old out in the winter cold for being disobedient, rejecting your children's hand-drawn birthday cards because they were not thoughtful enough, not letting your kids have play dates or sleepovers, threatening to burn your older children's stuffed animals if she didn't improve on the piano, keeping your younger daughter from dinner, getting water, or going to the bathroom until she perfected a piano piece. Just give us the logic of all of these tough love measures.

CHUA: OK. Yeah. You know, all the examples are a little bit different. And some of them actually are not so tough, like the birthday card example. This story is when my kids were maybe four and seven, my husband had forgotten about my birthday and we went to a mediocre Italian restaurant and he said, OK, the girls have a surprise for their mom. And my little daughter

Lulu handed me a piece of paper folded in half with a smiley face on the front.

And I knew that she couldn't have taken more than three seconds to make this thing. And I said, you know, Lulu, this isn't good enough. I want something better than this. You know, when you have a birthday party, I take my whole salary and I hire magicians and I make the cakes and I buy party favors, and I deserve better than this. And people are saying, oh my gosh, did you damage her self-esteem?

I've talked to my daughters about this, and—they, well, first of all, they find it a little bit comical, but they also said, we felt much better after we made you better cards.

MARTIN: Part of your point here is that you say in the book that the Chinese model seems harsh to Westerners but your argument is that self-esteem comes from actually doing something. And that's part of the premise of the question here.

CHUA: I think you're right. I am critical. If you just tell your child, you're great, you're great, you're perfect, I'm not sure that's the best way, because eventually your child's going to have to go out into the real world. Suddenly they don't do well at school or they don't make the sports team, or God forbid, Westerners—I'm using these terms loosely, as you know—Westerners talk a lot about, I want my children to have choices and to pursue their passion.

Well, I used to resent my parents when I was little, but I feel like their being strict and having high expectations in me coupled with love, always love, that's what allowed me as an adult to have these choices. I felt like, oh my gosh, I get to pursue my passions now, right? When you can't get the job you want, I think that's when you really lose self-esteem.

MARTIN: Part of it is you're talking about raising your kids loosely the way you were raised. And you talk about how in the book when you were 14, your dad made you dig a swimming pool with a pick and a shovel and you emphasize it wasn't a really big swimming pool.

CHUA: Oh, it was so fun.

MARTIN: But you said that you enjoyed digging that. And you go on to say, look, I know people with kids who don't do chores, they can't even carry their own bags. I grew up working, I had a paper route. And that you feel that you got something from it and you wanted to carry forward what it is that you got from that.

CHUA: Yeah. I think it's also funny that some of the things that I'm talking about have been kind of labeled "Chinese" or "Western," because if you go back to Western parenting, 100 years ago or even 60 years ago, people did chores. People were proud of building things. And my favorite books are *Caddie Woodlawn* and *Johnny Tremain.* Boy, those families were a lot like mine, you know?

MARTIN: Well, you didn't apparently demand that your kids do hard physical labor, but one of the things you strongly demanded was that your kids master the piano and the violin. Your daughter Sophia ended up playing at Carnegie Hall. Your daughter Louisa, or Lulu, got into a very competitive program at Juilliard . . . . You made them practice for hours a day. Why was it so important to you that they master these instruments?

CHUA: You know why? I've seen this track where people will start with a hard instrument, and three months later maybe one will say, oh gosh, the violin was hard, I'm switching to the oboe. But three months later you'll discover the oboe's hard, too, so I'm going to the guitar. And sometimes I just worry that what we're calling, "it's my child's choices," is really just kind of letting them take the easy way out.

Once when my daughter Lulu did poorly on a math test, I think she was about 10, she came home and she said, "I hate math, I'm bad at math." Well, I went the quote-unquote "Chinese way," I made tons of practice tests. We drilled. I had a stopwatch. And guess what? A week later she did really well on her math test and she came home and she liked math. So I think in some ways a part of the parent's job is to help their child see what they're capable of.

MARTIN: . . . One of the interesting things about your story is that you're part of a mixed marriage, what we call a mixed marriage, and your husband is a white Jewish American. And one of the things I was curious about is you point out, he was raised in a very different way, but you both ended up in the same place. You're both professors of law at Yale. Both successful, doing very well. But you were adamant about—at least initially, about doing things your way.

And I was curious, the data would suggest that you had an equally good chance of showing up in the same location doing things very differently. He did have that kind of more relaxed upbringing where if he didn't want to do something, he didn't really have to do it.

CHUA: Yeah, you're right.

MARTIN: So why do you think you were so insistent on doing it your way?

CHUA: Well, my husband supported me always, but he was so crucial all along in bringing a kind of balance to the family, like insisting that we go to these dangerous water parks, while I was horrified. . . . He's a huge Redskins fan. Sports, apple picking, hiking—so, we did have a lot of fun.

MARTIN: Well, to that end, though, I want to go back to some of the comments you have gotten for your book. On the one hand there are people who are saying, right on, about time somebody sort of says "enough with the whole empty self-esteem." On the other hand, there are those who really think your behavior was abusive, and have said so.

CHUA: I completely agree, Michel, that some of the same things, some of the same practices in other contexts, where there's not a foundation of love and respect, could be abusive. But that is one thing I will not accept. My household was not abusive. You should meet my daughters. I'm just very proud. There are a few things I would change, and probably a little bit more choice, including choice of instruments.

MARTIN: You came to that realization in kind of a painful way. And I want to ask you to tell us that story.

CHUA: When Lulu was 13, she rebelled. She was studying with a Juilliard teacher. She was practicing three hours a day. We were driving into New York. There was no free time. She just started to hate the violin.

MARTIN: It came to a head in a confrontation, which was very painful for you both.

CHUA: Oh yeah. And painful, disrespectful, and she threw a glass on the floor. And, here I am, so proud of my kids and I just could not control her.

MARTIN: She threw a glass on the floor in public.

CHUA: Yes, absolutely. And it was kind of cold turkey. After years of fighting I said, "OK, let's stop the violin." And it was the best thing I could do. I just didn't want to lose my daughter, and I saw that this method I thought I was so confident about wasn't working here.

So I let her play tennis, which is what she wanted to do. Even though you can't start tennis at 13 and—but she loves it and she's applying the same values I instilled in her, which is whatever you choose, that you're applying dedication and tenacity, don't give up. You can do it. And I think she applies that to herself.

MARTIN: But to that end, though, you are tough in the book. And I do want to emphasize, again, as you have here, that it's funny. It's self-mocking in a lot of ways. It's meant to be tongue-in-cheek. I just want to clear that up for people who might not be clear on that. But you are pretty tough on these different sort of cultural styles.

And even though you did come to a place of feeling that maybe you could sort of bend on some things, you do ask some really tough questions that a lot of parents are asking themselves, which is kind of rigor and sticking to a plan and sticking to a program versus a lot of choice, a lot of freedom and a lot of creativity.

For example, here's one of the lines from the book a lot of people are passing around and repeating to each other. You talk about how your kids went to this progressive school where the educators made learning fun by making the parents do all the work, which I think a lot of parents found very funny. But what do you think is the broader lesson here?

CHUA: There are, of course, broader implications. To me, I'm still struggling. I don't have the answers. I think that's what's causing so much anxiety, in some ways why there's a furor, because it's tapping into something. We all want to do the right thing for our children. We all don't know what that is and we all— you know, you won't know until the future.

I guess where I'm coming at now is, it would be great if we could combine, let's just call it Western, but it's sort of this emphasis on independence and challenging authority with a little bit more rigor and self-discipline, instilling those things that will create people who can be self-reliant in the end.

MARTIN: You are, though, tough again on this whole question of the Western style as you experience it. You know, the West hasn't done too badly—the Declaration of Independence, the U.S. Constitution, Bill Gates. We have a lot of things to show for the Western style.

CHUA: I'm with you here. I want to turn it around on you. Because the last lines of my book, I'm on a rant. I say, I don't think the Founding Fathers had sleepovers and play dates. I think the Founding Fathers had Chinese values. And of course, my oldest, funny, smart daughter says, "Mommy, if the Founding Fathers had those values, then they're American values." And that's really one of the points of my book.

I think it's so ironic that we're calling hard work, striving for excellence, don't blame others, don't give up—that we're calling these, quote, "Chinese values," because I always thought of them as American values.

MARTIN: But American values also value choice, you know, freedom . . . not having the piano chosen for them if they want to play the oboe, or tennis.

CHUA: There are so many ways to end up in a good spot. So I don't think you should say "I'm promoting this way." But there are a lot of kids that are raised with more strict, rigorous, loving immigrant parents who come out pretty well too. . . .

Asian-American Dilemma

GOOD NEWS IS BAD NEWS

Eric Liu

In 2012, the Pew Research Center released a comprehensive report titled "The Rise of Asian Americans." The report asserted that Asian immigrants had overtaken their Hispanic counterparts as the fastest growing immigrant population in the United States. It further maintained that Asian Americans were the highest-income, best-educated, and fastest-growing racial group in the United States. While seemingly positive, the report drew much criticism because it confirmed the monolithic tenets of the model minority myth and did not take into account Asian ethnic groups that had historically struggled (e.g., Southeast Asian Americans, undocumented Chinese workers, and refugees). Eric Liu, former speech writer for President Bill Clinton and author of The Accidental Asian *(1998), offered a critique of the report with the introductory heading "Our binary way of thinking about race prevents us from openly discussing the challenges that still exist." (Eric Liu. "Asian-American Dilemma: Good News Is Bad News." Time, 26 June 2012. Online at ideas.time.com/2012/06/26/asian-american-dilemma-good-news-is-bad-news/. Reprinted with permission from the author.)*

Last week, the Pew Research Center released a report called "The Rise of Asian Americans," offering a portrait seemingly full of good news. Asian Americans, Pew said, are on the whole more educated, affluent and happier than other Americans. They hew more strongly to family values and an ethic of hard work. And, quietly, these 17 million Asian Americans have surpassed Hispanics as the largest and fastest-growing cohort of immigrants to the U.S.

The report made headlines everywhere: "Asians Top of the Immigration Class" was a typical, if somewhat ham-handed, one. The leading advocacy groups for Asian Americans were silent for a beat. Then they decried the report. It was "disparaging," "shallow," "disturbing." It perpetuated a patronizing stereotype of Asians as dutiful nerds, a "model minority." It overlooked the true cultural diversity of the Asian population and obscured the struggles and pain of countless Asians.

Rarely in either the Pew report or in the advocates' response was this possibility raised: both the good and the bad could be true at the same time.

Welcome to race in America. It may be 2012, and we may have a black President, but public discussion of race remains inexorably, insanely binary. American race talk used to be literally black-and-white, leaving no room for other colors. Now the problem is it's *figuratively* black-and-white. For all our rainbow multiculturalism, there are still basically two choices—in or out, mainstream or opposition, powerful or powerless. Sometimes the labels *white* and *black* are used, but they signify more than hue or actual demography—they signify polarity—and any cognitive dissonance must be resolved to one or the other.

This is why those Asian-American advocates felt they had to blast the Pew report. When forced by the media to choose between telling an achievement story or an injustice story—Is yellow white or black?—they felt compelled to choose the latter. That's understandable. There is privation and injustice in Asian America—from high poverty among Hmong refugees to forgotten elders in Chinatowns to the health struggles of Pacific Islanders—and if activists privileged enough to have a voice use it to express complacency or self-congratulation, then they aren't doing their job. Moreover, Asian Americans rightly resist being used by whites to criticize other groups who aren't deemed "model."

Yet this binary is a box. It limits the freedom of Asian Americans to call progress *progress,* or to discuss openly the causes of the challenges that persist. It makes it harder to unpack the fact that in Asian America, as in America at large, widening inequality and the cult of meritocracy has created more anxiety for both winners and losers. It means we all keep speaking a language of race when we are trying to communicate about issues of class.

Consider Chinese Americans, the largest Asian-American subgroup. Pew tells us that on average the 4 million Americans of Chinese descent have *both* more college attainment *and* more poverty than other Americans, *both* higher incomes *and* less optimism about race relations. As China grows stronger, Chinese Americans are going to be cast as *both* valuable bridge-building citizens *and* aliens of uncertain loyalty. Are we ready for both?

We may be. Last week, as the Pew report and its backlash broke, two other Asian American story lines unfolded. First was the commemoration of the 30th anniversary of the killing of Vincent Chin, a Chinese American who was beaten to death in Detroit by resentful white autoworkers who assumed he was Japanese. Those assailants never spent a day in jail. Meanwhile, thanks to Chinese-American Congresswoman Judy Chu, the House of Representatives last Tuesday passed a historic apology for the 1882 Chinese Exclusion Act, the "yellow peril" law that for decades banned the immigration or naturalization of people from China.

Both good news *and* bad. Complexity is here, and it's not going away. If we must have a binary in our reckoning with race, then, let it be between those who know how to navigate complexity and those who don't. And let Asian Americans be at the forefront of the first group, showing their compatriots how to embrace diversity and contradiction: how to be truly American.

Abercrombie & Glitch

ASIAN AMERICANS RIP RETAILER
FOR STEREOTYPES ON T-SHIRTS

Jenny Strasburg

In 2002, the retailer Abercrombie and Fitch included in its product line Asian-themed T-shirts that featured stereotypical representations of Chinese labor (laundrymen) and the Buddha. As this article from the San Francisco Chronicle *suggests, at stake in the controversy was the use of racist "coolie" caricatures that disremember the histories of violence and exclusion that circumscribed the experiences of Asian immigrants in the nineteenth and early twentieth centuries. The shirts were quickly recalled after the company received hundreds of complaints. (Jenny Strasburg. "Abercrombie & Glitch: Asian Americans Rip Retailer for Stereotypes on T-Shirts."* San Francisco Chronicle, *18 Apr. 2002: 1. Reprinted courtesy of the* San Francisco Chronicle.)

Days after hitting store shelves, new Abercrombie & Fitch T-shirts featuring caricatured faces with slanted eyes and rice-paddy hats had Asian Americans in the Bay Area and beyond demanding a public apology from the retailer.

The Midwestern clothier, which targets the young, affluent and active, said it was surprised by the mounting controversy over the T-shirt designs.

One has a slogan that says, "Wong Brothers Laundry Service—Two Wongs Can Make It White." Beside the prominent lettering are two smiling figures in conical hats harking back to 1900s popular-culture depictions of Chinese men.

"We personally thought Asians would love this T-shirt," said Hampton Carney, with Paul Wilmot Communications in New York, the public relations firm where Abercrombie referred a reporter's call.

"I wouldn't know how they could think that," said Austin Chung, 23, of Palo Alto, business manager for the quarterly Asian-focused magazine *Monolid.* "Abercrombie & Fitch is producing popular culture, and they cater to the views of the majority. You have to ask yourself, who benefits, who gets empowerment, from these kinds of images? It denigrates Asian men."

As word of the new T-shirts in Abercrombie stores spread yesterday among university students and on far-reaching e-mail lists, plans shaped up for a late-night meeting in a Stanford dorm lounge.

The subject: What to do about the series of themed T-shirts the retailer—known for edgy advertising and skin-bearing advertising—introduced Friday in stores and on its Web site, www.abercrombie.com.

"Wok-N-Bowl—Let the Good Times Roll—Chinese Food & Bowling," one design reads, with a stereotypical image similar to the figures on the Wong Brothers shirt.

"Abercrombie and Fitch Buddha Bash—Get Your Buddha on the Floor," reads another shirt that shares display space in the youth-oriented, casual-clothing store.

"Truly and Deeply Sorry"

The shirts were designed to appeal to young Asian shoppers with a sense of humor, Carney told *The Chronicle* yesterday.

The shirts were available for sale yesterday in the Abercrombie store at San Francisco Shopping Centre on Market Street. Whether they will remain on the shelves was unclear yesterday, the spokesman said.

"We are truly and deeply sorry we've offended people," said Carney, adding that he had spent much of the afternoon returning calls of complaint, many of them from Stanford students.

"We never single out any one group to poke fun at," Carney said. "We poke fun at everybody, from women to flight attendants to baggage handlers, to football coaches, to Irish Americans to snow skiers. There's really no group we haven't teased."

Abercrombie might consider rethinking that approach when marketing to—or representing images of—racial and ethnic groups, said Michael Chang, vice chairman of Stanford's Asian American Students' Association, organizers of last night's meeting on campus.

"It's really misleading as to what Asian people are," Chang said. "The stereotypes they depict are more than a century old. You're seeing laundry service. You're seeing basically an entire religion and philosophy being trivialized."

Abercrombie should apologize publicly, starting with a message from corporate headquarters, Chang said. The Asian students' association at Stanford yesterday was encouraging calls to the company.

Even Store Manager Surprised

Chang said Stanford students who complained to individual Bay Area store managers quickly realized that was futile because the merchandise decisions were being made at a higher level.

Stanford senior BJ Lee, 21, said one store manager acknowledged even he had been surprised when the T-shirts arrived at his store. "We tried to get them pulled, but we weren't successful," Lee said. "Managers don't have authority."

The online chat about Abercrombie doesn't stop at Stanford.

"This story is going around the whole Asian e-mail circle," said Kevin Choi, a 21-year-old student at the Massachusetts Institute of Technology, who said the chorus of angry voices was growing at MIT and near the campus. Some students organized public protests in front of Abercrombie stores, he said.

"I think they need to apologize, to make a public statement, but I also think they need to start looking at their whole strategy for how they portray people," Choi said. "Maybe it sells in the suburbs . . . but their whole national marketing image is buff, tanned male and female models without any Asian representation."

Last year, Abercrombie & Fitch caught flak from some activist groups, and even state governments, for what they viewed as sexually suggestive advertising campaigns and catalog photos.

Sometimes that kind of publicity can help a retailer more than it hurts, said retail analyst Jennifer Black with Wells Fargo Securities in Portland, Ore.

"In all honesty, I think the controversy (over sexually charged advertising) is kind of a marketing thing—the teens love it," and they're crucial to Abercrombie's customer base, Black said.

But pushing controversial racial or ethnic depictions is different, said Black, who added that the best damage control might be "to come out with an immediate apology."

Company to Discuss Response

Carney said company executives would discuss a formal response today to the complaints they had received. He said he did not know how many of the T-shirts had been distributed or whether they had reached stores in all regions yet.

"They're part of a fashion line that moves in and out of stores," he said.

Abercrombie, a company that started with one small New York City outdoors store and factory in 1892, sold $1.36 billion worth of upscale clothing, accessories, shoes and related casual merchandise in the fiscal year that ended in February. The heavily mall-based retailer has headquarters in Columbus, Ohio.

Recommended Resources

Bow, Leslie. *Partly Colored: Asian Americans and Racial Anomaly in the Segregated South.* New York: New York University Press, 2010.

Bulosan, Carlos. *America Is in the Heart: A Personal History.* Seattle: University of Washington Press, 1973. Originally published in 1946.

Cheng, Wendy. *The Changs Next Door to the Diazes: Remapping Race in Suburban California.* Minneapolis: University of Minnesota Press, 2013.

Chin, Frank, Jeffrey Paul Chan, Lawson Fusano Inada, and Shawn Wong, eds. *Aiiieeeee! An Anthology of Asian-American Writers.* Washington, DC: Howard University Press, 1974.

Chiu, Monica, ed. *Drawing New Color Lines: Transnational Asian American Graphic Narratives.* Hong Kong: Hong Kong University Press, 2014.

Choy, Catherine Ceniza. *Global Families: A History of Asian International Adoption in America.* New York: New York University Press, 2013.

Choy, Philip P., Lorraine Dong, and Marlon K. Hom, eds. *Coming Man: 19th Century American Perceptions of the Chinese.* Seattle: University of Washington Press, 1994.

Chuh, Kandice. *Imagine Otherwise: On Asian Americanist Critique.* Durham, NC: Duke University Press, 2003.

Davé, Shilpa, LeiLani Nishime, and Tasha G. Oren, eds. *East Main Street: Asian American Popular Culture.* New York: New York University Press, 2005.

De Genova, Nicholas, ed. *Racial Transformations: Latinos and Asians Remaking the United States.* Durham, NC: Duke University Press, 2006.

Desai, Jigna, and Khyati Y. Joshi, eds. *Asian Americans in Dixie: Race and Migration in the South.* Champaign: University of Illinois Press, 2013.

Eng, David L. *Racial Castration: Managing Masculinity in Asian America.* Durham, NC: Duke University Press, 2001.

———, ed. (with Alice Hom). *Q & A: Queer in Asian America.* Philadelphia: Temple University Press, 1998.

Espiritu, Yên Lê. *Asian American Panethnicity: Bridging Institutions and Identities.* Philadelphia: Temple University Press, 1992.

Fujino, Diane C. *Heartbeat of Struggle: The Revolutionary Life of Yuri Kochiyama.* Minneapolis: University of Minnesota Press, 2005.

———. *Samurai Among Panthers: Richard Aoki on Race, Resistance, and a Paradoxical Life.* Minneapolis: University of Minnesota Press, 2012.

Ignacio, Abe, ed. *The Forbidden Book: The Philippine-American War in Political Cartoons.* San Francisco: T'boli, 2004.

Imada, Adria L. *Aloha America: Hula Circuits Through the US Empire.* Durham, NC: Duke University Press, 2012.

Isaac, Allan Punzalan. *American Tropics: Articulating Filipino America.* Minneapolis: University of Minnesota Press, 2006.

Iwamura, Jane. *Virtual Orientalism: Religion and Popular Culture in the U.S.* New York: Oxford University Press, 2011.

Kim, Claire J. *Bitter Fruit: The Politics of Black-Korean Conflict in New York City.* New Haven, CT: Yale University Press, 2003.

Ku, Robert Ji-Song, Martin F. Manalansan, and Anita Mannur, eds. *Eating Asian America: A Food Studies Reader.* New York: New York University Press, 2013.

Kurashige, Scott. *The Shifting Grounds of Race: Black and Japanese Americans in the Making of Multiethnic Los Angeles.* Princeton, NJ: Princeton University Press, 2010.

Lee, James Kyung-Jin. *Urban Triage: Race and the Fictions of Multiculturalism.* Minneapolis: University of Minnesota Press, 2004.

Lee, Julia H. *Interracial Encounters: Reciprocal Representations in African American and Asian American Literatures, 1896–1937.* New York: New York University Press, 2011.

Lee, Robert G. *Orientals: Asian Americans in Popular Culture.* Philadelphia: Temple University Press, 1999.

Leong, Karen J. *The China Mystique: Pearl S. Buck, Anna May Wong, Mayling Soong, and the Transformation of American Orientalism.* Berkeley: University of California Press, 2005.

Leong, Russell. *Asian American Sexualities: Dimensions of the Gay and Lesbian Experience.* New York: Routledge, 1996.

Lin, Jan. *Reconstructing Chinatown: Ethnic Enclaves and Global Change.* Minneapolis: University of Minnesota Press, 1998.

Lowe, Lisa. *Immigrant Acts: On Asian American Cultural Politics.* Durham, NC: Duke University Press, 1996.

Lye, Colleen. *America's Asia: Racial Form and American Literature, 1893–1945.* Princeton, NJ: Princeton University Press, 2009.

Maeda, Daryl J. *Chains of Babylon: The Rise of Asian America.* Minneapolis: University of Minnesota Press, 2009.

———. *Rethinking the Asian American Movement.* New York: Routledge, 2012.

Maira, Sunaina. *Desis in the House: Indian American Youth Culture in New York City.* Philadelphia: Temple University Press, 2012.

———. *Missing: Youth, Citizenship, and Empire After 9/11.* Durham, NC: Duke University Press, 2009.

Manalansan, Martin F., IV. *Global Divas: Filipino Gay Men in the Diaspora.* Durham, NC: Duke University Press, 2003.

Mannur, Anita. *Culinary Fictions: Food in South Asian Diasporic Culture.* Philadelphia: Temple University Press, 2009.

McClain, Charles J. *In Search of Equality: The Chinese Struggle Against Discrimination in Nineteenth-Century America.* Berkeley: University of California Press, 1994.

McKeown, Adam M. *Melancholy Order: Asian Migration and the Globalization of Borders.* New York: Columbia University Press, 2008.

Nakamura, Lisa. *Cybertypes: Race, Ethnicity, and Identity on the Internet.* New York: Routledge, 2013.

———. *Digitizing Race: Visual Cultures of the Internet.* Minneapolis: University of Minnesota Press, 2008.

Nguyen, Mimi Thi, and Thuy Linh Nguyen Tu, eds. *Alien Encounters: Popular Culture in Asian America.* Durham, NC: Duke University Press, 2007.

Nguyen, Viet Thanh. *Race and Resistance: Literature and Politics in Asian America.* New York: Oxford University Press, 2002.

Okihiro, Gary. *Margins and Mainstreams: Asians in American History and Culture.* Seattle: University of Washington Press, 1994.

Ono, Kent A., ed. *Asian American Studies After Critical Mass.* Malden, MA: Blackwell, 2008.

Palumbo-Liu, David. *Asian/American: Historical Crossings of a Racial Frontier.* Stanford, CA: Stanford University Press, 1999.

Prashad, Vijay. *Everybody Was Kung Fu Fighting: Afro-Asian Connections and the Myth of Cultural Purity.* Boston: Beacon, 2001.

Sharma, Nitasha Tamar. *Hip Hop Desis: South Asian Americans, Blackness, and a Global Race Consciousness.* Durham, NC: Duke University Press, 2010.

Song, Min Hyoung. *The Children of 1965: On Writing, and Not Writing, as an Asian American.* Durham, NC: Duke University Press, 2013.

———. *Strange Future: Pessimism and the 1992 Los Angeles Riots.* Durham, NC: Duke University Press, 2005.

Spickard, Paul R. *Mixed Blood: Intermarriage and Ethnic Identity in Twentieth-Century America.* Madison: University of Wisconsin Press, 1989.

Tchen, John Kuo Wei, and Dylan Yeats, eds. *Yellow Peril! An Archive of Anti-Asian Fear.* London: Verso, 2014.

Teng, Emma Jinhua. *Eurasian: Mixed Identities in the United States, China, and Hong Kong, 1842–1943.* Berkeley: University of California Press, 2013.

Wei, William. *The Asian American Movement.* Philadelphia: Temple University Press, 2010.

Williams-León, Teresa, and Cynthia L. Nakashima, eds. *The Sum of Our Parts: Mixed-Heritage Asian Americans.* Philadelphia: Temple University Press, 2001.

Wu, Cynthia. *Chang and Eng Reconnected: The Original Siamese Twins in American Culture.* Philadelphia: Temple University Press, 2012.

Xu, Wenying. *Eating Identities: Reading Food in Asian American Literature.* Honolulu: University of Hawai'i Press, 2008.

Yang, Kao Kalia. *The Latehomecomer: A Hmong Family Memoir.* Minneapolis: Coffee House Press, 2008.

Yung, Judy. *Unbound Feet: A Social History of Chinese Women in San Francisco.* Berkeley: University of California Press, 1995.

Index